You can return this item to any library but please
note that not all libraries are open every day.
Items must be returned on or before the due date.
Failure to do so will result in overdue charges.
Items may be renewed unless requested by
another customer, in person or by telephone, on
two occasions only. Your membership card
number will be required.
Please look after this item – you may be charged
for any damage.

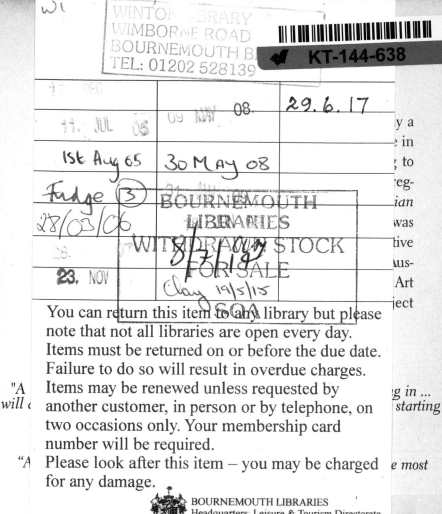
"A
will (*g in ...*
                                                          starting

"A   *e most*

                                                          er is
                                                          lian

*twenty-something back-packer's romantic liaison with a very
French Frenchman and the howling differences in language,
customs and expected behaviour."*
What's On In London

*"Turnbull pulls no punches when it comes to describing life among her
new countrymen and is refreshingly direct about her own failings
as perceived by the Parisians.
Required reading for anyone contemplating a spot of French leave."*
marie claire

Almost French

A new life in Paris

SARAH TURNBULL

NICHOLAS BREALEY
PUBLISHING
LONDON

This paperback edition first published in Great Britain by
Nicholas Brealey Publishing in 2003

Reprinted 2003 (twice), 2004 (three times)

3–5 Spafield Street
Clerkenwell, London
EC1R 4QB, UK
Tel: +44 (0)20 7239 0360
Fax: +44 (0)20 7239 0370

100 City Hall Plaza, Suite 501
Boston
MA 02018, USA
Tel: (888) BREALEY
Fax: (617) 523 3708

www.nbrealey-books.com

ISBN 1-85788-316-0

British Library Cataloguing in Publication Data
A catalogue record for this book is available from the
British Library.

Printed in Finland by WS Bookwell.

For Mum and Dad

Et, bien sûr, pour Fred

Prologue

I left Australia hoping to cram a lifetime of adventures into one unforgettable year. Instead, I ended up with a new life. I'd taken one year's leave from my job as a television reporter in Sydney to travel around Europe. If I didn't go now, I never would, warned a nagging voice in my head. Though, at twenty-seven I wasn't much interested in hanging around youth hostels. The idea was to immerse myself in fascinating foreign cultures, to work as a freelance journalist in Eastern Europe, which in my mind bubbled with unwritten, hard-hitting stories.

It was in Bucharest, Romania, that I met Frédéric. His English was sprinkled with wonderful expressions like 'foot fingers' instead of toes and he seemed charming, creative and complicated—very French, in other words. When he'd invited me to visit him in Paris, I'd hesitated just long enough to make sure he was serious before saying yes. Why not? After all, this is what travelling is all about, isn't it: seizing opportunities, doing things you wouldn't normally do, being open to the accidental?

That trip to Paris was more than eight years ago now. And except for four months when I resumed my travels, I have been living here ever since.

It was a city and culture I was familiar with—at least that's what I thought back then. When I was a child my family had toured France in a tiny campervan and my eyes had popped at the chocolates and the cheeses. At secondary school I studied French and saw a few films by Truffaut and Resnais which had struck me as enigmatic and European, although I couldn't have said why. When I was sixteen we lived in England for a year and I came to Paris several times. In my mind, these experiences added up to knowledge of France and some understanding of its people. Then, a little over ten years later, my meeting with Frédéric drew me back, and when the time came to actually live in Paris, I figured belonging and integrating would take merely a matter of months.

Now, remembering my early naiveté draws a wry smile. The truth is, nearly all my preconceptions of France turned out to be false. It hardly needs to be said that living in a place is totally different from visiting it. And yet this blatantly obvious statement does need to be said, particularly about Paris, the most visited city in the world. A place I imagined to know after a few nights in a closet-sized hotel room as a teenager and one summer holiday with a Frenchman sipping *kir* on café terraces.

At times the learning curve has seemed almost vertical. The social code I discovered in France wasn't just different from my Australian one, it was diametrically opposed to it. For a long time, I couldn't fathom the French and, to be fair, they couldn't fathom me either. My clothes, my smile—even how much I drank—set me apart. During my first year, dinner parties turned into tearful trials. There I was, a confident twenty-eight-year-old with the confidence knocked out of me, spending cheese courses locked in somebody's loo, mascara streaming down my cheeks.

It hasn't all been tears and trials, of course. The truth is, if

France failed to live up to some of my expectations, in other ways the reality has been far richer, a thousand times better than my clichéd visions. My work as a journalist has enabled me to meet people ranging from famous French fashion designers to master chefs. On a personal level I'd taken a headlong plunge into new territory as well. Put a very French Frenchman together with a strong-willed Sydney girl, and the result is some fairly spectacular—and sometimes hilarious—cultural clashes.

If I had to pick one word to sum up my life in France, it'd have to be 'adventure'. Every moment has been vivid, intensely felt. No doubt many people who live in a foreign country would say the same thing. But there is, I think, something that sets this country apart from many other parts of the world. I know of no other place that is so fascinating yet so frustrating, so aware of the world and its own place within it but at the same time utterly insular. A country touched by nostalgia, with a past so great—so marked by brilliance and achievement—that French people today seem both enriched and burdened by it. France is like a maddening, moody lover who inspires emotional highs and lows. One minute it fills you with a rush of passion, the next you're full of fury, itching to smack the mouth of some sneering shopkeeper or smug civil servant. Yes, it's a love–hate relationship. But it's charged with so much mystery, longing and that French speciality— *séduction*—that we can't resist coming back for more.

From where I write in Paris today, I see a foil shimmer of rooftops, a few orange chimney pots, quaintly crooked windows and lots of sky. Although by this city's standards it's nothing special, to me it is precious, this view. It makes me think back to a time when we didn't have it, when we were living in a different apartment where I wasn't nearly as happy.

Those early difficult years in France seem a lifetime ago now, as though they were lived by someone else. So much has changed since then, including me, probably. The truth is, when I started to write this book I had trouble taking myself back to that time. I don't know why it should have been so difficult. Either I'd forgotten or subconsciously didn't want to remember or, being a journalist, I was paralysed by the idea of writing in the first person. Probably a combination of all three.

For days and weeks, I sat staring at my rectangle of pearl-grey sky. For inspiration I looked at old photos, read my early articles and Mum sent me all the letters I'd written from France, which she'd carefully kept. The memories came back gradually, growing sharper and brighter until I could see myself on that summer's day almost eight years ago, excited but nervous, arriving in Paris in my safari shorts and flat, clumpy sandals, oblivious to the horror my outfit would inspire in any self-respecting Frenchman.

And suddenly it seemed as though it had happened only yesterday.

One

This isn't like me.

The queue for passport inspection at Charles de Gaulle airport surges impatiently. My flight from Romania has coincided with one arriving from Mali and I curse the rotten timing because at this rate it'll take all day. The French police scrutinise the passports from Eastern Europe and Africa, ask lots of questions. The queue isn't really a line but a claustrophobic knot and I am somewhere in the middle of it, surrounded by women in bright headscarves and cumbrous robes, and tall, athletic men. Their blue-black faces shine: it's hot and stuffy. More passengers pour from planes and we squash together tighter and tighter, our clothes and skins sticking together.

I'm not the sort of girl who crosses continents to meet up with a man she hardly knows.

I'd intended to give the passport officer a piece of my mind when it was my turn at the window—a few helpful suggestions. Like, how about concentrating on the task at hand instead of idly chatting with your colleagues? And haven't the French ever heard of those rope railings which arrange queues in neat snake configurations? But he stamps my pass-port with barely a glance, smiling charmingly as he says, '*Bonne journée, Mademoiselle*,' and after all that waiting sud-denly I'm through the bottleneck and officially in France.

Paris hadn't even been part of my travel plan.

I'm in a space ship. Terminal One is a galactic sphere tra-versed by transparent tubes which are speeding people in different directions. I take one going up. The impression of breathtaking modernity is dashed by the general rundown appearance of the place. If this is a space ship, it's a pretty out-dated model. At the top, luggage is being spat onto a conveyer belt which keeps stopping and starting. After another inter-minably long wait, my tattered blue backpack tumbles out.

Yet here I am, coming to see—no, stay with—a Frenchman with whom I have conversed for a grand total of, oh, maybe forty-five minutes.

Glass doors slide open. I push the luggage trolley down the ramp into the arrivals lounge. I wonder if I'll recognise him straightaway. A couple of months have passed since we met. But to my surprise, there's no-one in the crowd who even remotely resembles my mental snapshot. I steer the trolley over to an exposed seat near the glass exit, apprehension squeezing my chest.

This is mad.

The doubts had started festering after a series of bad phone calls, gnawing at my excitement until I'd almost forgotten what had attracted me in the first place: the impression that he was different, unlike any man I'd ever met. The worst was one week ago when he'd called to confirm my arrival time. It had been another awkward telephone conversation punctuated by long pauses and misunderstandings which made me wonder if the problem was deeper than just language. Of course, it doesn't help that his English is pretty basic and my French is awful. We can't even communicate, for god's sake, I'd thought. What are we going to talk about for a whole week? At the end of ten excruciating minutes I'd said goodbye and he'd said, 'I kiss you,' which made me cringe. What a sleaze! Had I paid more attention during French classes at school I might have remembered that in France this is the sort of farewell you could say to your sister or grandmother but all I can think now is how weird it sounded.

The air inside Charles de Gaulle airport is stale and smoky. It's like being in a giant school toilet block after a student smoking session—the chipped white floor tiles are covered in butts. Tired passengers dribble through the sliding doors. I try not to scan the crowd too often. The minutes limp by, my mind relentlessly replaying our two encounters, assessing them from every angle.

He'd been sent to Bucharest for a few days in his job as a lawyer. I was doing some freelance television stories there and had met up with an old friend, Simon, from university who'd moved to Romania for work. On my third day, Simon announced that a couple of French guys from his firm's Paris office were in town, advising on some privatisation project. Would I like to join them for dinner?

Ten of us had crowded around the table outside the Lebanese restaurant, a favourite haunt of expats in Bucharest. As it turned out, I was next to one of the French guests.

'I'm Frédéric, from France,' he'd said politely by way of introduction, and I had to stop myself from saying 'no kidding', because there was no mistaking this man's nationality. Trim sideburns slid down his cheeks. His jumper was slung nonchalantly around his shoulders and he had that perennially tanned look of many Europeans. A faded silk scarf, knotted at the neck, made him look like some nineteenth-century French painter. Over dinner, I noticed the unusual yellowy-brown colour of his eyes; the smooth, manicured hands which made my wrinkled, nail-bitten paws look like something out of science fiction. After we'd finished eating, he lit a pipe, which struck me as hilarious. 'I didn't know anyone under a hundred smoked pipes,' I teased and his face had fallen.

The following night was the Frenchmen's last evening in Bucharest before returning to Paris. Again we all went out for dinner, this time to an Italian restaurant. They were the last to arrive and they wore their lateness stylishly, circling the long table like suave diplomats, shaking hands with each bloke, kissing the girls on both cheeks. Frédéric seemed to give me a meaningful look or did I just imagine he did? We talked some more. A few personal details emerged, hanging in the air like question marks. Thirty-six and newly single, I learned. I didn't ask more, didn't want to appear nosy: *interested*.

By the time we all ended up at an Irish bar, it was clear the groomed, continental exterior concealed a rather eccentric character—a lawyer who preferred painting even though he's seriously colour-blind. A slightly absurd sense of humour flashed through his well-brought-up politeness. He told me he loves practical jokes, adores fancy dress parties and making elaborate costumes.

'Like what?' I'd asked.

'Well, one year, we made a New Year's Eve party, the theme was *esprits de la forêt*, forest spirits, yes. I wanted to do something that looked real but also extraordinary.' Frédéric told me how he went searching in the woods, where he found a giant, dead tree trunk. It was winter, nature was sodden and the trunk weighed 'at least one hundred kilos'. When Frédéric and a friend finally got it home in a borrowed truck, he spent four days hollowing it out and trying in vain to dry the inside with a hair dryer. But it remained far too bulky and heavy to shuffle around in it in the way he'd envisaged so he picked up an old wheelchair from an antique shop. On the night of the party, Frédéric sat on the chair, wrapped in the wet blackness of the hollowed trunk which was still crawling with bugs and spiders.

I laughed, although this didn't sound like my idea of a great party. 'Did you enjoy yourself?'

'Oh yes, it was *terrible*! Everyone thought I was part of the décor, nobody talked to me!' Frédéric chuckled at the memory and I recall that in French 'terrible' means great. 'It was so *terrible*,' he repeated, stumbling slightly over the word in his effort to pronounce it in the English way, with a short 'i' sound instead of 'terreeble'.

Chatting, we discovered we share a love of travelling as well as an absentminded habit of turning up to airports minus the required paperwork (tickets, passports, money). But I don't go anywhere without a guide book, whereas Frédéric's adventures are amplified by a pathological dislike of planning and preparation. This plays havoc with his life, he'd told me, causing him to run out of petrol on autoroutes, leave his credit cards in automatic teller machines and embark on mountain treks in Kashmir wearing filthy socks on his head and hands in the absence of beanie and gloves.

As we were about to say goodbye Frédéric turned to me, his expression disarmingly earnest all of a sudden. It was then he'd popped the question. Would I like to come to Paris?

Now France wasn't on my itinerary. The idea of this twelve-month trip was to discover new places, and I'd been to Paris before. After Romania, I was planning to fly to London to try to get some casual work through some television contacts people had given me in Australia. I would stay with my old friend Sue, who'd moved there a year ago. But faced with Frédéric's invitation, I quickly changed my plans. The truth was I wanted to see him again. We'd both felt the spark, it was obvious. London and work could wait.

'Well yeah, I'd really like that. I mean, that sounds great.'

As the weeks rolled on in Romania, Paris began to look attractive for reasons other than Frédéric. It's not that I didn't enjoy being in Bucharest—in fact I loved it. The city is an absorbing kaleidoscope of sashaying gypsy skirts and stray dogs, proudly cultured people, raffish artists and unreliable lifts. I spent days exploring the cobbled passages of the old Jewish quarter, poking around state-owned art galleries knee-deep in dusty oil paintings. Through Simon I met a great crowd of people. We went out every night, revelling in Romanian red and the freedom which comes from finding new friends far from home, in an out-of-the-way place.

But in Romania, even the simplest of tasks involves hurdling a long line-up of bureaucratic brick walls. My twenty-minute television story on the fight for the restitution of homes and land seized under the communists took almost three months to research and film. And towards the end of the project, the post-communism melancholy of the people started to wear me down. Just around the corner from Simon's apartment loomed Ceausescu's monstrous palace—the biggest building in the world after the Pentagon, apparently. It looked like a Stalinist wedding cake, fitted inside with kilometres of Italian marble and cascading crystal chandeliers. It started to grate, the disparity between this in-your-face waste and the street kids with pleading eyes and skinny, twisted limbs. Many of the Romanians I interviewed seemed resigned, crushed. By the time my television project was wrapped up, I felt ready for a holiday. The Paris invitation winked like a diamond in sunlight, dazzling and indulgent. Yes, London and work could definitely wait.

Thirty minutes. I've been waiting thirty minutes!

Still there's no familiar face among the crowd. I open my Lonely Planet guide to Mediterranean Europe and start reading the history of France summary, feigning nonchalance. In reality, my seize-every-opportunity backpacker's bravado has all but evaporated. Thoughts swirl around my mind like snowflakes in a blizzard, jumbling irrationality and reason. Ever since the I-kiss-you phone call, I've been seriously wondering about the wisdom of coming to Paris. It has started to seem totally imprudent, given how little I know this guy. What if his suave appearance is a front? He could be a psychopath, a serial rapist, how would I know? He'd even admitted he had a problem. There we were on the second evening in Bucharest, casually chatting about the trials of being innately messy, rather forgetful people when Frédéric's tone had suddenly turned solemn.

'No, I was awful, really insupportable,' he'd said. And then his face had brightened—weirdly brightened, I realise in retrospect.

'I am maniac now,' he'd told me. They were his exact

7

words. At the time I'd dismissed it as a language thing. Unsure how to respond, I'd just said, 'Sounds pretty complicated', and he'd beamed, as though this was a compliment.

At least Sue will be in Paris in a few days' time, I comfort myself. She will save me, or, if necessary, report my disappearance (that is, if he ever turns up). One week before my departure, I'd called her in London. At the mature age of twenty-seven, I needed a chaperone. Meet me in Paris next weekend, I'd begged, calculating that'll only leave me five days alone with the French freak. She'd sounded surprised — the last time we'd spoken I'd been excited. She was having trouble keeping track of my flip-flopping sentiments.

Cries of joy from the arrival gate suddenly startle my train of thought. A family is swarming around a girl—about my age—smothering her with kisses. She's obviously been backpacking for a while, you can tell by her unkempt appearance. Which reminds me—I'm not exactly looking like model material either. The day before I left Bucharest the city's water supply had been cut. Apparently the authorities had forewarned the public but, of course, I wouldn't have understood the announcements even if I had heard them. I haven't had a shower for forty-eight hours and my hair—which I'd held off washing until the day of my departure—is pulled in a limp ponytail. So much for making a stylish entrance into the world's glamour capital. But I'd done my best with limited means, putting on a bit of makeup and even ironing my denim shirt. And at least my shorts are clean. I'm also wearing my favourite sandals—flat brown things that reveal my weakness for comfortable, orthopaedic-type shoes. Right now they're not looking too good, though: my feet and shoes are covered in dust and grime from Bucharest's streets. It occurs to me my legs could do with a waxing.

In the Lonely Planet guide the history of France is condensed into four and a half action-packed pages. Practically each line announces a world war or a revolution or some tremendous tragedy. I get to 'De Gaulle', struggling to concentrate. My eyes flicker involuntarily to my watch.

FORTY-FIVE MINUTES!

The anger that had been mounting in me over his tardiness abruptly dissolves. Reality hits me: it's time to face facts. Frédéric's obviously had a change of heart. I've been stood up. A rush of disappointment engulfs me. Despite my fears about barely knowing him, despite the bad telephone conversations, I realise now how much I'd wanted to see him again. Instead, my romantic Paris rendezvous is over before it's even begun. Faced with my changed circumstances, I'm thrown off balance, uncertain what to do next, and feeling so pathetic irritates me. The month before arriving in Bucharest I'd travelled through Eastern Europe, learning a new level of self-reliance as I'd grown comfortable with little things like eating out on my own. Breaking through the pain barrier had felt like an accomplishment. And now look at me! Coming undone because of a no-show at the airport.

The reunited family leaves the airport through the glass exit, chatting and laughing, the girl cocooned by parents and siblings. Including my stopovers in Kuala Lumpur and London, it's been four months since I left Australia. And suddenly I feel lonely—even more lonely than humiliated. I'd like to be with *my* family. Should have gone straight to see Sue in London instead of changing my plans for a dodgy stranger. Still waiting on a cheque for my Romania story, at this stage I can't afford to go blowing my savings on expensive

Paris hotels. Clutching the guide book opened at 'Places to Stay', I start fumbling pointlessly with a public telephone that demands a plastic card I don't have.

'Er, 'allo.' The voice behind me is flustered, apologetic. Breathless. Before I've even had time to turn around, Frédéric is spewing excuses. His trip to the airport has been besieged by obstacles ranging from traffic jams to a metro strike and being told the wrong arrival terminal by airport information. His face is furrowed with worry. I try to look casual not cross, which doesn't actually require a lot of effort. He looks just how I remembered him, maybe better. His continental tan has deepened several notches, if that's possible, enhanced by his smart summer suit which is some colour between grey and light brown.

We head to the lift which goes to the underground carpark, Fréderic dripping style with every step. Suddenly I'm excruciatingly aware of my dishevelled appearance. My stained shirt front where fruit salad juice spilled during the flight. My feet, my clothes, my spiky legs. He looks like he's just stepped off the set of a French film. And me, how do I look to him, I wonder?

Like an Aussie backpacker in need of a bath, probably.

Two

'Be quiet.'

Frédéric's stern command when I offer to help prepare lunch wipes the polite smile off my face. Stung, I sink back into the sofa. Registering my shock, he scrambles for a better translation of *'reste tranquille'*.

'Be still. Relax,' he tries. His tone is reassuring.

While Frédéric is in the kitchen, I poke around his apartment. Bright sunlight spills through tall windows overlooking a quiet, leafy lane. Levallois, he'd said the area was called. Driving through it seemed nice, more trees than I'd expected to see in the city. My fears begin to subside: this doesn't look like the home of a dangerous or disturbed man. It looks like the home of someone creative, someone who loves travelling and beautiful things: a collector. For a few minutes I just circle and stare. His taste is eclectic. Colourful papier-mâché masks pull faces at me from above the doorway. He picked them up in Sri Lanka, he'd told me. A contemporary nude watercolour hangs near an oil painting of cows in a field that looks like something I might have studied in art history at school.

The room's centrepiece is an imposing wooden model of an old sailing ship, standing on a marble-topped console table. The mast is nearly a metre high. This must be the

11

model he was telling me about in Romania, the one he had to fight to bring back from Mauritius. At the time, Frédéric was doing his military service in the navy and the ship's captain lambasted him for trying to sink the vessel with the oriental carpets, African masks and ancient swords he picked up at different ports.

An enormous gilt mirror leans against one wall, its glass mottled and smudgy with age. It looks like it belongs in a castle, it's too huge to hang in the apartment. Obviously practical considerations don't enter the equation when it comes to his treasures—he's the buy-now-worry-later-about-how-to-get-it-home-or-where-to-put-it type. I sense a kindred spirit. In Bucharest, I'd struggled awkwardly onto the plane with kilos of Romanian ceramics and three paintings, two for me, the other for Sue, all of which is presently cluttering up Frédéric's entrance.

When he comes back into the room I ask about the mirror and he tells me he bought it at an auction—on a hunch; from a distance he couldn't tell whether it was authentic because the elaborate frame was covered in horrible green paint. To his delight, there was gilt underneath and not wanting to damage it, he carefully scratched off the paint with his thumbnail. It took two weeks, working every evening, he tells me. I try to picture myself doing such a task. My patience wouldn't be up to it. I'd have attacked it with chisels and paint stripper.

'Did you do any of these?' I point to a grouping of water-colours.

'My grandfather did that one, during the war.' He indicates a lovely, wistful still life of lustrous pears and fleshy grapes. 'And this is mine.' He grins. 'My Turner phase.'

It is a large painting of a port, obviously done in the late afternoon because the shadowy blue fishing boats are wreathed in golden light. 'Boulogne-sur-Mer, my home town,' explains Frédéric.

'It's wonderful,' I say, meaning it. 'The colours seem pretty good for someone who's colour-blind.'

This makes him laugh, the fact I'd remembered this quirk. 'I've labelled all the colours in my paint box very precisely so I don't make crazy mistakes,' he reveals.

Frédéric disappears into the kitchen again and my eyes scan the bending bookshelves behind the dining table, searching for clues about their owner. Next to the handsome leather spines embossed with gold flourishes are a lot of dull-looking contemporary covers, devoid of decoration. From the look of them, in France plain egg-shell-coloured jackets must signal Serious Literature. Tea-coloured scraps of paper fan from many of the books. There are titles by Shakespeare, Hemingway and Graham Greene but mostly the authors are French and except for a few names—Jean-Paul Sartre, Albert Camus, Voltaire—they are unfamiliar to me.

More shelves stretch along the hallway, only these books don't look nearly so highbrow. Hardcover comics. Literally hundreds of them. I flip through one. It contains lots of bare bottoms and breasts. Opening another, I stumble straight into a sex scene. Pornographic comics? From the kitchen, Frédéric sees me standing, staring open-mouthed at it.

'Do you like *bandes dessinées?*'

It sounds obscene: 'Bond what?'

'*Bandes dessinées*, comic books,' Frédéric patiently explains. I must look horrified because he stops what he's doing to come out. 'In France they're very popular. They're considered a form of art. I drew one myself.'

I glance at the Barbie-like heroine, who on this page is

13

totally starkers. Fear flares again. Maybe he is weird after all. His taste isn't eclectic: it's schizophrenic. I mean, one room is all classics and culture and now here's a corridor of sexist cartoons, all tits and bums, which he's trying to pass off as art. Worse, he's even drawn one himself!

'Really?' I can't conceal the doubt in my voice. I want to ask how much nudity his comic featured but instead say, 'What's yours about?'

'Sherlock Holmes. It hasn't been published, though. It's a hobby, I worked on it with a friend.' The subject matter sounds harmless enough although who knows—his Sherlock Holmes might be some Casanova character who runs around in spangly G-strings. Promising to show it to me later, Frédéric pulls more *bandes dessinées* from the shelf. Far from acting embarrassed, he seems determined to flaunt his strange obsession.

'Who reads these bond thingies?' I ask, after a short pause.

'Oh, all ages. Children, twenty-year-olds, thirty-year-olds, forty-year-olds. Everyone.'

He resumes his chopping, leaving me to ponder what's happened to literature in the country that produced Proust.

The bathroom is equipped with a bidet. I try to remember exactly when you're supposed to use it: after you've been to the toilet or after sex? Right now, the low basin comes in handy for scrubbing my feet and shins. My eyes fall on the folded towel and lavender soap, which have been carefully laid out for me. Coming from a man, such attention to detail seems funny and foreign. And touchingly thoughtful.

The impression of hotel-like order snaps the second I step into the toilet, which appears to be doubling as a dishwasher. Crockery and cutlery swim in the open cistern. Plates lean against bowls, which are propped between a cup and a fork.

A stray spoon has sunk to the bottom. I search for a chain, a handle or a button—anything that looks familiar and flush-like. Bewildered, I call for instructions. 'How do you flush the toilet?'

Frédéric shouts directions from the kitchen but I don't understand them and in the end, he has to come in to show me. Mortified by this unscheduled intimacy, I quickly slam the toilet lid. Frédéric is apparently oblivious to my embarrassment: in fact he looks absurdly pleased with himself. The flush broke a few days ago but he managed to fix it, he explains in a way that suggests he's not accustomed to fixing things. There is a hint of pomp in his manner as he demonstrates his remarkable invention. Flushing is a simple matter of dipping your hand into the cistern to pull the fork which levers the plates. *Et voilà!* He lifts the lid so I can admire his DIY genius. Water rushes triumphantly around the bowl.

When I come back into the living–dining area, the table is set for lunch. I stare, astonished. It looks picture-perfect, like it's been carefully laid for a special occasion—Christmas or some fancy dinner party. Yellow and white impatiens flowers spill from a ceramic bowl in the middle. Linen napkins and silver cutlery mark our places. I struggle to picture my outdoorsy older brother knowing what to do with crystal knife rests. We have two elegant wine glasses each, one slightly bigger than the other. Formality in any form has always made me nervous and I beg Frédéric not to go to any trouble. Now it's his turn to look astonished. And then it sinks in: by his standards this isn't going to any trouble. The pretty soap and folded towel, the beautifully decorated lounge, it all starts to make sense. This must be how things are done in France. Everything arranged to look as aesthetically pleasing as possible.

Lunch is a salad topped with fresh tarragon, walnuts and crumbly goats' cheese, tossed in Frédéric's own vinaigrette. I am impressed. For me, 'homemade' dressing means buying a bottle of Paul Newman's special sauce. He opens a bottle of Provençal rosé and starts explaining that he has a motorbike for getting around in Paris. Much more 'amusing' than taking the metro, he says. I have to agree. The prospect thrills me—I've never been on a motorbike before. Conversation flows easily over lunch and I realise with a pang of guilt that communicating over the phone in English must have been very difficult for him—hence the awkward silences, the misunderstandings.

It suddenly occurs to me that during our last awful telephone conversation he'd suggested I stay a fortnight and I'd replied emphatically, 'No, really, I'm just coming for a week.' Back then, seven days with a virtual stranger seemed interminably long. But sitting opposite Frédéric in this room full of books and art (I've conveniently forgotten about the dubious comics), my feelings have done another U-turn. Incredible, really, how capricious emotions can be, how quickly fear and doubt can switch to excitement. Now, a different, far more intriguing possibility crosses my mind. A week might not be long enough.

Three

'You can't come to Paris without visiting the Louvre.'
Frédéric is adamant. So am I.

'It's too big. I hate crowds.' For someone who studied Fine
Art at university, my lack of enthusiasm for the world-famous
museum is shameful. But queues and colossal attractions
have always put me off. Just thinking about all there is to see
at the Louvre makes me feel tired.

'We'll keep the visit short, no more than two hours, okay?'
He sounds like a frustrated parent trying to strike a deal with a
recalcitrant child. A couple of hours. That sounds survivable.

'Okay.'

We begin in the sculpture galleries, among mythical men
with bunched muscles and graceful maidens in draping
robes. You have to stop yourself from reaching out and touching their smooth hands, the supple folds in their clothes, so
skilfully have they been rendered. Light pours abundantly
through glass ceilings, dancing on the marble figures. The
rooms burst with lyrical beauty and brightness. I love it here.
I want to stay.

But Frédéric hustles me up an escalator, along some
corridors and in an instant we're surrounded by crowded can-
vases of alarming dimensions. Chariots charge through the
air, cherubs somersault from skies, young kings dress for war,

breasts burst randomly from tight bodices. There is too much melodrama in the Rubens room to take it all in.

But there is no relief in sight. From here we enter an interminable stretch of galleries devoted to death and devastation. Mary sobs at the feet of Christ. Foaming seas capsize boats. Men are impaled on lances, corpses rot, battle scenes and severed heads swim in blood. Catastrophes blur before my eyes. I start to feel tired.

Frédéric, on the other hand, is becoming more and more engrossed. Entering a room of Flemish paintings, his expression elevates to rapt elation. To me these bleak landscapes are only marginally less depressing than what we've just seen. But to Frédéric—who grew up in northern France right next to Flanders—they represent his roots. He calls me over to a painting of thundery skies and foggy fields.

'Look, Sarah,' he raves. 'Can't you see the poetry in the damp, dark earth?'

I need air. I need to sit down. My stamina has been heroic but you have to recognise your limits (one hour, twenty-seven minutes). We take a break at Café Marly overlooking I.M. Pei's glass pyramid. An apathetic, handsome waiter in a smart suit eventually brings us two glasses of *kir*. The terrace has a glamorous, exclusive feel—partly because the staff treat you as though you're incredibly lucky to be here. I certainly feel lucky to be here. For me, the visit has been salvaged. I perk up enormously, knowing all that exhausting art is somewhere safely beneath my feet.

'That was great,' I say.

'What?'

'The Louvre. I really enjoyed it.'

Frédéric stares at me, baffled. 'You mean it's finished— you don't want to go back in?'

I'm baffled too. 'You mean you do?'

Until now, everything has been going very smoothly during our first few days together. Sure, we've had a few minor misunderstandings but nothing that has led to conflict. Just the sort of incidents that deepen complicity and quickly become sources of jokes and teasing. For example yesterday, when I'd complimented Frédéric on his 'olive' skin he'd looked confused but didn't say anything. This morning, after stewing over it all night, he demanded an explanation. 'Why did you say I was green?' he asked, his tone slightly indignant. I burst out laughing.

After I'd explained it was actually a compliment we started talking about the vagaries of the English language. Frédéric finds it difficult, full of exceptions to rules and words that sound confusingly similar. He made up sentences to illustrate his point. 'The *poodle* stepped in a *puddle*.' 'I *hunt ants* with my *aunt*.' Peeved by the thoughtlessness of the language, he kept repeating the suspect words. 'Hunt. Aunt. Ant. They sound exactly the same!' For the next half hour I tried to teach him the aspirated 'h' and the subtle phonetic difference between 'poodle' and 'puddle'. In vain. The English lesson ended in peals of laughter.

But my indifference for the magnificent Louvre is not a laughing matter, it seems. Incomprehension is etched on Frédéric's face. Chatting on the lovely terrace, our different attitudes to the Louvre reveal a wider culture gap.

'I've been going to museums since I was four,' he states. 'They were the highlight of family holidays. Whenever we arrived in a new town the first thing my parents did was take us to an art gallery or museum.'

'Weren't you bored?'

'Oh no, I loved it,' Frédéric enthuses. 'I found it interesting.'

'Kids in France must be a lot different from kids in Australia.' And I describe our family holidays when my parents took my brother and sister and me camping—not in camp grounds but usually in the bush, near lakes, rivers or beaches. The action-packed days waterskiing and swimming, the myriad, mindless ways we would amuse ourselves in water for hours on end. I describe how we'd cook over campfires, how we'd carefully shake our T-shirts or shoes—anything that had been lying on the ground—before putting them on. He is captivated, and I realise with surprise that to him my holidays sound exotic, dangerous even. He asks lots of questions about sharks, snakes and spiders. And why do I say 'the' bush if there are many bushes? I smile at his mental picture of a dry, barren continent inhabited by a valiant, solitary shrub. Overlooking the spectacular glass pyramid, we laugh at the sharp contrast between our childhood holidays: that while one of us was trailing maturely through museums the other was in serious sibling competition to see who could keep their balance longest standing on a floating Lilo. And so our disagreement over the Louvre is swept aside by the flow of conversation. But that moment of mutual incomprehension had allowed us to get to know each other a little better and I don't think either of us had forgotten it.

On previous visits to the French capital I'd rocketed up the Eiffel Tower and climbed the Arc de Triomphe and the stairs to Sacré Cœur. But with Frédéric as my guide, we mostly avoid the main monuments, spinning around them on the motorbike so that they seem merely a stunning backdrop to our adventures. Instead we revel in details. He takes me to the Marais, pointing out the dark, sculpted doorways and quaint, crooked shop fronts. He indicates the engraved plaques on façades announcing that Colette lived in the apartment above, or that on this spot in August 1944 three members of the French Resistance were shot by German soldiers. I soak up these fragments of history.

Simple discoveries seem extraordinary. Like the lovely private courtyards sealed from the street by thick wooden doors. Although at night you need the door codes to go in, during work hours you can enter by simply pressing the shiny silver buttons which are usually to the right of the entrance. One day during a stroll around the Left Bank we pass a particularly imposing, ornate entry. Although it looks resolutely closed and inaccessible, when Frédéric pushes the button the door unlocks with a soft clicking sound. It's so massive we have to lean on it with all our body weight before it creaks open and we step into a leafy courtyard: an oasis of cool calm after the street noise and heat. Virginia creeper tumbles down the walls. These apartments were for nobles, Frédéric explains, pointing to the towering arched entranceway we came through which was built big enough for carriages. He indicates the mansard roof, the tall windows whose many square panes are artisanal and dimpled and so different from modern glass with its glossy sheen. Looking through them we can see high moulded ceilings. It all seems so refined. 'L' élégance française,' Frédéric says, explaining that the essence of French elegance lies in the balance of romance and restraint.

It is August and every self-respecting Parisian has already fled to a crowded coastline. The city is full of tour groups and coaches. Seeing them only makes me more grateful for my personal guide: a Frenchman letting me in on the secrets. Who cares if his motorbike is an unglamorous old Honda? Certainly not me. Now ordinary outings are exhilarating. To

Frédéric, obeying road rules is only for the uncreative and we hurtle onto pavements, tackle one-way streets the wrong way, weaving wildly among traffic, alert and alive. Most thrilling of all is riding at night when millions of winking lights wake the city's monuments. The Eiffel Tower loses its metallic flatness and glows a lovely amber. Illuminated from within, the glass pyramid at the Louvre looks like a giant Scotch on ice.

I guess the circumstances are perfect for falling in love. Every skidding stop on the motorbike, each intimate garden, every candlelit café terrace conspires to spark romance. But is it the scene, the city or the man I'm succumbing to? A combination of all three? These questions don't even enter my mind. Who cares when it's all so much fun. Yes, I admit, I'm carried away on a kaleidoscope of clichés straight out of a trashy romance novel. It is magic.

One evening we go for a stroll along the Pont des Arts, whose looping iron arches connect the Louvre with the gleaming gilt domes of the Institut de France. A *bateau-mouche* steams towards us on the river below, its deck crowded with waving tourists. The colours and light are Monetesque—smudged golden-pink skies and soft violet shadows. Now I see why artists and writers have compared Paris light to champagne. The evening air does have an effervescent quality. On the *quai* below, couples fall into each other's arms. I don't think I've ever seen such a meltingly romantic setting.

But Frédéric's thoughts are not on romance. He is beginning to wheeze, a signal he's about to say something he finds hysterically funny. 'I would really love one day to stand here and peess on the boats,' he cackles, pretending to wave his willy at the unsuspecting families enjoying their river cruise. 'Imagine, all those poor tourists, nowhere to run or hide!' He turns to see whether I've got the joke. 'It would be so funny, no?'

Well yes, I mean I guess. Sort of. I smile vaguely. Evidently the Gallic powers of seduction are somewhat unpredictable. Unpredictable is good, of course—up to a point. But his joke takes me by surprise. Its bawdiness seems at odds with the refined appearance of the man who cracked it. Just as those comics weirdly contrasted with his shelves of highbrow books, it is hard now to reconcile the two images. Is this typically French, I wonder, this mix of culture and schoolboy coarseness? The romantic moment ricochets into the night.

By the time Sue arrives at the end of the week, I've forgotten all about needing a chaperone. My early fears about the French 'maniac' now seem neurotic. Frédéric had laughed when I confessed my panic a few days ago. He thought it was hysterical that Sue was supposed to be my lifeline in case he turned out to be psycho. The situation seemed to appeal to his imagination: he sensed comic potential. 'Let's play a practical joke on her,' he'd urged. 'I'll pretend I've taken you prisoner, that I am *maniac* after all. Let's tie you up in the cellar so that when she arrives . . .'

By now I'm getting familiar with his warped sense of humour. The way it pops up when you're least expecting it. This idea had to be quickly and firmly squashed.

'No.'

Sue and I have been friends from the age of thirteen, when we started high school together in baggy green tunics and brown stockings. She is the sort of person who can make you laugh with her sharp wit or just by clowning around and pulling stupid faces. In the past, boyfriends have occasionally felt uncomfortable about our closeness, not sure how much one has told the other (everything), not always liking their place in the general scheme of things when the two of us are together. She'll be gagging with curiosity about the Frenchman. Maybe she's worried I've lost my head. Maybe I have.

I'm a bit nervous as we sit down to our first dinner together as a trio. It's important to me that Sue likes him. Frédéric is relaxed, apparently delighted to meet my closest friend. He is affectionate and attentive towards me, leaning over every so often to brush my cheek or hand. Then, to my horror, he starts telling Sue about his planned joke.

'I proposed to tie Sarah in the cellar,' he begins. 'Like a prisoner. Naked, yes, naked.' He is chortling and embellishing as he goes along. 'Imagine your face when you saw her! All your worries come true. You would have thought I was so weird!' He pronounces this 'weed'. 'Yes, the Weed Frenchie!'

I am mortified. What will she make of him? After all, they've only just met and now here he is swinging through the civilised scene with all the subtlety of Tarzan, telling one of his bizarre jokes. Uncharacteristically, Sue seems lost for words. After a moment, she smiles uncertainly and says, 'I think I would have found that a bit upsetting.' There's a pause in the conversation. I feel awkward, wondering what Sue must be thinking. But Frédéric appears entirely oblivious to my embarrassment over his little joke, perfectly at ease with the momentary silence and soon he starts chatting about something else.

By the next day, though, she is won over. Figuring it would be fun for us to have some time on our own, Frédéric has tactfully arranged to leave for the weekend. He is going to northern France to see his father, who has lived alone since the death of Frédéric's mother four years ago. The plan suits

Sue and me perfectly: the truth is I'm dying to have some time alone with her, to tell her about the fantastic past five days. Gallantly, he waves goodbye, leaving us the keys to his apartment, his car, and his wine cellar. We are like pigs in a puddle—our own Paris pad to play in! We splash some syrupy cassis into the bottom of glasses then fill them with white wine from the refrigerator. For the next few hours, we don't move from the sun-soaked lounge.

∽

After farewelling Sue, my first week in Paris draws to an end. It seems to have passed in a flash. When Frédéric returns from northern France the subject of my departure is not broached. A hot spell hits the city, sending temperatures into the low thirties. Cafés cram even more tables and chairs onto pavements creating configurations so serried they would cause an outcry in many other countries. Customers are sandwiched in like sardines, elbows sticking into neighbours' ribs, cigarettes practically taking out eyes as they're waved through the air. No-one complains; obviously they're used to it. The atmosphere in Paris is surprisingly Mediterranean. Nobody seems to be working—not even the few remaining Parisians who've heroically stayed behind to keep the country running. The days are incredibly long and night doesn't fall until almost eleven. Only then do we stop meandering or vacate our bench in a pocket-sized park to look for somewhere outside to eat. Miraculously my stomach clock has adjusted: in Sydney if I didn't have dinner by about eight I'd be starving.

Amid the close clamour of café terraces, we discover more about each other and the places we come from. Statements that seem matter-of-fact to one of us can seem absolutely extraordinary to the other. Like the evening I happened to mention the words 'school' and 'fun' in the same sentence. Frédéric pounced on this absurd impossibility straightaway.

'You mean you had fun at school?'

I thought about it. The secondary school I went to was a privileged private one in tree-lined Canberra. Although it was not all games and gaiety, the image that immediately sprang to mind was of sitting on the grass in the sunshine with our lunch sandwiches. 'Yeah, we did have fun, I guess. I mean not every day. But I have lots of good memories.' As I described the green playing fields, the sports carnivals, drama and music classes and the well-equipped art room, his disbelief grew. It took some explaining for him to grasp the concept of Friday afternoon 'Extra Activities', when lessons would stop for students to pursue the activity of their choice—anything from car maintenance and bush walking to life drawing.

'Is it *serious*? I mean did you get a serious education with so much pleasure?' he asked sceptically. I laughed.

'Serious enough, I guess. Why, what was your school like?'

A cheerless, dark brick building with few windows, apparently. The asphalt playground was tiny, speared by two sickly chestnut trees which were the only vaguely green things on the premises. It was a private Catholic school and the priests practised tough discipline. Sport was condensed to a weekly hour of gymnastics. There were no drama classes, no public speaking and debating. Art lessons were taken by the maths teacher and after the first year of secondary school they stopped altogether. Creativity and imagination were considered frivolous.

'The only subject that counted was maths,' he rued. 'It's the same all over France. And I was very bad at it. It didn't matter that I was good at French, history and philosophy. If you're bad at maths, you're considered stupid. For a long time after, I felt bad because of it.'

I was floored. Coming from a man who has a doctorate in law this complex seemed inconceivable. I was crap at maths, too, I told him. And I couldn't have cared less. Maths was for swats. No teacher ever made me feel dim because of my lack of aptitude. But despite his unhappy memories, Frédéric also expressed pride in the French education system, the Republican principles which oblige every student to study the same texts with the goal of ensuring a common foundation and equal opportunity. Perhaps his schooling *was* more 'serious', as he put it—at least in subjects like history, philosophy and classical literature. But our discussion made me glad for the fun I had, grateful to the god of good fortune that I never had to struggle through anything as laborious as Kant's *Critique of Pure Reason*.

One evening towards the end of my second week, an old friend of Frédéric's calls. When he gets off the phone he is beaming. The friend and his family are staying in their summer cottage in Allier, a region in the centre of France, apparently. Frédéric must have told him about me because the invitation extends to the two of us. We've been asked to join them.

Hurtling down the A10 autoroute in his car, Frédéric gives me some background on where we'll be spending the next six days. Allier is a sparsely populated, rural region. It's really *la France profonde*, he says, explaining this is a loaded expression which refers to the mythic rural idyll that the French still consider the true essence of their country. The house where we'll be staying is little more than a pile of old stones. His friend is . . . He pauses. Unable to find the right words in English, Frédéric switches to French. *Un vrai personnage*. A real character. Four hours later, we arrive at the village of Saint-Léon where we stop at the little stone church as arranged, waiting for Jean-Michel to show us the route.

A few minutes later a dodgy-looking truck rattles straight for us. It has barely skidded to a stop when a bear-like bloke leaps out, bellowing at the trail of kids and dogs that tumble out after him. Before I can breathe *bonjour,* two massive hands clamp my face, practically lifting me off my feet. Loud, smacking kisses land on either cheek, amidst a babble of French endearments—*ma petite puce, ma poulette.* My little flea, my baby hen. Then Frédéric disappears in a huge hug, which is followed by more kisses and affectionate backslapping. 'What are these ridiculous things?' teases Jean-Michel, tickling his friend's neatly trimmed sideburns. 'You look like a bloody Parisian!'

It would be difficult to imagine a more unlikely pair. They strike a comical, Laurel-and-Hardy contrast: Frédéric, somehow chic in a shirt and shorts, alongside Jean-Michel, who on this day is exposing half his bottom. A white belly pokes between slipping shorts and a filthy, ripped T-shirt. While Frédéric smells lightly of Davidoff aftershave, Jean-Michel's personal aroma is flavoured by ripe armpits. Showering is something he does on Sundays.

They've known each other since they were fourteen and their friendship is as solid as ever, even though one has chosen to pursue a career in the capital working for a large law firm, the other a serene existence as deputy mayor of a quiet village in northern France. While Frédéric's lifestyle is rushed and urban, Jean-Michel has ample time for hunting and fishing. In France, the friends you make at school remain mates for life. You're bound by a shared past and in this country, it seems history is everything.

The house sits at the end of a potholed track overlooking a gentle valley sprinkled with cows so content and motionless they look as though they've been painted on the landscape. Empty and abandoned when Jean-Michel bought it, the former farmhouse has recently been subject to some erratic restoration. The toilet, I note in dismay, has no door and looks straight onto the dining table. Chortling, Jean-Michel promises to erect a curtain for the 'soft Parisians'.

For me, *la France profonde* is like sliding back fifty years in time. Allier has a rough-hewn authenticity: its villages are charming but devoid of the postcard prettiness which draws tourists. The boxy silhouettes of Citroën *deux chevaux* wobble gamely along skinny roads edged with poplar trees. Jean-Michel says the region is pretty much undiscovered, although to his chagrin, a neighbouring farm was recently sold to Parisians. (To Jean-Michel, all Parisians are pretentious snobs.) They plan to restore the place and use it as a holiday house.

I can understand why. It's so peaceful here. There are similarities between the way Australians and the French view their rural regions, I discover on this holiday. In both countries, the land is a powerful element in the national psyche. And as in Australia, in France youth are fleeing rural areas for cities and many villages are dying. But listening to Frédéric and Jean-Michel, it's clear there are also fundamental differences. There is a gentleness to the French countryside that contrasts starkly with the rural idyll I'm familiar with—the mythic outback.

For the French, the countryside is a vital refuge. They snatch time there whenever possible, as though they still haven't fully adapted to the idea of city living. Every French person dreams of retiring to the countryside, Frédéric tells me. On weekends, his Parisian friends flee to family houses in the provinces. But for most Australians the outback is an awesome, unforgiving place. You go there to be over- whelmed, for adventure, not to relax. Many of us know it only from books or films—rarely from sweet childhood holi- days. The outback might fascinate and inspire us, it might have shaped our national identity, but it's hard to imagine Sydney-siders rushing to buy second homes in Bourke or Broken Hill.

There are seven people (plus a dog and a slovenly cat) squashed into the two-bedroom cottage—us, Jean-Michel, his wife Nathalie, their kids Louis and Natacha and then ten- year-old Victoria from Ukraine. The family is looking after her following an operation in Paris to remove her thyroid gland which was cancerous as a result of the Chernobyl nuclear accident. Her presence underlines the generosity of our hosts, who are not loaded with money. With its frayed, sagging couches, paneless windows and lack of hot water, the house gives new meaning to the word rustic. But it radiates gaiety and convivial disorder, and perhaps because I'm used to roughing it camping, I feel right at home. Frédéric and I sleep on sofa cushions on the floor of the lounge. Jean- Michel and Nathalie speak some English and patiently explain the jokes or entire conversations I've missed. But there is no standing on ceremony for a foreign guest—I'm expected to fit in and lend a hand like everyone else. Which is pretty much how it's always been in my family with friends and visitors.

There are a few culture shocks, though. Jean-Michel, who turns out to be a Gallic version of an Aussie bushman, has an impressive arsenal of knives and guns with which he fre- quently slaughters dinner. Early morning, he heads out to hunt hare and wild boar. By breakfast, the carcasses are stripped to the bone. On several mornings I arrive in the kitchen for croissants and coffee to find it transformed into a bloody battlefield strewn with bright red meat and purple animal organs.

Fascinated, I watch him make chunky terrine using an old-fashioned, labour-intensive meat grinder. Why not use a modern mincer? Delighted to have an interested audience, Jean-Michel sets down his tools. His face is a pantomime of professorial patience. 'Ecoute poulette,' he begins importantly. The ensuing explanation includes many unfamiliar words but with the help of his hand gestures I eventually understand that electric mixers crush the meat into nothing, whereas with traditional hand grinders the meat retains its structure, its fibres and full flavour.

In a blackened fire oven beneath the stairs Jean-Michel bakes oval loaves of crusty bread. We scour bushy banks of quiet lanes for blackberries to make jam. He pours the crimson cascade into old-fashioned glass pots and seals them with wax. 'La méthode traditionnelle,' he beams, wiping berry-stained hands on his T-shirt.

Under Jean-Michel's tutelage, my French acquires personality. Instead of a 'verre de vin' (glass of wine) he teaches me the slangy, untranslatable expression 'coup de pif'. Around the table, they talk 'cul'—which literally means 'bum' but in colloquial language refers to sex jokes. A lot of the time I'm content to listen and observe, transfixed by the array of expressions which scud across their faces. I'd always assumed Gallic characters in films were wildly exaggerated. Mais non! Here they are Oh-la-la-ing, pouting to show doubt or disagreement, shrugging in resignation or indifference. They are natural ham actors, embellishing their own stereotypes to such effect that a simple dinner conversation looks like performance.

On our second last day we go to buy cheese from a nearby farm. The owners don't look very different from some of the people I met in rural Romania. He has a mouth of gold and black gaps; she wears an old-fashioned, floral smock, her abbreviated legs plugged into gum boots. Our request for cheese sparks a hum of excitement. What looks very much like an argument breaks out but in fact it's only a lively discussion—emphatic hand gestures and raised voices are standard features of conversation in *la France profonde*, apparently. Eventually, we're led into a barn, where through the dimness I can just make out bird cages containing small, pale discs. We gather around the goats' cheese, heads shaking at the *mauvais temps* which has produced a lot of *vers*. There is a lot of heavy sighing happening and it seems appropriate to join in, although I have absolutely no idea what they're talking about.

Later, the source of their concern becomes all too apparent. Poised to slice into a *chèvre* on my plate, I notice the rind is wriggling with maggots. Unphased, Jean-Michel is shaving off his crawling crust. Revulsion rises in my throat and I try to overcome it, not wanting to offend. No-one else appears shocked. And so I copy Jean-Michel, telling myself that I've eaten worse. Once, in northern New South Wales where I'd gone to do a television report, a group of Aboriginal kids presented me with a six-centimetre long, raw witchetty grub. Bush tukka, they'd giggled, bright eyes daring me. My weak, white, urban sensibilities were on trial and it would have looked bad to refuse, I'd thought. The liquid explosion in my mouth had almost made me retch.

I wipe some cheese onto my bread and bite.

The table erupts in peals of delighted laughter. It had been a test, and quite unwittingly I'd passed with flying colours. In fact, except for Jean-Michel, the others had been feeling squeamish just contemplating the plate. But used to foreigners wrinkling their noses at pungent, unpasteurised French cheeses, my new friends are immensely flattered by this gullible show of gameness. It's as though I have just leapt on the table and delivered a rousing rendition of *La Marseillaise*. *Anyone willing to eat wormy chèvre must be okay*, read their expressions. Even Jean-Michel is impressed. 'An American would never had done that,' he remarks admiringly.

❧

By the time we return to Paris, the gloriously long days are getting noticeably shorter. There is a sense of something reaching an inevitable end—and not just summer. Everything seems to herald change, the new crispness in the evening air, the shrinking queues, the city streets. The tourists with their shorts and cameras have been replaced by purposeful people with caramel tans and bright highlights in their hair. Parisians. Back from their holidays for the September start of the school and working year, known as *la rentrée*.

These changes seem to be a sign. Having already stayed far longer than I'd intended, my holiday in France is over too. I can't keep prolonging my departure. Besides, Frédéric is about to go back to work. It's time to hoist my backpack and pick up my travel plans: back to London, then Greece, then on to Turkey where Sue will fly over and meet me and from there perhaps an overnight bus back to Bucharest.

Everything seems to have happened so quickly. In one month, my relationship with Frédéric has shifted from holiday romance to something more serious. In retrospect, right from that second night in Bucharest I think I sensed that given half a chance it would. But now this seismic shift has occurred I feel the need to slow down the pace. To take some distance. A few weeks ago I'd felt carefree and unconcerned. Everything had seemed crystal clear—I was in Paris and in love! But our wonderful holiday together has raised the possibility of a commitment—and with it confusing questions about my future. *Do I want to live in France? What if I take the plunge and stay and then everything with Frédéric falls apart?* All clarity is clouded by a sudden premonition of the complications involved in letting this relationship run its course. As my departure day looms I become increasingly impatient to go.

Frédéric takes me to Gare du Nord station. My train will stop at Calais, connecting with a ferry to Dover, where I'll catch a bus to London. His face is long. At least I have my travels to look forward to, whereas he has only work. We talk about meeting up in the near future for a long weekend in London or maybe Istanbul. This is not really a goodbye, we reassure each other. But there is a poignancy to the moment, reflected in the clamour of comings and goings, the hurried movement all round us, the huge, hangar-like space which makes us feel tiny and uncertain.

As the train glides smoothly forward, I turn over my shoulder for one last wave. Frédéric stands on the platform, arm stretched high in the air. He stays like that for about thirty seconds, perfectly still, until the track curls away from the station and he disappears from view.

Several weeks later I'm a world away from Paris, stretched

across four seats on an overnight ferry which is cruising towards the far-eastern edge of Europe. The boat docks at the Greek island of Samos, which nudges—rather tensely—the Turkish coast. After a couple of hot days in Vathi, the main port, I take a bus to the pine- and oak-forested hills skirting Mount Ampelos. The sun beats on my back as I wind through orchards and vineyards, trying to follow a walking trail marked by contradictory arrows and the occasional mad map. Eventually, I arrive at the gleaming white, mountain village of Vourliotes, tired and sweaty.

The scene is surreal. Thousands of kilometres from home, plunged in the middle of nowhere, I suddenly step into what looks like a giant Australian souvenir shop dropped into a Greek setting. Children run playfully past, with koalas, kangaroos and 'I love Australia' splashed on their T-shirts. The local taverna is waving an Australian flag. In the shade, elderly men play a card game at the sort of pace which suggests they might take the rest of their lives to finish it. One of them has 'I've surfed Bondi Beach' emblazoned across his chest.

A charming, chatty villager solves the mystery. After the Second World War, much of the community emigrated to Australia. Over the years, some family members have returned. Most of them no longer know where to call home, the inhabitant explains. His own Australian-born children are studying to be lawyers and teachers. To them, Sydney is home. But for him, the choice is not so simple. Now in his fifties, with every passing year the pull of his village among the vines grows stronger. His life is a constant dilemma: in Australia he feels Greek; in Greece he feels Australian.

'It's a bitter–sweet thing, knowing two cultures,' he sighs. 'Once you leave your birthplace nothing is ever the same.'

The man stares at the glittering turquoise cradling the coast, thinking of his kids at the opposite end of the earth.

'It's a curse to love two countries.' He smiles wryly at his own melodramatic words. But there is sadness in his eyes.

Unable to relate to his experience, I can only sympathise in a limited sort of way. Besides, I'm in no mood for dark thoughts. A few days from now, I'll be meeting Sue in Istanbul. In the bursting sunlight, sucking in the island's jasmine-scented air, the future seems full of promise.

I had no idea then how radically my life was about to change and how well I would come to understand what the Greek had said.

Four

I return to Paris, of course. The way I see it, there is really no alternative.

After four months of travelling, I know only one thing with absolute certainty: if I don't go to France—and I mean to try to make a life there with Frédéric—I might regret it forever. I'll always be wondering about the love of my life that could have been, the entirely different future that might have been if only I'd taken the risk. Sure, there's no guarantee that it'll work out, but then *nothing ventured, nothing gained*. All I know is a chance encounter has thrown open an unexpected door. Instinct tells me to step through it.

On a winter's day in January under a watery sun, my plane touches down at Charles de Gaulle airport. Once again I'm struck by the ambivalent appearance of the place. I wonder if this rundown spaceship is a sort of metaphor for France; if this country is in some respects ultramodern and sophisticated yet in other ways behind the times. But a couple of things are different from my arrival here last summer. The weather, for starters. And this time Frédéric's punctual! Waiting for me with a spare, thick woolly jumper because it's an especially cold day and he's worried I'll freeze outside. We met up for only one weekend in the last four months but we spoke a lot over the phone and

gradually going to Paris had come to seem like the only sensible solution. There'd been no talk of whether I'll give it two
months, six months, or a year. Like many life-changing decisions, the move to Paris was decided with little thought for
the consequences. I am totally ignorant of what lies in store.

Frédéric is not the sole reason for staying on in Europe,
though. The truth is, I'm not *ready* to go home. And feeling
ready is hugely important when your country is so far away
from the rest of the world. No Australian or New Zealander
wants to end their working holiday in London only to be
haunted later by the thought of unlived adventures. Because
once you go all the way back, you're there to stay, goes the
logic. Oh sure, you'll travel and go abroad again but future
trips will not stretch towards infinity like this one, they won't
contain so many possibilities. Heading home is the fullstop
marking the end of adventure; the beginning of a responsible
life. And despite twelve months of travelling, I am not ready
to be responsible.

The television network I worked for in Sydney had given
me one year leave without pay from my job. Sitting at the
dining table of what is now my new home, I write to say I'm
not coming back. This is not an especially difficult decision.
I'd spent five good years at the Special Broadcasting Service,
the national television network set up to serve Australia's
ethnic communities. But now, in my late twenties, I'm wary
of getting stuck in a professional rut. The time seems right to
take a risk. In my mind, Europe is simmering with exciting
opportunities for a journalist. It's just a matter of finding them.

Still, the prospect of living in France is daunting. I have
no job, no friends here and I barely speak the language.
Frédéric and I are living together after little more than
a month in each other's company—by any reasonable

standards a ridiculously short time for such a serious move. This recklessness is both scary and sort of exciting. It's also totally out of character—in Australia I'd have thought this was mad, shacking up before the relationship has even got off the ground. What a recipe for disaster! But risks seem less alarming in a new and foreign environment where you can't measure your behaviour by familiar yardsticks such as family or friends or society in general. Besides, it's not like we have another option. Even if I had enough money (which I don't), renting my own apartment would be almost impossible. Having entered the country as a tourist, strictly speaking I'm not allowed to remain in France longer than three months.

But none of this can dampen my overriding feeling that somehow all of this is *right*: Frédéric; being in France; taking a professional risk. The lack of certainty only seems to underline new possibilities. The challenges ahead seem surmountable. Frédéric doesn't seem worried by any of it, not even my lack of a long-stay visa which he shrugs off as a detail that will be resolved, somehow. Buoyed by his confidence, I too am optimistic.

It takes me a few days to adapt to this new, wintry Paris. It's totally different from the sunny holiday city I fell in love with last summer. Gone are the café terraces, the dewy glasses of *kir* and Sancerre. By four in the afternoon, darkness has swallowed the day. The cold weather heightens the appeal of cafés and restaurants, whose glowing interiors contrast with the exterior greyness. On my first Sunday, we resume our habit of strolling around the city. In the smart St-Germain district we stop at Les Deux Magots—a Paris institution, Frédéric explains, where Hemingway once hung out.

Inside, it is lovely and warm, with luminous mirrors,

creamy walls and velvety crimson curtains. The crowd is diverse. A young fellow opposite is reading with a certain fervour, his impenetrable concentration something of a feat among the gossip and frisbeeing drinks trays. Staring, I see his large, thin book is actually sheet music: he must be a musician or a composer. In a corner, an elegant, cigar-smoking gentleman taps away on a lap-top computer. A writer, Frédéric guesses. The area was once full of them but soaring rents mean that starving poets and artists have long since shifted to neighbourhoods in the city's east. At a nearby table, a group of sleek girls with solarium suntans sit down. They're carrying bouquets of shopping bags and their leather jackets come in luscious ice-cream tones—cappuccino, chocolate and deep raspberry. St-Germain has become a haven for luxury boutiques. At another table Japanese tourists make shy attempts at hailing a waiter. Maybe they were hoping to soak up a vestige of the bygone intellectual era. Or maybe they came to shop.

At Frédéric's insistence we order hot chocolates—the speciality of the *maison*, he promises. It arrives in two steaming white jugs and you can tell just from the smell that this is an intense brew made with cream and *couverture* chocolate. We fill our cups. The liquid pours slowly like an oil slick of dark, molten mousse. I take a mouthful—and nearly die of pleasure. Every other hot chocolate I've ever tasted suddenly seems like a powdery imitation. I marvel at the French *art de vivre*: their civilised attitude towards consumption. They know how to indulge in a cigarette without guilt, a glass of wine at lunch or a cake without counting calories. In the middle of this thought stream I happen to glance at the ice-cream-coloured girls: they're drinking slim glasses of sparkling water and bobbing lemon.

When the new week begins I start considering what I'm actually going to do in France. Now that I'm no longer travelling, I'm impatient to establish a routine. I need something to do, I need work. Without it, I'm in limbo—no longer simply a tourist but not a proper resident either. Also, although Frédéric seems totally relaxed about supporting me financially, I am uncomfortable with the idea. I don't want to be dependent. And my cash situation is getting desperate.

Given that I'm not supposed to be in France long-term, working for a French company (at least legally) is out of the question. The only option is to freelance for foreign media. The idea of being autonomous appeals to me enormously but having only ever been a salaried employee, I've no idea how to get started. Frédéric does everything he can to help. A second-hand computer arrives at the apartment, which he bought from our neighbour upstairs who works for a computer company. My stationery supplies soon take on warehouse proportions. Frédéric brings home rainbows of highlighter pens, colour-coded paper files, fancy pencils, notepads, transparent plastic covers, a tower of in and out trays, rows of fat folders and—most ambitious of all—an invoice book to record my future payments. My office takes over the dining room table. Equipped to the eyeballs, I am ready to start. But on what?

I contact a few television networks in Australia but the prospect of regular work looks unpromising. Hiring camera crews in France is too expensive, they tell me. I mull over another idea, one which would mean a new career direction. After leaving Frédéric last summer, I'd continued travelling and eventually returned to Romania in October, partly to see the fun group of friends I'd met there during my first stay but also to work because I needed the cash. It was

41

during this second stay that I wrote a few articles for an English-language business magazine. An Irish journalist living in Bucharest with whom I'd become good friends had put me in contact with the editor in London. It was my first experience of working in print after six and a half years as a television journalist and at first I wondered whether I would be able to do it. Compared to television reports which only ever ran to a few paragraphs, the thought of writing enough to fill two or three magazine pages seemed inconceivable.

My first print story was a profile on an elderly Romanian artist who produced wildly imaginative paintings on glass. Not exactly headline material. And it wouldn't have mattered if I'd made it up, since there were probably no more than six people in the entire world who'd heard of the magazine, let alone ever read it. But I toiled over every word. I loved the novelty of interviewing armed only with a tiny tape-recorder instead of a crew and cumbersome camera equipment and lights. It was so satisfying just concentrating on writing, not having to worry about pictures.

And so in Paris the idea of embarking on a career in print journalism takes hold. It has been one of my dreams for a while now, I realise. I've always loved reading well-written profiles and news features and magazines like *Vanity Fair*. Seeing your byline in a good publication must be such a buzz, I've often thought. Somehow it strikes me as far more thrilling than seeing my face on television. I decide to give freelancing for magazines and newspapers a whirl.

Through the Australian Embassy I consult a media guide which lists the contact details of magazine and newspaper editors in Australia. I also track down a few names in London by calling switchboards. The weeks crawl by in a one-way flood of faxes pitching story proposals to editors who have never heard of me and do not care to, apparently. On a good day, I might receive a polite, negative response to an idea I can barely recall having.

Dear Sarah,
Thank you for your story suggestion. Unfortunately we do not take work from contributors . . .

(Wipe them off the list.)

Dear Sarah,
Thanks for the ideas but they do not suit the magazine . . .

(Honest at least, but not encouraging.)

Dear Sarah,
Thank you for your proposal. Unfortunately we have already commissioned a Paris correspondent to do the same story . . .

(What bad luck! What rotten timing! These replies go straight to the Try Again pile.)

But mostly, my painstakingly worded, desperately upbeat paperwork meets a crushing silence. Responses—even negative ones—are quite rare. *Be patient, it'll take time, something will come off eventually*, I reassure myself as the hours drag by. My days are spent waiting: first for a fax, then later for Frédéric. Parisians don't start work until about 9.30am but they also finish late and he is rarely home before nine. To keep myself busy, I do the grocery shopping and cook dinner. By the time he steps through the door, I am gagging to see him—to see anybody, actually. I need to talk, to off load, to laugh, to have a drink. Each night we open a new bottle of wine, which will be empty by the end of dinner.

Frédéric is extremely supportive. He clips articles from French newspapers that might make potential stories and in the evenings we workshop ideas for me to turn into a fresh battery of proposals. By the time we go to sleep, I feel recharged. But our days are totally out of sync. After a stressful twelve hours at the office, he just wants to unwind at home. I, on the other hand, am itching for a change of scenery, having spent all day at the dining room table. Let's go out for dinner, I sometimes suggest and to cheer me up Frédéric agrees. But usually it's an effort for him. The local restaurants cater for the business lunch crowd and mostly shut at night, and the last thing he feels like is jumping back on the bike and heading into town.

As a full-time employee I used to dream of having abundant spare time, imagining all the ways I could fill it. But now that it's limitless, it doesn't feel like freedom. More like I'm free falling. Some days the sensation is exhilarating and the hours hang before me like opportunities. But mostly I'm praying for the parachute to open, the moment when my feet will plant firmly on the ground.

'*C'est pour offrir, Monsieur?*'

We have stopped to buy flowers for Benoît and Sylvie, which is the done thing in Paris when you're invited to someone's home. My first Parisian dinner party. I don't understand the florist's question, but Frédéric says '*oui, merci*', and then explains to me that she wants to know if the flowers are intended as a gift. The pretty violet and yellow tulips are expertly arranged in a fan and wrapped in clear cellophane lined with lemon tissue paper. Raffia tightly binds it all together. The florist staples her gold card and more wheat-coloured curls to the outside. Although simple, the finished bouquet looks lovely.

But it doesn't stay that way. Flowers and motorbikes don't travel well together—not an altogether astonishing discovery. One hand clinging to Frédéric, the other clutching the tulips, I struggle to shield them but they are whipped and snatched by the bitter wind. Halfway there, we are suddenly pelted with a deluge of hard little rocks which ricochet off our helmets and limbs. Hail. Continuing for a couple of precarious kilometres, we eventually pass beneath a bridge where we shelter until the storm eases.

There are approximately five petals clinging heroically to the tulip stems by the time we reach our destination on the other side of Paris. Ushered inside like a pair of sad, soggy dogs, we are immediately invited to peel off our wet outer layers. Our hosts, apparently accustomed to Frédéric arriving in all sorts of weather-beaten states bearing bouquets of naked stalks, bring us a couple of thick jumpers. Crumpled, frozen and forlorn, I haven't travelled well on the motorbike either. My blue and white hands provoke a volley of 'Oh-la-la's' and 'Ce n'est pas vrai's!' from Sylvie and Benoît. She's got terrible circulation, says Frédéric—the expert explaining the exhibit. Sylvie pulls a pair of ski gloves from a dusty cupboard. I enter the sitting room like a bedraggled boxer after a fight. How chic! What a style statement I make at my first Parisian dinner party.

To my surprise, none of the other guests looks particularly smart either. Somehow I'd assumed all Parisians were imbued with that amazing style you see in the streets. But the description that springs to mind now is 'neat'. They all look terribly tucked in. The women are mostly dressed in well-cut blazers with skirts or pants, and two of them are wearing headbands. The men all have dark trousers on and wear almost identical shirts—blue with fine white checks or the other way round. I'm introduced to a Nathalie, an Anne, a Caroline. So far so good. But the boys are a barrage of seem-ingly reversible double-barrels. Jean-François, Jean-Luc, Jean-Marc. (Or is it Luc-Jean? François-Jean? Marc-Jean?)

A few of them are lawyers, one's an accountant, Anne works in publishing and Nathalie has a marketing job for a big French group. What surprises me is they don't really look Frédéric's type, these people. In comparison, he seems more youthful, far less formal. I tell myself this is all new: don't judge by appearances.

A tray has been laid with a line-up of alcohol and bowls of nibbles that look like Cheezels and taste like peanut butter. I happen to love Cheezels (and peanut butter) but I'd expected something more sophisticated from the French. Olives, at least, or some fancy pâté on little toasts. Offered a choice of apéritifs, a couple of the guys take whiskey and the rest of us opt for muscat or port, which the French apparently drink before dinner. Pulling off my gloves, I spy two bottles of wine near the dining table. I'd kill for a glass of red but it's obvious they are being saved to have with our meal.

'*Tu es anglaise? Américaine?*'

'*Je suis australienne,*' I manage to reply to the fellow next to me. A faint ripple of interest spreads across the room. Compared to the English and American communities in Paris, the number of Australians is small which makes us more of a curiosity. For French people, Australia looms in their imaginations like a mythical final frontier which they dream of visiting but never will because twenty-three hours in a plane would be *insupportable*. Still, while none of them have ever been there, this group seems pretty well informed about my homeland.

A slim fellow—Jean-Marc or Marc-Jean, at a guess—starts talking about something he read in *Le Monde* concerning the push for Australia to become a Republic. 'Why is Australia still tied to England?' he asks me, puzzled. As a staunch Republican, privately I am delighted for this opportunity to discuss the issue, to shed some light on it for a foreign audience. Taking a deep breath, I summon up my most eloquent French.

'Many want. Some they don't want. The old, for example. But I want.'

There is a buzz of rapid conversation as Frédéric scrambles to elaborate: 'It's just a matter of time . . . Sarah thinks most young Australians . . .'

'But why are you still loyal to the Queen?' pursues my interrogator.

Realising my first answer was hopelessly inadequate, I try to convey some passion.

'No, not true! The Queen, she okay, but not for Australia. Yesterday okay, but not tomorrow.' Pathetically, I look to Frédéric who again steps in to decipher my message. Thank god he was listening when we'd discussed all this last summer. The conversation about the state of affairs in my country continues without me. Jean-Marc-Marc-Jean addresses all further questions to Frédéric. Inside, I fizz with frustration at my inability to communicate. I love these sorts of discussions! Or at least I used to. But it was as though in trying to express myself in another language I'd suddenly plunged fifty IQ points.

For the next ten minutes I try to sink inconspicuously into

the sofa. Then another guest addresses me. Frédéric has to translate what they said.

'He said he's just finished reading *The Songlines*. He wants to know if you've read it.'

In fact I have read Bruce Chatwin's book. And in my own language I'd be delighted to admit it. But saying yes now will only open another Pandora's box. I'll be expected to give an opinion, maybe even asked to comment on the plight of Aborigines, their living conditions or spirituality. I'll only be doing Aborigines and my country an injustice.

'*Non*,' I say to save face.

Sylvie summons us to the table. Everyone hovers, waiting for Benoît to seat us, a process which involves rather a lot of indecision and debate. Only when everyone has been placed do all the guests sit down. The entrée of fish terrine is passed to me first, establishing a pattern that will be followed throughout the dinner. It's as though my foreigner status makes me the honoured guest. I push the platter towards the fellow next to me and he quickly passes it to the next girl, swivelling it expertly so that the serving spoons point in her direction. It conducts two orbits of the table: one for the women, the second for the men. Some people take their time serving themselves, letting the terrine sit in front of them while they finish a conversation. After what seems to me an interminably long wait, at last everyone is served.

The terrine is airy and delicious and I make the mistake of taking two helpings, unaware that four other courses will follow. A rabbit stew with chunks of potato and carrots is served next. It is bursting with flavour and I love the simple way it is served without any accompaniment. Green salad is a separate course. After, a platter of six cheeses is set in front of me and I stare at it nervously, unsure of the correct way to cut the different shapes. Dessert is a rich, layered chocolate cake which looks so perfect it must have come from a fancy shop. By the end of the meal, my trousers are slicing into my waist.

Throughout dinner, Frédéric tries to include me in the conversation, seizing any opening for me to contribute to the discussion: 'Oh your brother works in TV?' he says to his neighbour at one point. 'Sarah used to work in television too.' I am touched and amazed that after my earlier efforts he would encourage me to open my mouth again. But the conversation is mostly too rapid for me to follow, let alone worry about contributing to it. I only catch odd words and phrases. Something about a very 'poetic' book by Marie someone. A joke about De Gaulle which makes everyone laugh, so I do too. Now they're talking about virility and femininity and I'm frustrated not to understand more because this sounds interesting. It's only when they start examining the bottles of Burgundy on the table that it clicks—they're talking about the wine.

The conversation is, frankly, a bit intimidating. Although animated, this dinner is nothing like the garrulous mealtimes with Jean-Michel and his family in Auvergne—it's nothing like any dinner I've ever been to, actually. It seems so *practised*, as though the guests and hosts have spent centuries refining their respective roles, their manners and interjections. They all seem so articulate, so knowledgeable. Apparently it's okay to interrupt because everyone does. If only I could think of something worth saying. What illuminating pronouncements could I add to the wine discussion, for example? *C'est bon. Je l'aime.*

Just after midnight we move from the table to the comfortable chairs in the salon. Sylvie goes into the kitchen to prepare coffees and herbal teas and I wonder why Benoît doesn't do it—he's done nothing all night except seat us and pour the wine. All this smiling and concentrating and feigning avid interest in conversations I can't follow has been exhausting and I'm keen to go. Although surrounded by noise and people I feel apart. Alien.

We finish our teas. But no-one makes a move. For the next hour the guests stay talking. The scene is remarkable for the startling absence of alcohol: the wine dried up after dinner. I'm used to it flowing in reckless, bottomless quantities. It's not a lack of generosity on the part of our hosts—the Burgundies served with dinner were very fine, expensive *crus*. Maybe this is something I'll have to get used to in France: smaller, measured quantities of wine.

Finally, at almost half past one, someone makes a move to go. This seems to be the cue because then everyone stands up and the room fills with a buzz about leaving. Hugely relieved, I leap to my feet too. But the business of farewelling and thanking takes another fifteen minutes. I am astounded—a little impatient too. Why so much procrastinating? Why does everything seem to take ten times longer than it would in Australia?

A few days later, after telephoning to thank his friends for dinner, Frédéric tells me the impression I made.

'They thought you were nice.'

I pull a face. So much for being fabulously interesting or entertaining. 'Didn't they say anything else?'

'Um, no. Just that you seem the quiet type. Shy.'

'SHY?' I bellow in disbelief. 'I'm not shy!'

'But you *were* quiet. Anyway, don't worry about it. It doesn't matter what they think.'

But Frédéric hasn't grasped the measure of my frustration.

Actually, it does matter to me that I'm now perceived as quiet, nice and *boring* (that's not their word but, of course, that's what they meant). And the reason it bothers me is because it's true. Looking back, I'd said very little all night. When I did speak, it was to issue childlike statements or ask simple questions which made me cringe at my own dumbness. Most of the time, Frédéric was the only one actually listening to me — the others had already leaped two topics ahead. Eventually my nerve vaporised into the mushroom cloud of cigar smoke.

Things will be much easier when I can speak French properly, I tell myself. And this is true, of course. But instinctively I sense that language isn't the only problem. I'd felt totally out of place at the dinner. Everyone had been pleasant enough but no-one had been especially warm. In hindsight, even those two guys who'd politely asked questions at the beginning seemed to have done so more out of an intellectual curiosity for my country rather than a desire to get to know me. (Or could it be that this more impersonal approach is how the French show interest in someone?) Fitting in and making friends might be harder than I expected. It seems my first dinner party is a portent.

Five

The long days in the apartment begin to take their toll. After six weeks, my faxed story proposals have elicited either no response or negative ones. Being on my own for so many hours with nothing to do is proving more testing than I anticipated. Although I try to fill my head with upbeat thoughts, I feel lonely.

Realising I'm craving company, Frédéric calls regularly from work and often we arrange to meet near his office for lunch. One day at about one, he turns up unexpectedly at the apartment with some guys from work and a couple of takeaway pizzas topped with runny egg. On their way back to the office after seeing a client, they thought they'd stop and have lunch with me, he explains.

After we've finished eating, Frédéric pats his coat pocket, his eyes skimming the room, searching for something. This is a familiar routine. I now know that when Frédéric told me in Bucharest he was 'maniac' he meant he was obsessively tidy. Keeping everything in perfect order—shirts stacked in a colour-coded pile, the bed neatly made each morning—is his way of restraining his natural disorderliness. But it's as though he's still surprised by his tidy habits. Frédéric can never recall the thoughtful places where he puts things away.

I think I know what he's looking for—one of his pipes. '*Tu veux une pipe?*' I ask.

It takes less than a split second to realise that my question is not quite right. Not right at all, in fact, judging by the four male faces which freeze in surprise before cracking into hooting, helpless laughter. Without even meaning to, I have been fabulously funny. This is my first joke in French—the first time since my arrival that I've managed to make an entire table laugh—and it seems a bit unfair that I don't get it.

'Where can I find an Australian girlfriend?' wheezes one guest, appreciatively.

The French language is full of double entendre. Although toilet humour is considered poor taste in France, sex-related witticisms are acceptable in virtually any social setting. Sustaining linguistic volleys of naughty innuendo is a national sport. Sometimes these word games are subtle and sophisticated. But often the banter is ribald and silly—a bit like Frédéric's joke about peeing off the Pont des Arts. '*Pipe*' is the sort of word which ping-pongs across dinner tables. Although it shares the innocent English meaning, in French it also has a more risqué definition. Had I said *ta* pipe—*your* pipe—it might not have been so funny. But as it is, I have just offered Frédéric a blow job.

Linguistically, let's face it, the relationship is challenged. Progress is measured in small but significant steps. With much practice, Frédéric learns to say SAR-ah, with the stress on the first syllable instead of pronouncing it the French way with even emphasis. But the two 'r's' in his name are problematic. My throat can just about raise a respectable roll for the first but for some reason can't manage it for the second 'r'. 'They're too close together,' I growl ungraciously, as if the consonants have conspired to trip me up. Frédéric becomes Fréd.

Until now we've been speaking mostly English together because my French is limited to conversations I learnt by rote from school textbooks. Thus, I am brilliant at answering the telephone, as long as it is Philippe Ledoux calling to compliment my new red car. I'm also good at flattering someone in a skirt—*mais quelle jolie jupe!* Regrettably, opportunities to use these engaging lines are rare. When it comes to constructing my own sentences—stringing nouns, verbs and adjectives together in an intelligible order—I fall apart.

But my 'pipe' gaffe makes me more determined to improve. What's more, mastering the language will surely help ease my loneliness. And so Frédéric and I vow to speak only French together, a decision which eliminates all possibility of semi-adult conversation. The language remains a mystery to me—a gorgeous, mellifluous gabble which I can listen to forever without identifying where one word ends and the next begins. Those sliding liaisons and smooth syllables, the to-die-for accent and controlled cadence; together they make an incomprehensible verbal stew.

To speed up my progress, I enrol in a month-long French course at Alliance Française whose headquarters lie on Boulevard Raspail in the 6th *arrondissement*. It takes about thirty-five minutes for me to get there by metro because the trip means changing lines at St-Lazare—a manoeuvre involving a mini marathon through pee-scented corridors. The underground labyrinth is filled with surging crowds rushing to work. I love feeling part of them.

The Alliance classes are hugely entertaining. Our *professeur* is a lively brunette with a provocative twinkle and plunging décolleté who clearly understands that we'll probably never differentiate masculine from feminine nouns, let alone grasp the subjunctive. She flirts outrageously with the only male student, an awkward Hugh Grant sort of character with an Oxbridge accent who squirms and blushes under her persistent attention. *'Défends ton bifteck!'* she commands, urging us to argue our viewpoints in class debates. Argue? We can barely make ourselves understood in our awful, halting French.

Upon learning our discussion subject for day five, eleven backs suddenly straighten. This is far more fascinating than the imperfect or the imperative. As usual, the teacher starts the class by tossing us a topic. Today it's 'What Would You Do If You Walked in on Your Partner in Bed with a Lover?' Made up of mostly English and Americans, the class erupts in a babble of unanimous indignation. Such betrayal would end the relationship. No question — the erring other half would be out on his or her arse. There's a lot of girls' talk about lopping off male body parts.

'Ah, *les anglo-saxons! Vous êtes tellement puritains!'* The *prof* is delighted by the quaint naiveté of our moral right-eousness. The French don't bother with such hypocrisy, she explains. They understand affairs put the frisson into mar-riage. In France, everyone seduces everyone — *la séduction* is the essential spice to life. Why do we think village shops shut tight for three hours at lunch? She winks wickedly at Hugh Grant. 'So the butcher can sleep with the baker's wife and the florist can seduce the *fromager.'*

Although my French improves only marginally, the course is a huge success. There are some fun students in the class and afterwards we sometimes go out for a coffee and a chat. Most of them are only in Paris temporarily, though, and one by one these new friends soon leave. But the greatest thing about my French course is that for one whole month I have something to do.

∾

'I thought you were living in Paris. Then I saw your postcode on the back of the envelope . . .'

This innocent observation in a letter from a Sydney friend comes as a complete shock. Two months have passed since my arrival and all this time I too thought I lived in Paris. It had never occurred to me that Frédéric's apartment lay beyond the *périphérique* ring road which neatly separates the city from the sprawling suburbs. The rapid fifteen-minute motorbike ride into town had made me assume we were part of the fabulous capital.

It might sound mad but this revelation makes me look at our neighbourhood differently. It provides a concrete explanation for niggling doubts I'd begun to have about Levallois—feelings which until now had been only abstract, nothing I could articulate. All this spare time on my hands doesn't help matters, naturally. During long days alone, I dwell on my doubts and they flourish under my attention. They give me something to do; a focus. No wonder living here wasn't turning out to be the Parisian dream life I'd envisaged—it's not even Paris! My friend is right. When it comes to Paris there is no middle ground—you're either in or you're out. Slowly the truth sinks in: we are two metro stops too far.

It occurs to me my friend may be right about another thing. In Paris, postcodes matter. Whereas in Sydney they are purely functional, their purpose simply to ensure mail ends up in the right place, here they're evocative and, yes, even romantic. Paris postcodes begin with 75 and end in one of the twenty *arrondissements*, or numbered districts which spiral out clockwise from the city centre. These last figures are numerical indicators loaded with information and significance. The final five in 75005 conjures up nostalgic images of smoky student cafés full of Audrey Hepburn look-a-likes and dark brooding boys. The 8th *arrondissement* signals pomp and palaces, smart business lunches and famous French fashion houses. Neighbouring 75016 is all about poodle parlours and stiff cocktail parties with caviar canapés. The four in 75004 transports you to the ancient village streets lined with gay bars and Jewish bakeries in the vibrant Marais quarter.

But 92300—our postcode—is a numerical no-man's-land. Like the area it designates, it is devoid of magic and sex appeal, sandwiched between Paris and the luxurious mansions and modern apartments of nouveau-riche Neuilly-sur-Seine. Levallois is lovely and leafy. It is also dull. There are no lively cafés, no decent restaurants open at night. At first I'd thought the area was fabulously multicultural, a hotbed of mixed marriages. During the day the sidewalks are crowded with African and Asian mothers pushing prams. But then it clicked—these women are not related to their pale-faced charges. They are nannies, or *nounous* as the French call them. The real parents can be seen after school finishes on Saturday, loading children and dogs into cars, off to family homes in the Loire or Normandy.

Frankly, if I'd wanted trees and blond Labradors that badly, I would have headed home to Sydney's North Shore. What I want is to live in one of those old white apartment buildings run by a grumbling concierge, round the corner from a crowded café where I could read the newspaper each morning while the barman banters with a regular line-up of red-wine raconteurs. Nearby, there'd be a couple of trusted bistros serving melting *chèvre chaud* at lunch, heart-warming *cassoulet* for dinner. I want to step out my front door and be amid the buzz, the bohemian poets, the brasseries, the bums, the crooked boutiques, the achingly beautiful window displays, the chic *mesdames* with spaghetti legs and neurotic terriers. In short, I want to live in Paris.

It's the suburban inertia of Levallois that creates the first tension between Frédéric and me. Although pretty in a well-maintained, middle-class sort of way, for me, cooped up in the apartment day after day, Levallois starts to seem like a prison. The city centre is a twenty-minute metro ride away—longer if you have to change lines—and so it's not something you do for a quick coffee. I feel stranded and that only exacerbates my loneliness.

But for Frédéric, Levallois is a refuge. After all, he has an office to escape to, one that is conveniently located ten minutes away in the modern business district of La Défense. 'We're lucky,' he insists. 'We're so close to the city centre and yet we can wake up and hear birds singing every morning.' He doesn't understand my frustration with where we live. Before moving to Levallois he spent ten years in Paris and although he loves the city, he is stubbornly opposed to the idea of moving back there. 'Here we've got the best of both worlds,' he repeats.

He's right, of course—we *are* lucky to live here. It *is* a lovely area. But even if it's only just beyond the city limits, Levallois is not Paris. Intuitively, I sense that life would be much more fun and interesting living in the thick of things. That I'd feel less alone in the pulse of urban energy. Moving into Paris becomes my dream, although Frédéric seems so resolved to stay put I'm pessimistic about the chances of it happening. In my heart I desperately hope he comes round to the idea.

The stretch of hours between breakfast and dinner becomes a rollercoaster of optimistic peaks followed by plunges into despair. At first I seek comfort in the thick Côte d'Or bars of black chocolate that Frédéric keeps in the apartment. In my state of frustration, demolishing however many I can lay my hands on gives me a sense of achievement. But he takes to hiding them in cunning places, locking them in antique chests or sandwiching slabs between the pages of one of Jules Verne's extraordinary adventures. Unable to fathom my lack of control, Frédéric beseeches me, 'Where is the pleasure in eating it *all*? Why can't you just have one or two pieces?' I take no notice. I've had enough of this French restraint when it comes to indulging in everything from wine to chocolate. If anything, his self-righteous tone only strengthens my resolve. When there's no more chocolate to be found, I resort to the jar of Nutella, ploughing through fudgy spoonfuls, sick and satisfied.

At times the decision to give up my secure job and stay in Paris seems insane. There are moments when my convic-tion that everything will work out wavers. Sure, being with Frédéric is fabulous but what about my life? What about my income? I want a career, not this self-punishing routine of pumping out faxes like some obsolete production line. It's all very wonderful having the whole day to do dinner, but this frustrated housewife routine wasn't part of my plan. Where oh where is the glamorous Paris life I envisaged?

Memories of my previous job come back to me, the images brighter than the reality ever was. At work, the noise in the open plan newsroom used to drive me mad. Forty journalists all talking on the phone at once against a background hum of twenty televisions tuned into different channels (and often different languages) made concentrating on writing almost impossible.

But now I'd kill for a bit of office noise. I miss the conviviality of working in teams, gossiping over cappuccinos, discussing stories with camera crews and editors; pooling ideas. Maybe if I had colleagues to share ideas with I'd have more of them? I miss my friends. I miss sun and light and can't help wincing when someone at home tells me what an incredible summer Sydney is having.

'You need to get out of the apartment,' Frédéric urges, when he senses my head is about to implode. And so I take the direct metro line into Opéra and sit reading my newspaper at Café de la Paix, trying to eke out my exorbitantly priced *café crème* for as long as possible. After, I go for a wander, my melancholy mood inexplicably deepening with every step. You'd think the sight of beautiful Place Vendôme would lift my spirits but oddly the arc of luxury jewellers—so obviously beyond the means of a jobless person like me—only depresses me more. I plod on feeling confused, guilty even, that I should feel unhappy in a place that looks like paradise.

Six

The biggest shock during these first months is how different France is from my romantic imaginings. In my mind it was a country of rolling revolutions, peopled by anarchists and communists who brave police truncheons and tear gas to fight for their cause. If they were a bit on the violent side, this lack of discipline only heightened their appeal. For me, the French were passionate and progressive and unafraid of change. France conjured up thrilling images of radical philosophers and cobblestone-throwing students into marijuana and all sorts of sex.

No doubt many factors helped shape this opinion, beginning with the French Revolution which we covered in one lesson of head-rolling drama at school. Seeing a television documentary about the 1968 riots; reading Simone de Beauvoir, whose uninhibited characters seemed to spend their lives having amorous adventures. This impression of sexual and social freedom was only confirmed after seeing late-night French films on SBS which featured precious little dialogue and lots of nudity. The French were the very last people in the world I imagined to be conservative or socially repressed.

And yet . . .

One evening we're invited to a drinks party in Neuilly, the suburb next to Levallois which is home to famous actors, television personalities, politicians and wealthy business types. We pull up outside a *hôtel particulier* which belongs to our host, a successful entrepreneur whom Frédéric knows through another lawyer friend. Already, the serious, stately exterior signals that the evening will be very different from the breezy barbecues I am used to where you turn up with ten friends and twice as many bottles of wine. We are self-consciously fluffing up our helmet hair when a hired butler opens the door, ushering us into an entrance with a sweeping stone staircase and teal tapestries.

The party is upstairs, in a *salon* lined with sculpted wooden panels which once decorated a Burgundy château. The round drinks table is crowded with perfectly buffed champagne flutes and bottles of expensive bubbly. But, curiously, no-one is drinking it. Although there are about fifteen people gathered, the room is oddly quiet. Everyone seems strangely inhibited—although by what or whom I can't imagine. Couples stand together, voices discreetly lowered as if anxious not to disturb. No-one offers us a drink or tells us to help ourselves. After a brief hello our hosts have both disappeared. Although we're surrounded by unfamiliar faces, no introductions have been made.

'Is this a *party*?' I mutter to Frédéric, incredulous, trying to spot someone who looks like they're having fun. The scene is terribly grown up—too grown up for any of the grown-ups I know.

'It's a *cocktail*,' he whispers back.

Surveying the uptight scene in the imposing room, I wonder if it is a typical French '*cocktail*'. Surely the surroundings must be grander than most. Compared to the guests at my first dinner party, the crowd here is more how I imagined Parisians would look at soirées. The women are in chic, short black dresses, the men in sleek suits. Among the understated elegance and high heels, I feel out of place in my black pants and Doc Martens (even if I did polish them for the occasion). According to Frédéric, the guests are mainly lawyers, business and public relations people. Everyone appears ill at ease and it occurs to me that maybe the French are better at dinners than stand around drinks parties. No-one seems to want to be the one to break the ice. The guests are all hanging back. Bewildered by this cool distance, I make the mistake of trying to bridge it. 'We can't just stand here talking to each other,' I whisper to Frédéric. 'I'm going to introduce myself.' He looks doubtful for some reason but after a tedious week of no work, I am dauntless, eager to make new friends.

'Hello, my name is Sarah.'

Surprise scuds across the faces of a crisp couple, who step back involuntarily before accepting my outstretched hand. Frédéric, in the meantime, has just seen someone he knows and goes over to say hello. For the next ten minutes I practise my best 'people skills', chit-chatting in the friendly, interested sort of way which can always be relied on to start conversation. What do you do? How do you know so-and-so? These people are proving to be much harder work than I imagined, though. While they answer politely enough they don't initiate any questions of their own. Unnerved, I try even harder, filling the silences with embarrassingly inane remarks. *Quel beau salon! Regardez les belles peintures!* Two heads nod impassively at me. It isn't working, I realise. Far from engaging them in conversation they seem to be shrinking away from me. God, don't they know the golden rule (show interest in others and they'll show interest in you)? Don't they know they're supposed to *make an effort*? A sudden wave of doubt rushes over me. Could the rules be so different in France? But then how else are you supposed to get the ball rolling if not with preliminary questions and conversation?

Eventually, to everyone's relief, I run out of things to admire. We're all surreptitiously searching for an escape. The champagne is still standing opened and untouched. If ten minutes ago I was keen for a drink, I'm absolutely gagging for one now. You'd think if our hosts bothered to get a doorman for the night they might have hired a barman. It seems incongruous in such a formal setting, but, well, I guess it must be a self-serve set-up.

'Who'd like a drink?' And without waiting for a response, I start filling flutes.

A pall of silence falls over the room as I attempt to distribute the champagne. The guests seem to be torn between a desire to accept and some sense of duty not to. Looking slightly faint, Frédéric takes a flute, prompting six or seven others to follow suit. The other guests stare from a distance, apparently not wanting to be associated with our renegade group.

'Was that wrong?' I ask Frédéric quietly, wanting to shrink behind a Louis-something chair.

'No, um, not really.' He smiles weakly. 'It's just that, it's stupid, but maybe we were supposed to wait.'

'What for?'

'For the other guests to arrive.'

Stunned, I say, 'But the bottle was already *open*.'

'I know. That's why it was confusing. No-one was sure what they were supposed to do.'

I am quiet for a while, too shocked to speak. All this protocol seems surreal. Why would people not know what they're supposed to do? It's a cocktail party for god's sake— surely you're supposed to chat and drink! As for this idea of waiting to serve the champagne until all the guests have turned up (if that is what our host was planning), talk about a disincentive to arrive on time! Sensing my confusion, Frédéric squeezes my hand.

As soon as we're out the door, I exclaim: 'That wasn't a party, that was another planet!'

'They've changed,' Frédéric says, disappointed at the way the evening turned out, not quite sure how to respond to my brutal assessment. 'They're more *madame-et-monsieur* since they moved to Neuilly.'

Back at the apartment, we carry out a post-mortem of the evening. Frédéric explains that among a younger, hipper crowd my champagne grabbing gesture wouldn't have been such a big deal. People might have found it refreshing or funny or been plain grateful that someone had taken the plunge. But to this 'bourgeois' gathering, my action had appeared shockingly forward he says. Especially for a woman, because in France, apparently, serving alcohol is very much a male domain. Even before my champagne gaffe my behaviour had been far too assertive. To me, spending an entire evening talking to your partner is antisocial but Frédéric says this happens all the time at parties in France. As for my bold introduction, to the couple it would have seemed like an intrusion; my clumsy questions cluttering up each comfortable silence. Far from building a rapport, my efforts only seemed to diminish me in their eyes, as though by showing interest in them I had revealed the depths of my own dullness. Enthusiastically admiring the paintings and the lounge was inappropriate too. 'In our culture it implies you don't have those sort of things at home and makes you seem a bit *paysan*,' Frédéric says. A bit of a peasant.

This last comment is almost too much to take. I might have

thought of myself as a sophisticated Sydney-sider but in that cool, urbane setting I was gauche—too smiley, too chatty, too *eager*. My clumpy Docs may as well have been gumboots, for all the grace I showed. For the next hour, I puzzle over the *cocktail* crowd. Frédéric had said it was typically Parisian, not the sort of gathering you'd come across in the provinces. Having never met people like them in Australia, I can't grasp them. They seem to defy classification, they're neither one thing nor the other. For example I assume 'bourgeois' means they are conservative in all senses, politically speaking as well. It certainly looked that way to me. But not necessarily, according to Frédéric; he says that some were *gauche caviar*—'caviar left' being the French equivalent of champagne socialists.

'Well whatever and whoever they are, they were pretty dull,' I declare finally.

'It wasn't *that* bad.' Frédéric's tone contains a tinge of reproach. 'There were some interesting people there.'

And although I manage to bite my tongue, I can't help wondering by what secret code he discerned who was interesting and who wasn't, given how little people talked and mingled.

And so the reality of France today slowly sinks in. Instead of being daring and reckless, the French people I've met so far have been rather restrained. Although the country's past is marked by violent upheavals, at heart its people are traditionalists, clinging to centuries-old rules and formalities which dictate everything from how they set a table to when they smile. This being a land of contrasts and extremes, there is still a core of leftie rebels who have maintained their provocative edge. You occasionally glimpse them on television, spicing up debates with their swearing and combative polemics. Frédéric tells me he has a couple of friends in their fifties—people I haven't met yet—who fall into this category. But their revolutionary fervour hasn't been passed down. The generation of thirty- and forty-year-olds is perhaps the most rigid—the most conformist—in France today. Too young to have been influenced by the radical liberalism of the 1968 riots, they are also too old to be among the dynamic, entrepreneurial French youth fleeing abroad to work.

The trouble is, I only ever seem to meet thirty- and forty-year-olds. Frédéric, after all, is thirty-six and most of his friends are around the same age. After a few months in France I'm dying to meet some people I can relate to. To have a real laugh with someone; to dispel the self-doubt that has seeped into my thoughts. *What am I doing wrong? Why can't I click with anyone?* I need to relinquish the tension that's building within, to joke about my lack of social success instead of stewing over it. Before each new outing my hopes are high: maybe this time everything will just fall into place.

During my third month in France we're invited to a Sunday lunch near Lille, two hours north of Paris. Many of the people going are friends from Frédéric's university days. Because they all live in the north and he lives in Paris, they don't see each other as much as they used to. This will be something of a reunion. They're completely different from the stiff cocktail crowd, he assures me.

At the end of a bumpy driveway straddled by a leaning pigeon tower, we pull up outside a partially restored farmhouse, half-hidden by shrubs and scaffolding. We walk past a barn where a bunch of kids are noisily constructing a cubby. As soon as we're through the front door, Arnaud, one of our hosts, thrusts a potent rum and lime cocktail into our hands.

There's a lot of backslapping and joking and jovial clinking of glasses amid regular choruses of 'chin-chin!'. They seem more easy-going than many of the Parisians I've met, and I wonder if Jean-Michel might have been right about Parisians being pretentious and snobby. But despite all the positive signs, I don't feel comfortable. It takes me a while to work out why.

I've become invisible. That's what's wrong. At least it seems that is what has happened, judging from the way everyone stares straight through me. They might be delighted to see each other but they don't appear very interested in getting to know me. Nobody asks me anything or tries to include me in a conversation. Then, to my dismay, Frédéric disappears for a spin on Arnaud's motorbike, leaving me on my own. When Arnaud's wife Marie-Hélène invites the other women for a tour of the house, I panic. Am I included in this invitation? No, I don't think so. *Oh come on, stop being so hypersensitive. What are you waiting for—a personal invitation?* Pushed by my own persuasion, I trot after the group, hanging on the edges, wishing someone would just glance my way to reassure me I exist.

By the time we return to the living room, another couple has turned up. Close friends of Frédéric's, Léon and Caroline live in Lille. They are also mates of Jean-Michel, who I haven't seen since that wonderful week in Auvergne last summer. I'd kill to see his friendly face right now. Behind his glasses, Léon's brown eyes sparkle. '*Enfin, le kangarou!*' he jokes, giving me two welcoming kisses. Frédéric introduces me to Caroline whose face immediately splits into a huge smile. Her sentences flutter over me, full of sweetness and warmth: 'I'm really pleased to meet you . . . heard so much about you from Jean-Mich . . . you'll have to come to Lille for a weekend soon.' I'm so grateful I could weep. Not only do I exist but Caroline is already hinting at a future friendship!

Unfortunately, at lunch we're seated at different ends of a long table. Opposite me is Marie, a petite woman in a short skirt and tiny top ensemble, which shows off her honey tan from a recent holiday in Greece. She hadn't been friendly during the house tour but now that we're across the table from each other I figure she'll warm up. Speaking in French, I ask which islands she visited on her holiday. She answers phlegmatically. I sense she'd rather be talking to someone else.

As the cheese platter is passed, Marie leans across to Frédéric, who is next to me. '*Et ta petite copine, comment va son français?*' Her words ring across the table, loud and patronising. How's your little girlfriend's French coming along? She doesn't so much as glance in my direction. Aware that I have heard and understood every word, Frédéric is awkward and embarrassed.

'Er, I think she can probably answer that herself.'

Now here is my opportunity to put petite Marie in her place. And the Sydney Sarah would have been up to the task. After all, Marie is asking for it. She knows damn well what my French is like—we've been discussing her dumb, dull holiday throughout the entire lunch. And what's with the 'little girlfriend' business? Couldn't she at least have called me by name?

But I am too stung to come up with a retort. Although buoyed by meeting Léon and Caroline, I still can't fathom the coolness of the others. Besides, two out of twenty isn't a fabulous success rate. To me Marie's question is a slap in the face. I take it personally. Suddenly I'm hit by a tidal wave of homesickness. It has been heading my way and gaining force for some time and now it engulfs me. I want to be in London with Sue or better still back in Sydney. Going out had never required such a thick skin in Australia. Instead of confronting Marie, I retreat to the toilet, sobbing pathetically, willing it to whisk me home.

Hurt turns to resentment, resentment to anger.

'Why were they so rude?' I challenge Frédéric on the way back to Paris.

'Léon and Caroline weren't,' he points out. 'Anyway, the others weren't rude. They were just . . .'

'What?'

Frédéric falters. How do you explain the nuances of the way people interact when you've never questioned them yourself before? How can you construct neat answers for customs and codes of behaviour you have taken for granted since birth? Although he seems far more open than many of the people I've met so far, Frédéric is immersed in this culture where even something as natural as making friends seems burdened by centuries of complications.

'They just need a bit of time to get to know you.'

My frustration erupts like a storm cloud, filling the car space with thunder and fireworks. 'TIME? How much time does it take to be friendly?'

We stare ahead in silence. Seeing France through the eyes of an outsider is a new experience for Frédéric. Later it will be enriching for us both but at the moment our cultures are colliding head-on. On one side there's me, with my Aussie expectation of easy-going friendliness and rapid rapport. On the other there's Frédéric, whose loyalties are torn in two. Neither one of us is objective. I'm too vulnerable. And Frédéric is defensive. Deep down I know he feels keenly my hurt and disappointment. Perhaps he even feels responsible. But this is his country, these are his friends and my confusion is coming out as criticism.

In desperation, I head to the English-language bookshop WHSmith, in search of something to help me understand. Apparently, I am not alone in needing guidance. An Irish shop assistant explains the best-known of these guides for expatriates, *French or Foe*, is a perennial bestseller, flying off shop shelves as soon as stocks arrive. I buy a copy.

The book contains helpful explanations and sharp observations. It's comforting to learn that almost every expat in the city experiences the same cultural confusion I am feeling. Don't take things personally, reiterates the author Polly Platt, which, of course, is exactly what I've been doing. But despite the upbeat, isn't-this-a-fabulous-adventure tone, some tips are deeply troubling. On going to dinner parties, for example, Platt advises readers to pretend they are chairs. 'Then, when no-one smiles at you or talks to you before dinner, you won't be surprised,' she writes. 'Who talks to a chair?'

Before, the idea of mixing with other expatriates hadn't appealed to me. Living in France I'd expected to have French friends, not a bunch of foreign mates. But this book confirms that the business of integrating is going to be a much longer process than I'd initially thought. Suddenly, seeking out other expatriates doesn't seem such an awful option. What harm is there in hanging out with other English speakers?

In the back of my address book is a list of contacts in Europe—friends of friends to call if ever I happen to be in the same city. One of the names belongs to an English girl living in Paris, Alice, who has set up her own language school teaching English to French executives. I call, feeling like someone with no friends, which I suppose is what I am. But Alice quickly dispels any awkwardness with her warmth. We arrange to meet one week later at a Montmartre fondue restaurant where she is going with some friends, plus a few newcomers to Paris who, like me, had been given her number.

Inside, diners are squashed along loud tables with chequered gingham tablecloths which line two sides of a small, skinny room. The scene looks quintessentially French in a rather clichéd way. But what are those things on tables, in people's hands and mouths? Baby bottles? I stare, amazed and repelled. No, I'm not hallucinating: everyone is sucking wine through baby bottles. Apparently it's a gimmick this restaurant has developed to amuse tourists. (They are obviously targeted at tourists because Parisians would not think this detail is funny. *I* don't think it's particularly funny.) The waiter waves towards twelve tight places sandwiched in the middle of the row, which have been reserved by Madame Aleeece, who hasn't arrived yet. The only way to get to our seats is by standing on the banquette and climbing over the other diners, so I decide to wait in the middle of the restaurant, the only space available.

Alice's friends trickle through the door. Introductions are made in the effortless, upfront manner I'm used to and when it's clear our growing crowd is getting in the waiters' way we climb over the other guests to our table. Alice eventually arrives, flushed and out of breath, creating instant gaiety with her exclamations about 'how nice it is to meet you,' and 'hello, haven't seen you in aaaages' and 'oooohh don't you look wonderful!'. Immediately I'm glad I came. This is more like it. Although she's up the other end of the table and we don't get much of a chance to talk, she soon has us all laughing at her mad adventures while travelling the world and working as a fortune teller.

Apart from Alice, most of my potential new friends appear to be in Paris only temporarily. Bringing us together had been a gesture of great kindness. But we make a motley group: our only common ground is that we speak the same language and that many of us are struggling to find our feet, somehow. Several people complain about the French and I cringe, hearing how I must sound to Frédéric. There's an underpaid English au pair with a slightly vulnerable air. One bloke is struggling to break into the Paris advertising world and spends his days making coffees for difficult art directors. There's the girl who has had it up to here with France and is so, so, sooo relieved to be leaving. And then there's me. What am I? Where am I going? I pray that no-one asks.

An accordion player bursts through the door and the tables of tourists who have poured from the coaches parked near Pigalle start clapping to 'La Vie en Rose' minus Edith Piaf's distinctive rasp. Someone orders more wine and we suck awkwardly through the teats of the baby bottles.

It has done me good to get out on my own and meet some new people. To be among a group that guzzles wine instead of sipping it in measured quantities. But surveying the scene I can't help feeling dismayed by the ridiculous baby bottles, the grating gaiety of the accordion player, the clapping tourists.

Nothing—but nothing—could have been further from the sophisticated Paris of my dreams.

That evening leads to another dinner a few weeks later.

This time the venue is Alice's boyfriend's apartment. Frédéric has a work function that night so I make my way to the 11th *arrondissement* by metro, pleased to have my own social engagement, looking forward to seeing exuberant Alice again, reassured that this time there'll be no baby bottles.

There's quite a crowd gathered in the lounge room by the time I arrive. Obviously it's a big dinner party. I'm introduced to an English lawyer called Rupert, who asks politely what I do. I'm a freelance journalist, I say, trying not to sound despondent.

'Oh, you must meet my wife, then,' he replies. 'Alicia. She's a freelance journalist, too.'

I know he means well, but privately this doesn't seem like such a great idea. Alicia is probably some big name writer, rolling in pounds and prosperity. Still faxing forests each week to editors, I'm in no mood to meet someone who has the whole freelance scene sewn up. I resolve to wildly exaggerate my own writing success.

Wrapped in a pair of Dolce & Gabbana leopard-print trousers, Alicia is in the kitchen, emptying a bowl of chips. Her sentences spill out in a rush of enthusiasm and energy that somehow fills the room. Quickly, I discover she arrived in Paris at the same time I did after Rupert—who, like Frédéric, is a lawyer—joined a French firm. The conversation turns to our work and Alicia explains she writes for fashion magazines. My casual tone rings fake and forced.

'Oh, how's it going?'

Alicia smiles sweetly. 'Really, really badly, thanks. Just awful.'

With those words, my flimsy defence barriers tumble. As Alicia describes her growing stack of unanswered story proposals, I try hard not to beam. I am not alone! What a relief! Like me, she spends desperate days longing for responses. Like me she is going stir crazy in her apartment. Details of our dreary existence blurt out in a reciprocal rush. Although we have all the time in the world, curiously, both of us have developed an irrational aversion to preparing lunch for one.

'My staple is rice and soya sauce.'

'I can't be bothered cooking. I just have stale baguette and butter.'

'I miss working with other people,' I say. 'I hate the silence.'

Alicia's eyes glitter with a mix of effervescent fun and English madness.

'I know! Let's do a tape of office noise! You know, something people working at home can play. It'd be like (and her tone turns urgent and office-like): SARAH, THERE'S A FAX HERE FOR YOU! SHALL I PUT SO-AND-SO THROUGH TO YOU? DO YOU WANT A COFFEE, SARAH?'

It is no doubt a telling indication of our delicate emotional states that we find this side-splittingly funny. In fact, everything suddenly seems a wonderful joke—even our sorry piles of rejection faxes. We have both reread these so many times we know them by heart. (Never mind that they are negative. These are our beacons of hope. At least the editors acknowledged our ideas and some replies are even encouraging.) Clutching kitchen benches to avoid collapsing on the floor, we now recite, word for word, the reasons why our carefully crafted proposals will never become published stories. *Thanks for the recent offer but we don't use contributed pieces.* What a giggle. *Thanks for the ideas. They're all interesting but don't suit the magazine.* Wheeze, wheeze. *Sorry, but our next twenty issues are full.* We can hardly stand up.

To the rest of the dinner party, it must have seemed a bit tragic—two grown girls laughing like lunatics over something as unfunny as failure. But even slightly hysterical laughter is wonderfully therapeutic. Meeting someone whose struggles and aspirations mirror my own is a lifesaving stroke of luck. Together we will discuss ideas, help each other write the ultimate fail-proof story pitch and empathise and encourage. We share our big hopes for the future—Alicia wants to make a name for herself as a Paris fashion writer. And I have just applied to Journalists in Europe, an eight-month course which is based in Paris. I'd first heard of it through a friend at SBS, who knew someone who'd done it. It sounds like an exciting solution to my work dilemma, even if it's only a temporary one. The program, which is designed for journalists with at least five years' experience, involves lots of trips across the continent to write stories.

Of course, I had people to talk all this over with before meeting Alicia. Frédéric. My parents, who have been wonderfully supportive. Sue, who has followed these first rough months of mine through regular soul-lifting phone calls. But Alicia represents a different sort of confidante. She doesn't have to imagine what it's like to be in my shoes: she *is* in my shoes, or almost. It is far easier to confide your despair in a friend going through the same experience than one who calls to announce a promotion or some new job perk like a company convertible.

By the end of the dinner we have resolved to spend culturally enriching afternoons at galleries and museums, instead of moping around our apartments. For special anti-stress treats, we'll head to steam baths and soothe our brittle nerves with mud and scrubbing. But despite our good intentions, these plans are rarely realised. Invariably, the route to our destination passes an empty, tempting café. Shamelessly, we invent excuses to justify our desire to drink. The paintings can wait, we can always catch the exhibition another day. We don't even make it to the steam baths. Instead, we plough through *pichets* of house red, workshopping our futures and devising extravagant strategies for success.

Seven

In April, my aunt Joannie arrives from New Zealand, the first of what will grow to be a steady stream of antipodean visitors. Far from being upset about me living on the other side of the world, family and friends seem only too delighted with the prospect of a Paris pad. Straight off a twenty-eight hour plane trip, Joannie is her usual boisterous, overexcited self. Within approximately sixty seconds of meeting Frédéric, she has done away with any preliminary formalities.

'My husband made me promise not to mention the Rainbow Warrior,' she tells him. 'But you know, Freddo, I think I'll feel a lot better if I just get it off my chest.' And shooting him a wicked wink, Joannie erupts in whooping, helpless laughter. Although momentarily taken aback, Frédéric quickly joins in. Soon the pair of them are swapping smutty, silly jokes which they both find hilarious. Before long she is on the back of his motorbike, her joyful shrieks ringing down the boulevards.

Far from being affronted by this easy antipodean familiarity, Frédéric seems to adore it. He loves having people to stay and seems to relish his role as host, getting up early to buy croissants and baguettes and squeeze fresh orange juice for breakfast. Inevitably he gets called 'Freddo Frog', and a packet of the so-named chocolate frogs even arrives from

Sydney friends as a joke. He seems to like the tickling, teasing humour. Although undeniably proud, the French can be excellent sports when it comes to poking fun at themselves. They can also be terribly self-critical, referring to '*les français*' in the third person as though they are a foreign, vaguely suspect people. *Les français sont tous des râleurs*, is one frequent refrain. The French are all whiners. Too individualistic; hopeless with foreign languages. The French are hypochondriacs, they say, citing the way people expect pages of doctors' prescriptions for a common cold. They seem resigned to their litany of French flaws, as though powerless to change them.

This self-deprecating honesty is not something I'd expected from the French. They seem to be able to view themselves and their country from afar, serving up frank self-criticism while remaining glaringly Gallic. It is another paradox in the puzzle these people represent. Frédéric's deep pride in his country doesn't prevent him from ridiculing the Republic.

Several months after Joannie's departure a parcel arrives from New Zealand. It's addressed to Frédéric. Inside is a card and a present—a white Greenpeace T-shirt with a commemorative message splashed across the front:

Rainbow Warrior
tenth anniversary of the sinking

It's from Joannie, of course. Frédéric wears it everywhere. The T-shirt is a reminder of the 1985 bombing of the Greenpeace boat in Auckland harbour, carried out by French secret service agents, no doubt on the orders of President François Mitterrand. The vessel was scheduled to sail for

Mururoa to protest French nuclear tests on the South Pacific atoll. France wanted to stop it. In the end, the international outrage over the sinking—which tragically caused the death of a Portuguese photographer—forced a moratorium on French tests.

The T-shirt arrives just after the tenth anniversary of the Rainbow Warrior sinking. Ironically, when the date of the anniversary came around, France was already at the centre of another nuclear furore. And oddly, it would have an unexpected impact on my future.

◌

Several months earlier, in May, I'd received a phone call which had delivered exciting news. My application had been accepted by Journalists in Europe! I was one of about thirty applicants who'd been selected. The idea of the eight-month course is to give journalists a chance to deepen their understanding of Europe through work experience. There are regular field trips to write stories and scholarships cover basic travel and living expenses.

The trouble is, I didn't get a scholarship. The apologetic French voice on the phone explained that funding cuts mean the school no longer offers them to applicants from wealthy, Western countries, including the United States, Canada, England—and Australia. It is left to the governments of these countries to cough up some cash. The program co-ordinator advised me to contact the Australian Department of Foreign Affairs. I tried to picture public servants in Canberra agreeing to sponsor Paris *séjours* for journalists. It seemed wholly unlikely. The government hadn't provided funding in previous years and it wouldn't help me either. Because of the trips, the course costs a steep $22,000.

Having blown all my savings on travel, I didn't even have one tenth of that sum sitting in my bank account.

But I desperately wanted to do the program. It seemed just the lucky break I needed. Not that I'd been entirely luckless on the work front lately. My persistent faxing seemed to be finally paying off: I had delivered my first commissioned story to a weekend magazine a fortnight before. It was on an Australian brother and sister who manage a bar and restaurant in Paris, although it wouldn't really have mattered what it was about—I was over the moon just to have had an article accepted. Two other editors had also responded positively to ideas and it looked like I would have more stories to write. But these last few months had left me with few illusions. Freelancing, by its very nature, can be precarious and never more so than when you're trying to get started. Establishing myself as a writer was going to take time. This first article represented a breakthrough but it didn't mean I was suddenly going to be swamped with ecstatic replies from editors.

The Journalists in Europe program would allow me to pursue my freelancing efforts and at the same time expose me to exciting new experiences. It might even help my journalism, because the stories we would write on course trips could then be sold to mainstream media. After four months of idling in the apartment, I was ready for a bit of excitement. I chased up former JE journalists living in Paris and I heard about their adventures in countries ranging from Moldova to Macedonia. Barely able to find these places on a map, to me these trips sounded thrilling. What's more, after four months working alone, being part of a group would be fun. Although the field trips are carried out individually, back in Paris journalists attend lectures at the headquarters on Rue du Louvre.

The schedule leaves plenty of time for coffees and *kirs*. It sounded perfect.

Somehow I had to raise the money. But how?

'I've got an idea! I know how you can do it!' Several weeks after learning of my acceptance to the course, Alicia was on the telephone, practically gagging with excitement. Twenty minutes later she was buzzing my door, breathless, having come to pitch her plan in person. A great believer in writing things down, she pulled out a pen and a sheet of paper and in big, bold numbers wrote £9,000—the required sum rounded up and converted into pounds. She underlined it.

The plan was simple and—according to Alicia—fail-proof. We will hold a raffle, selling tickets to family, friends and acquaintances on both hemispheres. Each ticket will cost twenty pounds. My jaw dropped in disbelief but Alicia was busy scribbling and dividing and she ignored me. 'So that means you just have to sell four hundred and fifty tickets.'

It was clear from her bright, suspenseful eyes that we were getting to the good bit. *La pièce de résistance*. The prizes, naturally. These had been given a great deal of thought. I could almost hear the drum roll beating in Alicia's head. For the Australian winner: a weekend on Sydney's northern beaches where my parents' home, which badly needs a paint job, will somehow be transformed into a luxurious B & B. Mum and Dad will be required to serve champagne breakfasts on the balcony. The European winner will be treated to a sightseeing tour of Paris by night on Frédéric's motorbike. Alicia was bursting with confidence.

'Everyone will be falling over themselves for tickets.'

I stared in stunned amusement. Could she be serious? (Apparently, yes.) Twenty pound tickets for the chance to ride on a motorbike or stay with my parents! Who'd fall for that? I tried to be tactful.

'You're off your head,' I laughed.

Unfazed, Alicia tried to persuade me. 'Go on, it'd be great! A friend of mine held a raffle to pay for some expensive college and he raised heaps of money.'

I was touched and buoyed by her enthusiasm—and who knows, maybe the plan would really work. But I couldn't ask for money from friends and family, I wouldn't feel comfortable. Besides, selling raffle tickets had never been my forte. When I was at school, Mum and Dad always ended up having to buy all my unsold booklets.

In the end, I decided simply to write to companies and ask for sponsorship. Because I needed to narrow my focus somehow, I targeted Australian companies which do business in France and French groups which have interests in Australia. It seemed logical given my nationality and the fact that the program is based in Paris. Breaking down the required total amount into more digestible bites, we decided to ask them for 'contributions' of about £1,500. All I needed was for six companies to say yes.

Although we didn't admit it, neither Frédéric nor I really believed this strategy would work. Companies receive hundreds of requests each year to support causes far more worthy than mine. But the alternative was to give up and forget about the program and I wasn't prepared to do that, not yet. All my hopes for the future were wrapped up in it and these hopes provided me with a purpose, a goal. We concealed our doubts under bouncy, brittle optimism. The business of letter writing turned into a full-time job—for both of us. But our approaches to the task turned out to be rather different.

'Can't you make it less flowery? I mean, it's not supposed

to be poetry.' Frédéric's French translation of my English letter seemed longwinded. Its wordy sentences, carved by commas, trailed onto a second page. On the computer, we fiddled with the font until eventually it squashed onto one sheet. In contrast with the airy original, the French version looked dark and compressed.

But as everyone knows from Proust's legendary page-long sentences, the French language doesn't lend itself to concision. Its beauty lies in the fluid rhythms of musical, meandering passages which express a multitude of possibilities and doubts before reaching any conclusion. Oblique messages are revered as subtle and sophisticated whereas direct language is considered too blunt—an appropriate writing style for a robot but not for an erudite human being. My English letter ended succinctly with 'Yours sincerely'. Signing off in French requires a two line formal flourish: *'Je vous prie de recevoir, Monsieur/Madame, l'expression de ma considération distinguée.'* Literally, 'I beg you to receive, Monsieur or Madame, the expression of my distinguished consideration.'

Thanks to the seventeenth-century philosopher and mathematician René Descartes, though, in France Latin flamboyance is tempered by method and reasoning. It's the French Yin and Yang, apparently. Frédéric's letter might have been long but each line led the reader through another step in his argument. Although I remained unconvinced about the length and wording of his translation, he was insistent. We were writing to some of the most important names in French business. They were most likely cultivated, highly educated people. Our message needed to be elegant, lucid.

By mid-June we had sent out about fifty letters and there were another thirty or so to be written. We hurried to get them done as quickly as possible. In a few weeks it would be summer and Parisians would start fleeing the city. My target companies would be operating on a scant staff who'd get to work late and take long lunches. Few decisions are ever made in July and August. Normal business in Paris would not fully resume until the first week of September, only one month before the start of the Journalists in Europe program. Most of the busy executives would not get my letter until after their holidays, when they'd have one million more important things to do. Meanwhile, responses trickled in from Australian companies, all minor variations of the same message. *I regret we are unable to provide any financial support . . .*

It was during my flurry of letter writing that France dropped a bombshell. Anxious to kick off his term to a decisive Gaullist start, the newly elected French President announced the resumption of French nuclear tests in the South Pacific. Jacques Chirac—who during his eighteen years as Paris mayor earned the nickname *'le bulldozer'*— planned a series of at least six tests on Mururoa Atoll. The decision had explosive repercussions for France's relations with the rest of the world, and nowhere was the protest stronger than in Australia. It also had direct consequences for me.

Suddenly, revealing my nationality sparked debate. Most French people my age appeared sympathetic to the anti-test stand. *'Il est con, Chirac,'* they shrugged. Chirac's a dickhead. But then media reports poured in from Australia describing French restaurant windows being smashed and—even more absurd—shops removing croissants from shelves. Although I shared my country's opposition to the tests, I was embarrassed by the extreme elements of the protest and tried to reassure those who asked that only a small minority of Australians were behind it. Meanwhile, interviews were aired with French travellers back from Australia, where some suffered gibes and even discriminatory treatment. The national mood in France turned from empathy to hurt. We've always liked Australia, people told me. Why are you taking out your protest on the French people?

It was a fair question. France is hardly the worst offender when it comes to nuclear tests, responsible for only one tenth of the world's total. Of course there was the thorny question of why, if these tests are so safe, the French government was conducting them far from its own shores. But even so, the virulence of the protest was revealing. France seems to trigger fiery emotions. The we-don't-give-a-stuff-what-the-world-thinks attitude of French politicians only exacerbated matters, cementing the country's reputation for contrariness and prickly pride. As international fury rose, France reminded me more and more of one of those starchy grand dames you see jumping queues in smart Paris boutiques. She has a rather inflated notion of her own importance and an unshakeable belief in being different from everybody else. Dark looks from the other customers don't faze her. She is utterly unapologetic about being difficult, considering it merely a sign of strong character.

The escalating tensions triggered a few outbursts in my own life. One day, sitting in a café with an Australian girl-friend, Brigid, I was accosted by two French academics. Having discerned our nationality from our conversation, they thundered on about Australia's hypocrisy—look how we've treated the Aborigines, how dare we give France lessons! A few weeks later, Frédéric and I were invited to lunch with some of his aunts and uncles. So far I'd met his sister and brother-in-law and his father, Alain, a charming, stern, widely read man with a passion for history who lives alone in northern France. These previous meetings with Frédéric's immediate family had gone well, I'd thought.

This was my first encounter with his extended family, though, and I hoped to make a good impression. The house was a lovely eighteenth-century manor burrowed in the hills a few kilometres from Boulogne-sur-Mer and because it was a fine day, lunch was outside, in an idyllic garden courtyard. But the aftershock of *les essais nucléaires* reverberated around the table, sending tremors through the perfect setting, conspiring against me. Our host was a highly successful, retired businessman. In his olive cords and freckled tweed blazer he epitomised the look the French call 'gentleman farmer', which is about the only fashion style they admit to borrowing from the English. But his sociable charm evaporated when the conversation turned to the tests.

'*Les australiens sont chiants!*' he roared, suddenly excited, from the head of the table.

'*Pardon?*'

'*LES AUSTRALIENS SONT CHIANTS!*'

Confused, I turned to Frédéric. He looked pained, focusing on a snail cruising around the garden bed, envying, no doubt, its peaceful endeavour.

'Umm, my uncle said that you Australians are shitty.'

I was speechless. These were the first words anyone had addressed directly to me in the two hours we'd been there and they were not exactly the welcome I'd expected. I wanted to tell Frédéric's uncle he was shitty too, but then we might have had an international incident on our hands. While I pondered a response, the conversation switched to the house next door which had been ruined by the *erreurs de goût* (errors in taste) of the new owners. The uncle's outburst was not meant as a way of opening conversation or seeking my opinion, I realised, but rather as a simple statement of fact.

'Well, that was a great success.' Afterwards I was despondent. It was as though I'd landed in the middle of a minefield and instead of nimbly negotiating my way out I was bumbling and tripping, triggering disaster after disaster.

'They didn't mean to be unfriendly,' began Frédéric, reluctantly recast in his meat-in-the-sandwich role. 'It's just they're not used to meeting foreigners. They're really fun, kind people, you'll see.'

The thing is, I already knew they were fun, kind people. It was obvious by the engraved laugh lines on their faces, the way they joked all the time. There was a lot of love around the table. But once again I'd felt invisible throughout the entire four hours. 'Pretend you're a chair,' the book *French or Foe* had advised as a way of steeling yourself for being ignored. Oh, if only I could. But I was too consumed by the effort of trying to adapt to my new home to see the reaction of Frédéric's relatives within the context of a culture. Instead, I did exactly what you shouldn't do, what I've been doing all along in France. I took it personally.

ᘐᘗ

The international furore over the nuclear tests brought me more work. Increasingly the messages from editors read something like this:

> *Dear Sarah*
> *I like your proposal. Can you do 1,200 words by the 11 August?*

There was an insatiable demand from abroad for articles relating to the tests and—as one foreign editor put it—'any story that makes the French look bad'. For one newspaper feature, I needed to speak to a top defence officer whom I could question about France's nuclear policy. The army chief was refusing to comment so I tracked down his predecessor. Although he was still a big brass with a bureau at the sumptuous Ecole Militaire, I thought he may be less constrained by protocol than the incumbent.

By now I'd learnt that in France, getting an interview is a more protracted procedure than the fairly straightforward system I was used to in Sydney. It's rare you can just ring an expert for a quick quote. Even telephone interviews often require a written request. The aim of your first call is simply to win the sympathy of the personal assistant and find out the fax number. Several days or even weeks may pass, during which you repeatedly blow extended story deadlines waiting for a response. Then, if you're lucky, the secretary will call back suggesting a day and time for the meeting.

I telephoned the Ecole Militaire hoping to just get the general's fax number. His secretary asked me to hold. Several seconds later an authoritative male voice curtly announceed his identity. It was the venerable general himself.

Far from being pleased by this easy access, I was appalled. I had not prepared. Logically, all I had to do was introduce myself and explain the reason for my call. The interview—if there was to be one at all—would happen later. But making yourself understood in another language is harder over the telephone than speaking with someone in person. My conversations have to be carefully choreographed, the sentences translated into French and written on a notepad which is kept in front of me throughout the call.

Unnerved, I stumbled straight into a foolish mistake. Instead of using the respectful word for 'you', *vous*, I addressed him with the casual, matey *tu*. In France, the military is the ultimate bastion of pomp and prestige and it's quite possible not even the good general's wife is permitted such familiarity. In my growing panic, I *tu*-ed him again. Then, after more nervous jabber, I said the unthinkable.

'Tu veux le faire ou non?' Do you want to do the interview or not? This sounds bad enough in English but in France—where the same question would require five minutes of poetic persuasion—such brusqueness is obscene. Forget about using his proper title, *mon Général*—I didn't even call him *Monsieur*. My French had been reduced to the sort of crude questions you'd expect from a five-year-old. The conversation had turned into an excruciating out-of-body experience. From my lofty vantage point it was obvious the babbling journalist had blown it. A faint feeling of hysteria squeezed my breath. Please oh please, let's just hang up and start again.

The general said he needed time to consider the interview, which under the circumstances seemed saintly, that he might even contemplate speaking to me again. Rushing to end the call, I said the first farewell that popped into my head.

'*Alors, à bientôt, uh.*' Well, see ya later. I may as well have said *bisou* and blown him a kiss. I put down the receiver, cringing, barely able to believe the conversation I'd just had. God that was awful. Pitiful. I was beyond help, out of control, hell-bent on self-destruction.

Half an hour later, his secretary called back. The general would like a word. I braced myself. After all, the French are renowned for their impatience with foreigners who can't speak their language.

But his tone was kind, avuncular almost. Yes, actually, he'd be delighted to be interviewed. Does such-and-such a day suit? Astonished and almost speechless, I wondered what made him agree to the interview. Was it simply his desire to state France's case? Or did my embarrassing performance earlier elicit an act of kindness? Whatever the reason, I was immensely grateful. At the end of our brief exchange, there was a small pause. Still unable to believe that he had said yes, I wondered what was coming. The name of a good French teacher? A request that a translator be on hand during the interview? (I planned to bring one anyway.) But no, it seemed he just wanted to say goodbye.

'*Alors, à bientôt, uh.*' It took a second or two for me to realise this was a perfect echo of my totally inappropriate farewell earlier. Beneath his grave tone you could almost hear him wink.

෴

By early September, the evening air has cooled. Nature is preparing for its long confinement. Chestnuts will soon fill the city's gutters, petals will fall. Leaves are curling, dying. I feel spent too. My pile of replies from companies answering my request for sponsorship now numbers more than forty. All of them are negative. The months spent researching the relevant people in the right companies—not to mention letter writing and embellishing my CV—have been futile. My hopes of doing the Journalists in Europe program begin to crumble, leaving an awful void.

Then, towards the middle of the month, a spate of replies from French companies fills our mail box. The business chiefs are back from their summer holidays. As with the letters from Australia, these answers are mostly variations of a theme. Only the message is entirely different. When the first one arrives, I have to reread it several times for the words to sink in.

'We would be very happy to assist you with your endeavour to do the Journalists in Europe program. Please contact so-and-so to arrange a meeting.'

I can't believe it. This isn't true. Each new letter sends me flying to telephone Frédéric, practically hyperventilating with excitement. He is stunned, ecstatic, speechless. By mid-September most companies have responded and we have a final, triumphant tally. Sixty-four negative responses. But six companies have agreed to meet the total cost of the course. All of them are French.

Without the nuclear tests my quest for funding would probably have failed. The truth is, Chirac's timing is incredibly fortuitous for me. As it turns out, the companies I targeted—French companies with business interests in Australia—are among those hardest hit by the fallout over the nuclear tests. Suddenly, Australia no longer wants their champagne, aeroplanes or water pipes.

In meetings with my sponsors to finalise the payments, the executives say the escalating furore made them sympathetic to my letter. To argue my case for doing the Journalist in Europe program, I'd mentioned the need for nations to have an understanding of each other's cultural and social contexts as well as at a political level. Giving journalists the opportunity to further their professional knowledge by living and working abroad will make the mainstream media more informed, I wrote. As incendiary anti-French headlines splashed across the world's newspapers, suddenly my bland message seemed meaningful. Except for correcting a couple of press releases in English, my sponsors don't ask for anything in return for their money. No doubt their private wish is for me to write balanced articles about the issue.

Another reason for their support emerges at these meetings. *La lettre.* Who wrote it? they enquire as tactfully as possible, having immediately divined from my spoken French that it couldn't possibly have been me. Heads shake in admiration over *les belles expressions* and *les mots bien choisis.* It is a powerful lesson in the importance of literature and language in this country. Frédéric's carefully crafted phrases which I'd attacked for being too long and flowery were, to these business chiefs, a thing of great beauty.

❧

And so my first autumn in France begins with great expectations. The season turns out to be more eventful than I expected—although not exactly in the way I imagined. In mid-October, a few weeks after the JE program begins, railway employees across the country stage a strike. Demonstrating in the street, they deliver a noisy forewarning: 'This is just the beginning, the beginning, the beginning!'

Autumn is often *chaud*, I learn now. Not 'hot' temperature-wise, but hot in ambience. After their long summer holidays, the French return to work with surplus energy. Rested and revived, they are ready. Not for work, though. The autumn of 1995 turns out to be one of the coldest and one of the hottest in a long time, the plummeting temperatures contrasting with the heat on the streets. Throughout November and December, the country is paralysed by the most severe rolling general strikes in twenty-five years. The one-day protest called by railroad workers snowballs into a nation-wide movement uniting the variously disgruntled—students, postal workers, teachers, employees at the Louvre, bus and metro drivers. Mostly, workers are livid about the conservative government's plans to cut France's extravagant welfare spending and overhaul the unprofitable railway system. Determined to retain generous health benefits and rights such as the ability to retire as early as fifty on a full pension, they aren't going to accept these heartless capitalist reforms without a massive fight. The battle makes Prime Minister Alain Juppé—perceived as clever but arrogant—the most hated man in France.

No sooner has my much anticipated journalists' program started than I can't attend it. There are no buses running, no metro. Short of walking almost two hours, I have no way of getting into the city centre to the Journalists in Europe headquarters. Our lectures have been cancelled. For the millions of people who live on the city's outskirts, getting into work has turned into a three-hour car crawl. Those who don't own vehicles simply don't go to work. The *grèves*, as strikes are called in French, become the country's sole news story. Every morning the papers publish fascinating *grève* trivia such as the total length of traffic-jammed roads into the capital from the day before (usually around 300km). The evening news shows aerial images of Paris by night, the stationary headlights forming pretty ribbons of golden beads.

At first, the *grèves* are a novelty. Rollerblade sales soar and the streets and pavements fill with skaters in work suits. Invited to a dinner at Bastille one evening, Frédéric and I cross the entire city riding the motorbike on footpaths to avoid the trailing traffic jams. Paris resembles a slightly surreal playground, and during demonstrations there's even quite a party buzz. The Australian wharfies and north England coal miners look decidedly dour compared to these French *grévistes* marching down the streets in happy, singing parades which radiate camaraderie. They are well organised and well looked after. Hot dog vans follow behind in case of hunger; a fleet of green street cleaning trucks sweep up their food papers and streamers as quickly as they can drop them. I attend several protests to write stories and every time I'm amazed by the gaiety, the spontaneous party mood which seems so at odds with the social restraint I've noticed at dinners. Even the poor people trapped in traffic jams remain remarkably good humoured. I'd expected pathologically impatient Parisians to be maniacal with rage but instead they are calm, sympathetic. Resigned. *C'est la vie. C'est comme ça.*

In the French press, the atmosphere in Paris is described as *prérévolutionnaire.* For a while anticipation builds as both the strikers and the government refuse to cede a centimetre. The city appears to be on standby, poised for something, although I don't know what. The tough-looking CRS anti-riot police who man every protest provide a clue. We are waiting for *événements.* Some cobblestone throwing and shop window smashing which will be smartly answered with truncheons and tear gas.

But instead of culminating in a repeat of May 1968, the strikes just drag on and on. The novelty wears off. The desire to see French history unfolding in front of my eyes is replaced by a craving for normalcy. I am fed up with being stranded at home, tired of this forced detention. Alicia is stuck too, only on the other side of the city. Desperate, we make ambitious plans to meet at a city café, halfway between our homes. Allowing for a leisurely lunch, for both of us the return trip will take pretty much an entire day. Travelling from the city's far east, she has a marathon journey on foot. Coming from the west, I plan to glide into Paris on my shiny new blades.

It is snowing when I set off around ten in the morning.

After skating moronically along a couple of boulevards, I swap my rollerblades for the running shoes in my bag. Head bent into the blizzardy wind, fresh blisters busily sprouting on my feet, I curse the fact that things have to get *chaud* just when the weather turns arctic.

I arrive at Le Café on Rue Tiquetonne in just under two hours, a few minutes ahead of Alicia. Noses streaming and cheeks flushed with icy roses, we are both in dark moods. Jugs of steaming, nutmeg-flavoured wine help us thaw. It's like being in a bloody war zone, we grumble. There are even rumours that some fresh food supplies might run out because of striking truck drivers. Alicia is worried about getting back to England for Christmas. Train travel is out of the question, of course. Even driving is fraught with hazards—what if the Channel ferry drivers strike? And I'm panicking about my planned Christmas trip to Australia. The thought of not being able to go is devastating; my ticket has been booked for months. But how can planes take off when the air traffic controllers are in the street instead of in their watch towers?

Finally, after almost five weeks of idleness, the metro—my lifeline to Paris and all things interesting—surges back to life. It's like opening prison gates, a passage to freedom from bourgeois boulevard induced boredom.

Eight

The most wonderful thing about the Journalists in Europe program is, quite simply, Europe. The chance to discover and write about this continent where so much that is marvellous and tragic has occurred, where so many borders have shifted and continue to shift; one corner of the world so drenched in history and diversity that unity seems utopian. I go to Sarajevo and Serbia, Seville, Northern Ireland, delightful Tallinn in Estonia and spend ten days in a remote, alcohol-soaked village in Romania's Danube Delta. I love these trips, the thrill (tinged with apprehension) of arriving alone in a strange place, absorbing the different language, the hand gestures, the coffee, the way the taxis drive, the hundreds of details that would elevate my stay to adventure. Just as I'd hoped, they also enhance my freelancing efforts. Suddenly I can offer harder news features from places where publications might not have a correspondent. A few times I end up being in the right place at an extraordinary time, like being in Belgrade when the Dayton Peace Agreement was reached and crazy crowds flooded the streets to celebrate the end of the war. I feel lucky, elated.

There are other reasons for my new buoyant mood. Lately, it seems as though I've had quite a bit of good luck. Although the strikes delayed my departure by a few days, I managed to get to Sydney for Christmas. The fortnight there felt like a shot of life-blood. Then, a few days after my return to Paris, Frédéric had actually raised the subject of moving from Levallois.

'What? You mean into Paris?' I asked, amazed when Frédéric nodded. Before leaving for Australia I'd tried to bring up the subject again and he hadn't even wanted to discuss it. As I'd become more entrenched in my views, Frédéric too had grown more adamant about staying at Levallois.

'Well, we could at least have a look at what's around,' he said. 'It seems like quite a good time to buy ...' And he started talking about the low interest rates and real estate prices. I'd wanted to leap into the air.

'Wow, but that's great,' I burbled, making a mental note to go away more often. 'I mean, where are you thinking, which *quartier*?'

'Somewhere central. I really loved Rue Lepic when I lived there but Montmartre is a bit far away. We can forget about the Marais, too expensive ...' Now that he'd made up his mind, Frédéric seemed enthusiastic about the prospect of life in the city centre. His words resonated like a symphony in my ears, joyful and uplifting.

The truth is I am touched. Although he is right—it *is* a good time to buy because of prices and interest rates—there was nothing to stop him from deciding to buy an apartment in Levallois or somewhere else outside Paris. I am the catalyst for moving into the inner city. I also know that his change of heart represents tacit understanding of the loneliness and difficulties I've experienced at Levallois. This decision to move seems to give our relationship a new solidity. It is a good omen.

It takes us three months to find an apartment. Our house hunting started unpromisingly, partly due to a poor choice of words by Frédéric, who declared we were looking for something *'un peu original'*. This was open to wide interpretation. And lucky us—the very first real estate agent we called on had just the perfect place! Never mind that it was among the neon nightclubs on Rue du Faubourg Montmartre—one of the most congested, noisy streets in Paris. 'Just wait until you see it!'

As it turned out, this place was more than 'a little original'. It was unique. I know of no other building in Paris sheathed in glossy black panels of fake marble. But the real surprise lay inside. The apartment didn't need 'light renovation work'; it was totally uninhabitable—pollution-stained walls, ceiling cracks like crevices, smashed windows and a filthy kitchen where a squatter had left an open jar of Nutella and a mouldy baguette sandwich. The real estate agent tried to draw our attention to the period fireplace, as though this one redeeming feature might compensate for the surrounding shambles. Frédéric tapped dubiously on an internal wall. 'What's behind here?' he'd asked.

'Mais voilà le côté original!' The agent was delighted we'd discovered it all by ourselves. In fact, the apartment contained an extra room, which some time in the past had been entirely walled in. 'Why would anyone do that?' our detective–agent had asked rhetorically. 'There could be skeletons inside, a cache of weapons, perhaps treasure! What a mystery! Imagine the intrigue!'

What an excellent reason to blow Frédéric's life savings on this miserable, overpriced dump. I was all scowls and sarcasm, unimpressed to have been dragged here by this upbeat idiot whose sentences all finish with exclamation marks. But Frédéric was enchanted—the possibility of finding skeletons had already taken seed in his abundantly fertile imagination. An engrossed—and, in my opinion, utterly pointless—conversation ensued between the pair, during which possible explanations for the walled-in room grew more and more extravagant. Leaving the building, Frédéric bubbled enthusiasm, oblivious to my irritation.

'It would be amusing, no?'

Then there was the place which we were told had ornate ceiling mouldings and tall, eighteenth-century windows. This turned out to be true. But many of the windows looked directly onto the unpainted concrete wall of the building next door: the bedrooms had all the natural light of prison cells.

More tempting was the apartment in a building that had one of those imposing entrances that led into a vaulted passageway and then an internal courtyard. The cobblestones shone as though they'd just been waxed. We passed two stately staircases on either side of the passage but the apartment we'd come to see had a more modest entrance at the end of the courtyard. As we climbed the steep twisting steps to the fifth floor, the real estate agent explained that this wing used to be for the servants employed by the noble families who lived next door. A developer had recently knocked out the walls and converted the tiny rooms into proper apartments. Inside, the place for sale exuded charm. Every surface was bent or crooked with age—the floors, the walls, the windows. But it was almost too cute for its own good. The exposed beams crowded the low ceilings like too numerous stripes, reminding me of a Swiss chalet. The quaintness was claustrophobic. It'd be like living in a medieval funhouse.

Out of the thirty-odd places we visited, the apartment we eventually buy—our apartment—is practically the only serious contender. It would not be everyone's idea of a dream home. For starters, it's on the sixth and final floor and there isn't a lift (although the real estate agent royally announces there's a *'projet'* to build one, which is no guarantee of a lift in our lifetime). The first three floors are occupied by noisy rag trade sweat-shops which will not be the most desirable of neighbours. And you could hardly call our entrance chic. In the past the building housed a school for problem teenagers and their grubby hand prints still smear the stairwell walls.

The kitchen is no more than a corridor with a workbench the size of a chopping board—dinner parties will be a challenge. The toilet is electric and flushing emits a thundery rumble which vibrates throughout the entire apartment. It is all noise and very little action. Directly across a courtyard is the other wing of our building whose cream painted façade is peeling like sunburnt skin. Next to it is another block of apartments; a geometric jumble of minute windows and tilting roofs. Although not without charm, it is not what you'd call a View.

But on first walking in, I knew we'd be really happy here. Even though the building is centuries old, the apartment has a fresh, contemporary feel which I find immensely appealing. Soaring ceilings make it seem airy and loft-like, and to my relief, this seems to satisfy Frédéric's criteria for something 'a little original'. At last we have enough wall height to hang his lovely big mirror—which sat on the floor at Levallois—above the console table. The advantage of being on the building's top floor is you see sky, a precious commodity in Paris where frequently you stare straight into another apartment. Light— *it has to be light*, I kept repeating to Frédéric—spills through windows and falls in bright shafts from skylights. After visiting so many dingy inner city apartments, this had become my foremost prerequisite. Instead of dark, heavy wood, the chunky beams which frame the spacious main room have been bleached the colour of sand. And then there's a spare bedroom which will be my office. I'm ecstatic. No more working on the dining room table.

A small staircase leads from the lounge room to a mezzanine level. This is where visiting family and friends will sleep, banging their heads constantly on the low, sloping ceiling. Directly beneath the roof, the mezzanine floor is framed at both ends by two crossbeams which you have to climb between to reach the central 'bedroom' area. It reminds me of a secret cubby-house—one which offers a panorama of Paris if you stand on the knee-high joist and stick your head out the skylight.

But the most wonderful thing about our new apartment is the location, smack in the city centre, within walking distance of almost everything—the Marais, the Tuileries gardens, the Left Bank, the Louvre. Most fantastic of all, we'll be just round the corner from the lively market street, Rue Montorgueil, a picturesque seven-hundred metre stretch of *fromageries*, fish shops, florists, bakeries and fruit and vegetable sellers who bugle their bargains six days a week. The street is the main artery of a rectangle-shaped *quartier* that's unique in the inner city because it is entirely paved and closed to regular traffic. This only heightens the villagey feel to the neighbourhood, the impression that it is somehow self-contained and separate even though it's an intrinsic part of Paris. I discovered the area through the Journalists in Europe program, whose headquarters are a couple of streets away on Rue du Louvre. Soon I was in love with it. It radiates life, it's the Parisian *quartier* of my dreams, rich in contrasts, characters and vivid colour.

Frédéric, as it turns out, knows it well: years ago he lived nearby and fortunately he is equally keen to move into the neighbourhood. The drawbacks of our apartment—the absence of a lift, the grubby entrance, the minuscule kitchen—seem a small price to pay for the joy of being close to Rue Montorgueil.

೧෮

It is late June by the time the sale has gone through and the tenants have packed up, leaving us free to move into our new home. After collecting the keys from the real estate agent, we decide to take some things over to the apartment now that it's officially ours. On the way there, my head spins with excitement. Before the car has even come to a stop, I'm fumbling inside my bag for the keys. This is it: the beginning of a fabulous new life in delicious 75002. Bye-bye dreary Nounou Land. Hello *le vrai Paris*.

The main move will take place on the weekend. Tonight we've just brought over a few fragile possessions—the mad papier-mâché masks, the wooden sailing ship that Frédéric bought in Mauritius and the large Flemish painting of grazing cows, which he rescued from a great aunt's barn (where I dearly wish it had stayed). But really, this preliminary carload is just an excuse to parade as proud owners and excitedly plan where the furniture will go.

We park in the loading zone just outside our building. Although we've come here many times during the day, in the darkness everything looks unfamiliar.

A couple of metres away, a man stands quite still, his back to us. He's peeing, I realise, into the untidy strip of lime trees which we'll soon dub the urinal because everyone from toddlers to businessmen in suits relieve themselves here day and night. A little further along, surrounded by beer bottles, someone is sleeping on the ground between the parked motorbikes. I try to think compassionate thoughts but it's no good; I hope we won't have to pick our way over drunks and broken glass every night.

As we're unloading the car, something catches my eye: a dark mass a few metres from our front door which appears to be moving, growing, *writhing*. The street lighting is dim and from a distance it's difficult to make out what it is.

I stop, appalled. 'Fred, look!'

Scores of seriously big rats are tearing at something shaped like a human head which in a calmer moment I would identify as a pineapple from the nearby fruit market. But who remains calm after spotting a pyramid of vermin on their newly acquired front doorstep? I count eleven of them, thirteen, fourteen, fifteen, there must be at least twenty. More arrive each second, busily squeezing through a metal grate covering the metro tunnel which leads from the Sentier station. Instead of fleeing as we approach they keep up their frenzied nibbling, cocky and concentrated.

This is hideous. Disgusting. Totally unhygienic. We'll have to write to our new *mairie* about this. Traps must be set, poison laid. What will family and friends think when they come to stay? Kaleidoscopic images from another life race through my mind. Sapphire Sydney coves glittering in the sunlight; fragrant frangipani trees; rainbow-coloured rosellas on bright balconies, hopping impatiently for birdseed. These crystalline snapshots are the antithesis of this sordid, snatching scene before me. I can handle the broken bottles, the drunks, the peeing on our (sort of) front garden. But not this. I search Frédéric for soothing words.

But he thinks this is hilarious. 'Who was desperate to leave

Levallois?' he teases. 'Who'd had enough of those clean, leafy streets?' Grinning, Frédéric gestures grandly towards the rats and the rubbish.

'You wanted the real Paris? *Voilà le vrai Paris!*'

As luck would have it, inside our building most of the stairwell lights have blown. The concierge is on holiday in her native Portugal and no-one has replaced the bulbs. The staircase is a spiral of dark doorways and dramatic shadows. My buoyant mood has been dampened by the rats. The darkness makes the stairwell look even more grubby and grim than I remembered. Before I'd been undaunted by the lack of a lift, making gung-ho declarations about the benefits for the thighs and the bum. But now I count every torturous step. There are one hundred and twenty. Plus five landings, three flat paces in length. I imagine struggling up the stairs with groceries.

Tonight's few possessions require only a couple of trips but by the end, our chests are heaving, our legs unsteady. Suddenly our decision not to employ professional removalists seems pure folly. Nervously, we itemise Frédéric's furniture. One massive oak chest. One incredibly fragile, two-metre high antique mirror that weighs a crushing eighty kilos. A marble-topped console table. Not to mention tonnes of heavy books, dozens of paintings. We think of the friends who have gallantly volunteered to help us move. This will put these friendships to the test.

Back at Levallois, Frédéric and I begin the serious business of preparing to move. I pride myself on a certain professionalism when it comes to packing up houses and apartments. Having a father who was an air-force pilot meant postings every couple of years, ensuring the family got lots of practice at moving, even if we were aided. At university, during several summer holidays, Sue and I had packed boxes for a Canberra removal firm. For a student, it was a well-paid job, if lacking in cool status and glamour. But the upshot is I'm uncharacteristically conscientious about details such as labelling boxes and the number of sheets of scrunched-up newspaper which are required for protective padding. Frédéric, meanwhile, has apparently forgotten his resolutions about being *'maniac'*: egg beaters are chucked in with books, unpaid electricity bills together with wine bottles. Jean-Michel is right. When it comes to moving house, his friend is *'une vraie catastrophe'*.

We are knee-deep in boxes, newspaper and kitchen utensils when we're interrupted by a boisterous barrage of buzzing and knocking. Our team of removalists is at the front door. Some of Frédéric's oldest friends from northern France have driven down to help us for the weekend: Jean-Michel, Léon, who with his wife Caroline had been so delightful at that lunch in the country, and Jean-René and his wife Corine. It's all part of a pact this group has maintained for twenty years, and the tradition is now part of their historical superglue. Every time one of them shifts house, the others help, transforming what is a tedious task into a source of hilarious memories and finger-pointing stories which will be raucously recounted at dinners decades from now.

Jean-Michel assumes authority the second he steps through the door. This is his shining moment. For the duration of the weekend he is our general, we his loyal troops. He swaggers around the apartment, sighing theatrically at the still open boxes and untidy piles of odds and ends. He fires a stream of interrogation at Frédéric. 'Have you organised the truck? It better not be like the last *camion de merde* you hired, the one that kept breaking down. Why isn't this stuff packed in boxes? What's for dinner? Omelettes? What? No *frites*?' He puts his arm around me, speaking in a confidential tone as though this is the sort of omission countries go to war over. '*Chérie, ma puce*, always, always serve *frites* with omelettes.'

I don't know whether this is a French rule or just Jean-Michel's opinion (I suspect the latter) but I laugh anyway. It is impossible to be offended by Jean-Michel, even if he is not joking about the *frites*. The presence of this group of friends fills the apartment with gaiety. Although we don't see them often because they all live several hours north of Paris, right from my first meetings with them all, we'd hit it off. Their constant joking and easy acceptance of me is an antidote to the formality of many Parisian encounters.

A year or two older than Frédéric, Jean-Michel has always played big brother to his friend, alternating roguish pranks with protective responsibility. As kids, one minute Jean-Michel would be on his *mobilette*, chasing his friend who only had a bicycle, until he rammed him straight into a prickle bush. The next he'd be smoothing things over, reassuring Frédéric's parents that *tout va bien*, when their son was slapped in an army detention cell during his military service in Djibouti for turning up drunk and patriotically painted to a morning parade. This weekend will be no different. Bullishly, Jean-Michel will grumble about Frédéric's 'château' taste in furniture which is a pain in the arse to move. Then, when no-one's looking, he will painstakingly wrap padding around the giant, sculpted mirror, careful that none of the tape touches the gilt.

Over a dinner of omelettes (no *frites*), pork terrine made by Léon's mother-in-law, cheeses and red wine, Jean-Michel outlines our battle plan. Tomorrow we'll wake at six. His voice rolls firmly over our squeals of protest. Not a minute later. This is a big job, a serious undertaking. He will be up even earlier to get our breakfast. We try telling him Paris *boulangeries* never open before seven but Jean-Michel holds up an impatient, silencing hand: leave it to me, he says. The morning will be spent getting the boxes and furniture down the narrow Levallois staircase and loading the truck. Then we'll break for a restorative lunch. We're going to need one almighty burst of energy for the afternoon to haul our belongings up six flights of stairs.

'ALLEZ, ALLEZ, ALLEZ!' Jean-Michel's booming reveille the next morning must have blasted through all five floors of our building. The apartment smells of croissants, fresh from the oven. He passes them around with a flourish. Apparently the *charmante* woman at the bakery (who has never been especially charming to me) obligingly opened the door a little early. The others dunk their croissants in their coffee, a French habit I have never been able to fathom because a) it seems a waste of all that delicious crispness, and b) it leaves soggy pastry flakes floating in your cup. We spend the morning doing as we're told, loading everything that will fit into the minuscule lift (not much), and lugging the rest down the four flights of stairs, into the truck. Exhausted, we arrive in the city centre outside our new apartment right on time; the move is running to schedule. Jean-Michel declares it's time for lunch.

But far from reviving us, stopping for takeaway chicken, potatoes, salad and beers has a soporific effect. The morning's work has wiped us out; muscles we didn't even know existed signal their soreness. Hot sunbeams stream through the skylights, sapping the last of our energy. We all want siestas. The jocular mood has sobered. Crashed out on the blond parquet floor, no-one can move. Even Jean-Michel's bravado appears broken by the knowledge that the worst is yet to come. Parked on the street six floors below us, the truck is waiting, crammed to the ceiling with furniture and boxes. Just thinking about it makes me want to weep.

And then four other friends turn up to help. Alicia, her husband Rupert, and some Australian friends Aileen and Brett, whom I have met only recently. When they'd gamely offered, I'd told them not to worry about coming—secretly hoping they would, of course. The timing of 'les anglo-saxons', as everyone broadly calls them, is miraculous. Prostrate, we stare at them as though they are angels.

Buoyed by the responsibility of more troops, Jean-Michel snaps back into command. We are to work in a chain: he and Frédéric will get the heavy stuff out of the van and up to the second landing. Léon and Jean-René will carry it up to the fourth floor, where Rupert and Brett will take over for the final leg. Corine, Aileen, Alicia and I form another chain, passing boxes.

In Paris, in an average year there are only a few days when the temperature nudges over thirty degrees centigrade. Today happens to be one of them. It is boiling and there's not a breath of a breeze. Before long the stairs are slippery with sweat and we have pink balloon faces. At one point I stumble over Jean-René, flat on his back, his sagging body following the contour of the steps, cartoon-style. As we struggle under the seriously heavy weights, I worry about someone falling. You could break a limb, even your neck. Our legs quiver like twigs about to snap. But between grimaces and groans, our team jokes stoically. By five, every last item is at the top. No-one has fallen down the stairs, even the massive mirror with its delicate gilt has arrived in one piece. Most amazing of all, these smiling people are still our friends!

That night, Frédéric and I take everyone out for dinner at La Fresque, a convivial bistro at Les Halles whose walls are covered in frescoes from its previous life as an oyster shop. Already the day has taken on legendary status—it is the Mother of all Moves. I am teased for cramming too many heavy books into my boxes. Frédéric is ribbed about his move-unfriendly furniture. Recklessly pouring more red, Léon proposes an amendment to their pact. Next time the workers will strike unless our place has a lift.

Squashed around the too-small table, surrounded by the happy banter of friends, I am in high spirits. Later, this evening will seem to occupy a pivotal place in time, like a bridge between two epochs. Looking back I'll reflect that my jubilance stemmed, in part, from the first stirrings of a sense of belonging. But right now I just feel glad to have trusted my early intuition: everything *is* working out in France, slowly. After dinner, Jean-Michel and the others will crash at our place. Tomorrow, Frédéric and I will start settling into our apartment, unpacking boxes and hanging paintings. From this very first night in our new home, the future looks a lot more fun.

Nine

One of the tasks I most relish in the first few weeks after our move is setting up my new office. After eighteen months of working from the dining room table, packing up my computer every time we want to eat, having a separate space of my own seems a luxury. By the time we left Levallois I could no longer contain my burgeoning stack of story and research files. They'd invaded the lounge room — clippings and papers were strewn like litter across book shelves, chairs and the coffee table. My mess became a bone of contention: Frédéric couldn't stand it. The French like their *salons* spotless, ever ready to receive guests. Having trained himself to be neat, to Frédéric it seemed unjustly ironic that no sooner had he achieved a perfect lounge room than I rolled up and wrecked it.

And so my new office, with its door that can be conveniently closed to hide the disorder inside, is an immense relief to both of us. We give the walls a fresh coat of white paint which makes the space light and bright. I buy a new desk and a filing cabinet which to our horror are delivered in boxes of parts you have to assemble yourself. The desk is pretty straightforward but the filing cabinet is a jumble of puzzle pieces. I try to make sense of the diagrams while Frédéric fumes about how scandalous it is to have to pay for such self-punishment. Although his patience is limitless for tedious tasks like scratching off the green paint which covered his gilded mirror, DIY sends him apoplectic.

Finally my office furniture is assembled. The desk wobbles and the filing cabinet ejects its contents every time I open a drawer but I am thrilled. We push the desk into the corner facing the window which looks across the courtyard to the other wing of our building and the rooftops beyond it. Sky fills the top half of the frame, ensuring I never feel enclosed. It is hardly an exceptional view but it is mine and to me it is special.

The truth is I really need my own office now. Work has become quite busy. When the Journalists in Europe program finished, I had already begun writing regularly for three or four cherished editors, who now not only answer my faxes but also frequently commission stories. Mostly they are feature articles; I avoid news reporting. News is scary. How can a lone freelancer compete with the speed and resources of agencies like Reuters and AFP? Jacques Chirac might be assassinated in Paris overnight and I wouldn't even know until I received an early morning call from a Sydney editor, who because of the time difference has had a whole day to find out the facts, so now wants the juicy details—preferably a scoop—and all within two hours. (This nightmarish scenario actually comes true when Diana, Princess of Wales, is killed in a Paris car crash.) This is not for me, these early wake-up calls, the impossibly tight deadlines, the sickly feeling in your stomach as you stare at a blank screen, knowing that any minute now the editor's going to call (feigning casualness) with the dreaded question: 'Um, how's the story coming along?'.

But I love having time to research and write. Feature

writing is incredibly varied. One day you're sitting in the palatial Hôtel Crillon interviewing Jeremy Irons about his latest film, the next you're on an RER train to a bleak Paris suburb to interview angry French–Algerian youth. And although it's a battle to find publications willing to pay travel expenses, some magazines do send me abroad. There is nothing glamorous about these trips. Commissioning editors always lament how they'd give me more money for expenses—of course they would!—if it weren't for their miserly editorial budgets. Invariably I end up in a modest hotel in a seedy part of town. But it wouldn't occur to me to complain; I'm grateful for every break.

These trips away exemplify the best thing about the job of a journalist. For short, intense periods you're welcomed into worlds that are completely different from your own. Ordinary people tell you their extraordinary stories. And although they will quickly forget you, you don't forget them. Their lives— touching, heartbreaking and sometimes uplifting—somehow stay with you. The handsome twenty-something boys in downtown Sarajevo—one Serb, one Croat, the other Muslim—best friends since childhood whose stirring story was simply the fact they'd remained best friends throughout the war. The Sicilian widow dressed in peasant black who broke the Omerta code of silence when she stood up in a courtroom filled with menacing Mafiosi and pointed to the men who murdered her husband. The tiny woman in Belfast who, two decades after her son was murdered during the Troubles, still says a prayer and lights a candle for him every night.

Once the office furniture is assembled and my clippings are all filed, I settle down to work. With no trips planned in the immediate future, for the next few months I enjoy writing in the peace of my new office. That is, until *la rentrée* in early September, the official start of the new school year, when all of a sudden a stir-crazy cacophony rips through my office window, tearing like a comet through my concentration.

Incredibly, we'd bought our apartment without knowing that a school wraps around the base of the building. Our visits had fallen on weekends or after hours when all was still and quiet. By the time we moved in, classes had already broken up for the long summer break. Not surprisingly, the real estate agent didn't mention the school when we'd enquired about our neighbours. Directly below us, it isn't visible without leaning precariously out the windows.

But oh how we hear it, I now discover. The playground is asphalt and ridiculously small because in France education is about filling heads with facts, not having fun (even if this is a *maternelle primaire*, which means the pupils range in age from three to eleven). Several times each day, one hundred under-exercised kids catapult out of class to run around something the size of a tennis court, squealing and screaming. The noise problem comes to a head soon after they start back. One morning, rushing to meet a deadline for a story on the far-right National Front party, I can't think for the whining wail of a little girl.

'Give me the ball! Give me! GIVE MEEE!' Her bawling is maddening—like a siren that can't be switched off. Then, after about five minutes, suddenly quiet. The ball crisis is over. Relieved, I turn back to my computer screen. Her next cry makes me jump, blasting through my window with all the operatic force her little lungs can muster: 'MAMAN, MAAMAN!'

I stick my head out the window.

'JUST GIVE HER THE BLOODY BALL! NOW SHUT UP THE LOT OF YOU!'

There is an astonished silence from below. Immensely satisfied, I imagine one hundred bewildered little heads swivelling to spot the screaming madwoman. But they can't see me any more than I can see them. Only later does it occur to me that I never would have done this in Australia; that this rather forceful approach to the problem is actually quite French. In our *quartier*, I've seen mothers lambasting toddlers for dirtying their clean clothes; adults—perfect strangers—roaring abuse at each other because someone's scooter is blocking someone else's doorway.

The silence from below doesn't last—within seconds the playground erupts in an excited babble of retaliatory *SHUT-UPS* which escalate until a teacher is finally forced to leave his lunch to establish some order. In time, though, I get used to this juvenile clamour and even grow fond of it. My work schedule adapts to the school day. I learn to avoid doing phone interviews during playtime. When the classes pour outside for lunch it's a sign for me to take a break too. Every now and then from my lofty, unseeing vantage point I adjudicate disputes. Like me, I sense the children quite enjoy our exchanges.

More worrying are the thumping *THWACKS!* which send tremors through our building several times a day. The neighbours' dog breaks into alarmed barking; the fourth floor babies wake and wail. The first time it happens I scamper down the stairwell, half-expecting to discover a semitrailer has crashed through our front entrance. But the cause of the quaking is rather more mundane. Fabric. Mammoth rolls of ordinary material are being delivered to the clothing sweat shops which occupy the first three levels of our building.

Reaching their destination, the workmen let the lead-weight cylinders topple and crash to the floor.

We live on the perimeter of two overlapping *quartiers*. Immediately to the south is the Montorgueil neighbourhood—quite a respectable, hip Paris address. But a few paces north is the heart of the city's rag trade district known as the Sentier. A maze of skinny streets, overcrowded workshops, poky passages and fire-hazard buildings, the area has been the launch pad for some major French labels such as Kookai and Naf Naf. Mostly, the businesses are owned by Sephardic Jews from North Africa. The secret of the Sentier's success is hard work and fast production—between them the several thousand workshops can handle huge orders and short deadlines, churning out beaded T-shirts or fringed pants in their hundreds. Sure, it's not Dior or Chanel but the clothes are fashionable and cheap.

Despite its central location, you won't find the Sentier listed in many guide books. When mentioned, it is usually to say that This is Not the Sort of Area Where Most People Would Like to Live. Although we weren't deterred by this widely held opinion, it is somewhat justified. The delivery trucks are responsible for some of the worst traffic jams in Paris. They block the narrow streets, nonchalantly loading or unloading while outraged drivers toot and shout abuse. Pedestrians have to dodge racing porters wheeling trolleys piled with fabric and rolling rails of clothing. Residents can forget about owning a car—you've got more chance of being kidnapped by an alien aircraft than finding a space big enough for a mini. Rather than risk the hassles and daily parking fines, we decide to leave Frédéric's car on a boulevard at Levallois while we work out whether or not to sell it.

The sewing machines in our building purr seven days a

week and in summer, with the windows wide open, we can hear them racing up seams and frantically spearing zippers. Frequently, leaving our building means fighting through five hundred cropped denim jackets or sliding down stairs sparkling with sequins, already falling off before the clothes even make it into the shops. Although there is wide opposition to the Sentier—from taxi drivers and city planners to environmental groups and residents—so far campaigns to move the district out of Paris have failed.

Over-the-top, in-your-face, a law unto itself, that's the Sentier for you. Illegal immigrants are paid by the garment to work outrageously long hours in workshops which breach the gamut of health and safety regulations. Swindling is carried out on a mythic scale. One audacious racket involved ripping off scores of financial institutions to the tune of about $150 million, through an elaborate network of money laundering and cheque kiting. After investigators swooped on the area, one hundred businesses were found to be directly involved. Before the case could be tried in 2001, a special eight-hundred square metre court room had to be built in the Palais de Justice to hold all the accused.

For a long time, merely mentioning the Sentier would likely elicit anti-Semitic remarks. Even the established Ashkenazim in the nearby Marais disdained the district, considering their North African brethren ostentatious and impious. But then *La Vérité Si Je Mens* hit French cinemas, proving such a success that it prompted an equally popular sequel. A satirical film set in the Sentier, it comically captured the stereotypes, camped them up, and made the whole country laugh and love them. We saw it at the Rex cinema, a Paris institution five minutes from home, and were surrounded by Sephardic youth who looked a lot like the characters on the screen. They roared at the young men in glossy convertibles cruising the narrow streets, talking on mobile phones above dance music booming from customised car stereos. The girls permanently dressed for clubbing in platform shoes and tight tops that show off cleavages. The flashy Deauville hotels. They revelled in the light-hearted characterisations, embraced the jokes, proud to own them.

Truthfully, I could do without the fabric scraps which litter our entrance. I go wild at the delivery men who stub out their cigarettes on our wooden stairs. If we don't go up in flames first, one day the reckless deliveries of fabric rolls are going to bring down the building.

And yet . . .

Somehow the Sentier has an appeal reminiscent of another era. *Le vieux Paris.* In the past, the entire capital was a clutter of commerce and residences which rose above narrow, canyon-like streets. Then in the mid–nineteenth century, Napoléon III appointed Georges Haussmann to carry out some urban planning. Much needed amenities were installed—sewers, water supplies, gas mains. But the new boulevards, however necessary, destroyed everything in their wake. The poor were moved out and the city's ancient heart was made to look more orderly.

The Sentier somehow escaped the clean up—and has resisted subsequent efforts. Among the gilded monuments of inner Paris, it has the audacity to be real. The district is strictly utilitarian: too consumed with the business of making clothes to care about appearances. Compared to the corporate blandness of many other city centres, the chaos of the skinny streets seems almost quaint. I like the Sentier's crowded cafés with their formica tables of sweaty barrow boys and serene Hasidim. The dishevelled little shops which sell nothing but zippers or skeins of gaudy flowers or *faux* astrakhan dyed olive or orange. It may be grubby, noisy and polluted but the quarter is also alive and oddly invigorating.

Eager to know more about the different *quartiers* in our area, I start reading books on central Paris and discover it has a fascinating, unique history. At the southern end of Rue Montorgueil is Les Halles, which aprons around the massive St-Eustache church. Despite the proximity of the two quarters, these days they are entirely different. Devoid of charm, Les Halles is the sort of place you avoid at night—beneath a park that attracts drunks and dealers is a cavernous underground shopping mall full of teen shops and takeaways. But the neighbourhood wasn't always so soulless, I learn.

For eight hundred years, Les Halles was home to a sprawling food market, teaming with racing barrow boys and tough men with towering baskets of fruit and vegetables bending their backs. Well into the twentieth century, the market exuded a medieval conviviality. At dawn, hundreds of horse-drawn carts and delivery trucks would roll in from across France, disgorging cattle, squealing pigs, geese, ducks and chickens. Stall owners piled their cabbages and cauliflowers into pyramids that were so tall they rose halfway up the buildings behind them. Locals joked the smell of seafood and tripe had permeated the cobblestones. Bowls of winey onion soup warmed callused winter hands. Deals were sealed over *pichets* of rough red in bistros and bars with names that sound straight out of old French films—Le Chien qui Fume, Le Pied de Cochon, L'Escargot. The Smoking Dog, The Pig's Foot, The Snail. Piano accordions pumped out popular songs on street corners. At night, the old zinc counters propped up everyone from prostitutes to poets. The 'belly of Paris' is how the nineteenth-century French writer Emile Zola described it.

Les Halles also had a seamy side: a thriving black market and an exploding rat population, not to mention the red light district which bubbled around its edges night and day for the wellbeing of the market men. On summer afternoons, the stench of rotting vegetables made passers-by gag. As the number of delivery trucks increased, the traffic tangles became untenable. Post-war Paris was anxious to be seen as progressive and modern and De Gaulle considered this unruly congestion unbecoming for the heart of the capital. In 1969, the first food pavilion was pulled down and the market was gradually moved south of Paris.

It was one of the biggest, most controversial demolition jobs ever undertaken in France and it quickly acquired mythical proportions. According to local lore, when the meat hall was dismantled, a black tide of vermin poured into nearby homes. For the market folk the relocation brought an end to the only life they'd ever known. Many plunged into depressions, refusing to move their stalls to Rungis—the modern replacement where produce is sold in air-conditioned steel hangars. Les Halles had been the city's heartbeat. Every Parisian old enough to remember it speaks wistfully of the colour and the characters, the coarse jokes and naughty repartee which rang through cobbled lanes late into the night. To many people, its closure signalled the loss of Paris' glorious gritty soul.

But a spirited splinter of the old market has survived. Rue Montorgueil was the oyster nub of the Les Halles market and it drew people from all walks of life. Monet painted the street, we learn. Balzac used to eat oysters at the café Au Rocher de Cancale. Although the *quartier*'s inhabitants were once resolutely working class, increasingly they're likely to be photographers, writers, professionals with young kids and gay couples with dogs. Fortunately, the recent arrivals haven't extinguished all the populist charm. The odours may be less pungent, the fruit and vegetable stands less grand, the prostitutes confined to Rue St-Denis. And there's only one oyster vendor left, a fellow who has been selling on the street for more than two decades, apparently. But in spite of these changes, the area has retained a sense of identity.

Like some of the other Paris 'markets', Rue Montorgueil is not so much a market as a street of speciality food shops, some of which wheel out stalls. It takes only ten minutes to stroll from one end to the other but the repetition of boutiques reveals something about French priorities. Nine cafés, six *boulangeries*, four butchers, four wine shops, three *fromageries*, two *chocolatiers*, two *poissonneries*, three fruit and vegetable shops and—for the truly carnivorous—one horse meat butcher. Queues of people waiting to buy cigarettes trail from two *tabacs*. Three pharmacies feed the French addiction to prescribed medicine, a dependence encouraged by everyone in the lucrative health care business from doctors to pharmaceutical companies.

It is almost impossible to describe the pleasure I derive from the rituals that will become synonymous with my new life in Paris. My favourite time of day on Rue Montorgueil is early morning—'early' in France meaning anytime before 9.30am. Even on overcast days, the white façades quiver with brightness. The *quartier* has an air of industriousness. Delivery trucks roll in. The armada of green cleaning trucks marked *Propreté de Paris* is inching forward, trailed by a team of mostly African sweepers. Often, when I step out the front door of our building, they're standing at the top of Rue Montorgueil leaning on their bright green plastic brooms, hands chopping the air in animated conversation. Water fountains from drains, rushing in rivulets down the street and leaving the pavement stones fresh and glistening.

My first stop is at the *papeterie* for newspapers. It would be much cheaper to buy a subscription and have them delivered but this place quickly becomes a morning must. The miniature shop is crowded with a chaotic conviviality which comes from having too many people and pets in such a small space. Customers linger to chat with the two friendly brothers who own it. Among the regulars is an elderly Italian with opera aspirations who every morning carefully reads the pages of *Corriere della Sera* before putting it back on the rack. Although his cream hat wouldn't be out of place on a beach and the gold buttons on his blazer have lost their lustre, this diminutive man is a walking testimony to old-fashioned pride and panache.

He struts down the street with princely deportment, singing the occasional LAAAA! at the top of his lungs. Anywhere else he'd probably be written off as a nutter but he's lived in this *quartier* for almost forty years and everyone knows him. His sonorous, rather limited repertoire draws indulgent smiles. One day at the *papeterie* I ask him why he sings and his reply is simple and philosophic: growing up in Verona, Italy, his two favourite pastimes were singing and soccer. Now he's too old for soccer, so he makes the most of his voice.

I should buy *Le Monde*. It is, after all, the chosen newspaper of *les intellos* and it remains the benchmark in France for good journalism. It is also excellent value for money if you judge by the number of words. It devotes an incredible amount of space to important, academic articles with headlines like 'Fight

Intolerance, It's Our Responsibility' and 'Is Philosophy A Monolith?'. Worthy though these subjects are, for me the scholarly tone, that spidery print uninterrupted by anything as plebeian as a photo, are too daunting. It would take all day to struggle through it. I don't buy *Le Figaro*, either. Not because it's a right-leaning paper but because I can't forgive it for 'Madame', its weekend magazine full of beauty and fashion, the very name of which, it seems to me, implies that lipsticks and liposuction are far more interesting to women than the main magazine devoted to serious news. 'Imagine *The Guardian* or *The Australian* calling a weekend supplement "Mrs!",' I rail, prompting astonishment from Frédéric who takes great Gallic pride in his country's political incorrectness. Instead I opt for *Libération* (easy headlines, big photos) and the *International Herald Tribune*.

Often I go to Centre Ville for a coffee and a croissant. The advantage of this café is the good coffee and its location—from here you can watch the market come to life. I sit absorbing the energy, unable to concentrate on my newspaper for the theatre in front of me. Beefy men shoulder giant carcasses into the butcher shop diagonally opposite. '*Salut chef!*' the driver shouts, seeing one of his market mates. While they stop to chat, a bright red side of something is left swinging from a hook out the back of the truck. I watch passing dogs straining on their leads for a lick, only narrowly missing the object of their frenzied desire.

Directly opposite the café, at the fruit and vegetable stalls, old biddies wheeling wobbly shopping trolleys stop for a sprig of parsley and a chat. Bright signs stab the radiant displays—everything is either '*extra*' (top quality) or '*en promotion*' (special offer) or both. Red and yellow capsicums are arranged in perfect pyramids; tomatoes are sold on vines;

clementines come on stems with glossy green leaves. They look beautiful, like a still-life scene you want to photograph or paint.

For a change, sometimes I head higher up the street where the cafés with their unpretentious zinc counters have retained a hint of workaday spirit. Among them is La Grappe d'Orgueil, run by Dehbia who inherited the bar from her Algerian father and Jewish mother. At night the crowd is multicultural, lively and interesting—a reflection of her mixed heritage. In the morning occasionally I go to Le Commerce, where the floors are sprinkled with sugar wrappers and cigarette ash. Smart executives in immaculate black toss back espressos on their way to work. Next to them stand blood-stained butchers and tough fruit sellers enjoying beers with meaty breakfasts, having already done a half day's work. The regulars mostly stand at the bar. 'Rouge ou blanc?' the barman René asks them. In the corner sits a flame-haired woman who starts each day with a cigar and a medicinal glass of white. The old fellows kiss cheeks and pump hands, 'Ça va mon gros?' How're things, my fat one? It is a fraternal French greeting—one of many which the likes of Jean-Michel use constantly. I'd love to be able to walk in and say 'Hi, my fat rabbit' too, but, of course, that would be totally inappropriate. Not only because it's considered very blokey but also because I'm not one of them. As much as I love this street and this neighbourhood, I am a newcomer—a foreign one at that—and as such the regulars regard me with polite indifference. How long will it be, I wonder, before I really feel part of it?

No matter where I go for coffee in the morning, I always catch sight of Napoléon, rattling up and down Rue Montorgueil on a bike which looks far too frail to support him.

A giant fellow with a big belly and a grubby grey beard, he belongs to the *quartier*'s cast of characters. Shabbily dressed in a brown coat, beret and leather boots with the tongues hanging out, he looks as though he's homeless but in fact Napoléon owns a spacious apartment a good deal larger than ours. According to the butcher, he inherited it from his parents and it is crammed floor to ceiling with the junk Napoléon pulls from local rubbish bins. By the end of each day, his bike basket is laden with treasures—broken toys, a left glove or torn umbrella—as well as fruit and vegetables which he's either been given or has pinched from the stalls.

He is the street stirrer, a *provocateur par excellence*, a genuine eccentric. Beneath errant eyebrows, his button eyes fizz with mischief. He'll sit on his bike, incessantly ringing its shrill bell in the hope of getting a bite. '*Ça t'énerve, toi?*' he challenges passers-by with a sly smirk, irreverently addressing them using *tu* and *toi*. Does this noise annoy you?

One morning walking down Rue Montorgueil I'm startled by insistent tooting. Beep-beep! Beep-beep! Turning around I see Napoléon, who to my disbelief is behind the wheel of a gleaming navy BMW. It's not unusual to see him doing odd jobs around the place to earn pocket money and this time it seems he's parking the car of a local rag-trade magnate. Suddenly Napoléon brakes. By now all eyes in the street are on him and he laps up the attention, cackling through the tinted windows. With an actor's appreciation of high theatre and timing, he reaches into his coat pocket and pulls out a pair of flashy purple sunglasses which he fits over his huge, vein-rippled nose. I recognise them—they are made of paper and earlier in the week people were giving the glasses away to promote some new 3D cinema. Grinning wildly at his purple audience, he resumes his royal parade.

Along with eccentrics like Napoléon, every Paris *quartier* has its *clochards*—homeless people who have been living on the same streets for so long that no-one can remember a time when they weren't there. Pierre has been in our neighbourhood for thirty years—most of his life, in other words. My first encounter with him is at the fruit and vegetable stall, where he is shouting drunken abuse and searching for targets. Pleased to have spotted a fresh one, Pierre smiles lecherously and offers me a filthy proposition, illustrated by crude hand gestures just in case anyone in the queue has failed to get the point. For the next few months I do my best to avoid him.

But in fact when he's sober (which admittedly is not often) he is genial and remarkably lucid. As my face becomes familiar he starts greeting me from across the street. '*Salut chérie! Ça va ma belle?*' he'll call, head bouncing to the beat blasting his ears through his Walkman. The headphones are just one of many second-hand items given to him by locals. Despite his sometimes belligerent presence and the noisy echo as he tears up and down the street on his clapped out scooter, most people seem to tolerate him with good humour—including the authorities. Whenever there is a drama on the street Pierre is first on the scene, importantly telling police his version of a crime he didn't even witness, insisting on holding the firemen's ladder as though if it weren't for him it might collapse, generally making a nuisance of himself.

At night Pierre sleeps on the street or else squats in an empty building which is being gutted and renovated. He earns money on weekends selling fruit and vegetables for one of the market shops. The responsibility transforms him. He stands behind his street stall, scrubbed, sober and clean-shaven. Everything is *'extra!'* he tells passers-by, bullying them into buying and you can tell by his swagger that Saturdays and Sundays are the highlight of his week.

One of the most appealing features of Paris is the rich diversity of life within a small circumference. A world away from Rue Montorgueil but less than ten minutes' walk from our apartment is the Palais Royal gardens. An oasis of calm beauty, it quickly becomes one of our haunts. One Sunday evening not long after our move, we take a bottle of wine and sliced *saucisson* there. In the twilight, the graceful buildings glint with gold. Beneath the vaulted arcades which frame the gardens—where revolutionaries once roared about *liberté*, *égalité* and *fraternité*—an opera singer is performing *Rigoletto*. Her beautiful soprano bounces off the stone columns; the acoustics are perfect. *'Bravo! Bravo!'* we cry when she finishes.

In Paris parks you're not allowed to sit on the grass—the pleasure of perfect lawn is to admire not use it. We open the swinging gate of one of the enclosed gardens where benches have been placed for quiet contemplation. Throughout the day the sun had drummed down with uncharacteristic intensity, making the city air dense and polluted. But here in the evening stillness, the carefully tended blooms release an exuberant potpourri of honeysuckle, rose and vanilla; the fresh sweetness is heaven. At first we are discreet about our bottle for fear of the barking *gardiens* who patrol the place. But they only seem concerned with keeping people off the grass and dogs out of the gardens. The little one just glares (this is a permanent expression), while his bigger colleague smiles amiably, looking sorry he can't join us.

Darkness comes quickly; lights blink on in the garden. We decide to take the long way home, *le chemin des écoliers*, meaning the meandering route of children who don't want to go to school. Through the southern end of the gardens, across Rue de Rivoli to the Louvre and the Richelieu passage where glass windows allow a view into the museum's magnificent sculpture courts. We pass the magical pyramid, piercing the blue-black sky like an incandescent crystal. Its fairyland beauty has won over most of the critics, who complained its modern geometry would disfigure the majestic museum which was once a royal palace. The fountains are still spouting and because it's a hot evening, children and adults dip bare feet in the glassy pools. Roller bladers slalom across the flat pavement stones.

In the adjoining Cour Carrée, a flautist is playing Vivaldi. It's a cliché, of course, but then Paris is full of them. The familiar notes ring sweetly through the silence. Less ornate than the main Louvre courtyard, the square has a sparseness that is rendered almost numinous by night, when thousands of tiny spotlights make the friezes float in an amber aurora. Somehow it calls for calm and couples whisper on the stone benches, a dad tells his children to keep quiet.

The main, western wing is the most elaborately sculpted of the façades, abundant with tangled vines and bursting buds, lions' heads, wise philosophers and angels. Cherubs gambol, their playful bottoms rendered in round relief, entwined with flowers and fruit and swooping swallows. It is a homage to nature and power, to royalty and religion, to literature and grand ideas. There is Homer playing a lyre, and next to him Virgil, pen in hand, a scroll of poetry falling over his knee. A majestic Moses brandishes the tablet of God's law.

It doesn't matter how many times we do this walk: without fail I'm struck by the heart-stopping beauty of Paris. You'd think the shock would wear off, that seeing it would no longer have the power to leave you wordless. But every sighting feels like the first. Frédéric is as captivated as I am.

I used to marvel at Sydney Harbour too, whenever I saw it. Sparkling blue carves the city with coves and inlets; it's a wonder of nature. But somehow in Paris the feeling of being awe-struck is even stronger. Perhaps because it is still relatively new to me or perhaps because it somehow seems preposterous that such beauty could be created by people. The city is a testament to civilisation. Of course, I know from the last year that living in a gorgeous environment isn't enough to make you happy. But breathtaking beauty of any kind is moving. It makes tourists of us all. It anchors your heart to a place. Just like Sydney Harbour, the wonderful sights of Paris inspire emotion, yes, even love.

Hand in hand in the courtyard, we tip our heads back to take it all in. Ridiculous though it sounds, I can't quite believe I don't have to pay to come here. That now I can simply walk out my front door and savour such places in private moments. It seems pure indulgence.

Ten

One of the consequences of this pervasive beauty in Paris is that it makes leaving your front door feel like you're stepping onto a stage. It calls for dressing up. Just like actors in a play, the pressure is on those who live here to look the part. Perhaps my most revealing lesson in French dress standards occurs one Saturday morning soon after moving into Paris. Rushing to the bakery to get a baguette and croissants, I chuck on an old, shapeless jumper and my tracksuit pants, which I'd rediscovered at the bottom of a wardrobe when we were packing up our place at Levallois. Catching sight of me, Frédéric looks appalled.

'Tracksuit pants?' He's never seen me wearing them before.

'What's wrong with that? I'm only going to the bakery.'

There is a second's pause. Frédéric's eyes implore me. Finally, he manages to speak.

'But it's not nice for the baker!'

I stare at him, incredulous, thinking, 'You can't be serious.' But he is. In fact, this is probably one of the most serious moments of his whole life. His girlfriend is about to step out in public wearing '*pantalons de jogging*' — an item of clothing he wouldn't even wear jogging. He can't fathom how I could do such a thing. I can't fathom why he is making

130

such a fuss. Head held high, I depart defiantly in my voluminous grey bottoms, more conscious than ever that from behind they make me look like a baby elephant.

For a long time, dress remains an issue between us. Underpinning Frédéric's reaction to tracksuit pants is a concept which to me is totally foreign: *looking scruffy is selfish*. Not only do you look like a slob but you let down the whole city. In Paris, failure to dress up leads to instant ostracism. Haughty shopkeepers don't want you in their beautiful shops, let alone to risk getting close enough to serve you.

Coming to terms with this emphasis on appearances is tough. Not because I don't enjoy buying and dressing in nice clothes. I really do. But trying to look perfect all the time has never been a priority. To me, it seems entirely normal to have good days and bad days. Besides, dressing down has an advantage: it makes you look extra good when you decide to dress up. It's the Before and After effect, a strategy I like to think achieves optimal impact (hopefully on the dressing up occasions).

But try telling that to a Frenchman.

In France, vanity is not a vice. Rigorous self-maintenance is imbued from birth—it's a mark of self-pride. Gallic women keep slim not through sweaty spin or pump classes but a strict regime which mixes steely discipline with self-pampering. They take little helpings of each course at dinners and watch how much they drink. To get their bodies back into shape (after giving birth, say) they lather themselves in anti-cellulite creams and book into 'thalasso' therapy centres where they spend a week bobbing about in warm tubs of sea water. They have regular pedicures and eyebrow pluckings and weekly 'brushing' sessions at the hairdressers. Men are expected to pay close attention to their appearances as well.

The loaded phrase '*se mettre en valeur*' is used all the time. It means 'to make the most of yourself'. This is not something the French do when they feel like it: they do it every day. Sloppiness in appearance is considered a fatal disease. Once it takes hold, you're on an irreversible downhill slide. You've committed the unforgivable. *You've let yourself go.*

Faced with my laxity, Frédéric has resorted to pleading refrains. 'Can't you brush the hair at the back of your head?' he says every morning, pointing to the triangle of tangles and tight curls which somehow my brush always misses. (This is a general habit—I only worry about the bits I can see.) Or, 'Your feet are like leather!' to which I invariably reply, 'Good', because doesn't he know that leathery soles are very handy when you're barefoot on burning bitumen and hot sandy beaches? A giant pumice stone arrives one day in the bathroom—apparently all by itself, because, despite all evidence to the contrary, Frédéric denies buying it. But revenge is sweet when my aunt Joan was in Paris and noticed his silky feet: 'They're disgusting Freddo, you should toughen them up!'.

I'd arrived in Paris with a pared-down wardrobe stuffed into my backpack: jeans, T-shirts, tracksuit pants, a couple of jumpers, summer sandals, black Doc Marten's and one 'good' outfit—black trousers, two decent shirts and a black jacket. One week into that first summer holiday, Frédéric was offering—more like insisting—to buy me some new clothes. We traipsed from the Agnes b. boutique to Et Vous, to Tara Jarmon and then in desperation to the fail-proof department store selections at Printemps and Galeries Lafayette. And we couldn't agree on anything.

'What about this?' he'd said holding up a petite dress which stopped mid-thigh. I pulled a face. 'Or this?' It was a skimpy skirt—very cute but not my taste.

'This is nice,' I enthused, showing him a long sarong style skirt with a casual, slightly hippy look that appealed to me. Frédéric frowned.

'What about something more *structured*.'

Flick, flick, flick. Our fingers rifled through more racks of clothes searching for The Outfit that would please both of us.

'I like these,' I'd said at last, holding up a pair of tailored, bootleg trousers.

'Black?' He looked baffled. 'But it's summer—no-one wears black!'

The shopping expedition ended, unsuccessful.

To get an idea of what Paris style is all about, you only need to go to London. London fashion is everything that Paris isn't. One November, as we've done many times, we went there for a weekend and as usual it took me a while to get over the shock. It was a Friday night and after disembarking the Eurostar at Waterloo station, we headed straight to Soho to meet some friends. I couldn't believe what I saw. Noisy crowds spilling out of pubs with pints. Noisy, happy, *drunk* crowds partying in the street! The only drunks you see in Paris are *clochards*—people like Pierre in our *quartier* who live on the street. It wasn't just the drinking that seemed surreal compared to Paris. 'Look at what they're wearing!' I exclaimed to Frédéric. There were vintage skirts mixed with silver S & M-style belts and shrivelled T-shirts which looked as though they'd been dragged from the bottom of wash baskets. Tatty trousers with lacy designer tops and tattooed arms. Sleek black leather teamed with clumpy trainers in shocking pink or purple. Every eclectic combination, every clashing colour exuded attitude. The latest trashy trends were worn with confidence. Compared to the city I'd left a few hours ago, London seemed like another planet.

In Paris there is no such edginess. Paris fashion is not about blindly following trends irrespective of whether they suit your body shape. It's no coincidence that movements like punk and grunge never really took off here. How unattractive. The French don't dress to make political statements. They don't like wild innovation or irony when it comes to their appearance. They don't want to stand out for looking funny or different or eccentric.

Take a look at your average *parisienne*. No matter how long the skirts are on the international fashion runways, *hers will always be short*. She will wear a beautifully tailored jacket, suggestive of the curves it covers. A snug Petit Bateau T-shirt shows why spending pay packets on padded, push-up bras is an investment. Her colours match, her choice of clothes is coherent. Petite, with lovely shapely legs, she wears very little makeup because she doesn't need it. Just a smear of lip gloss, faint colour in her cheeks and naked dark eyes. Her look is brilliantly balanced—*soignée* but natural, sexy without being tarty.

Elderly *parisiennes* are more excessive. The city is full of formidably glamorous grannies. They sweep into places such as the gilded Paris tea-room, Ladurée, on spiky heels, with trailing fur coats and fairy-floss hair that has been coloured a deep mahogany. Eyebrows are pencilled into dark crescents, mouths accentuated by lip liner. Twig legs poke from skirts. The occasional flamboyant accessory shows individual flair—a thin leopard print belt or a red felt hat tipped at just the right angle with a caramel plume tucked under the band. Fancy leather leads stretch like umbilical cords to dainty terriers who sit on seats. These women are awesome.

The essence of French style can be summed up in two words, which linked together are loaded with meaning: *bon goût*. Good taste. The concept has far more to do with the dazzling court of Versailles than this season's trends. It emerged during the seventeenth century, when Louis XIV built a culture of beauty, etiquette and elegance which still dictates almost every detail of French life, from the exquisitely decorated Paris shop windows to *l'art de la table*. In France, the expressions '*bon goût*' and '*mauvais goût*' and '*erreur de goût*' are used a lot. Said about your apartment, your outfit, your anything, the former is the ultimate compliment. Being told something is 'bad taste' or an 'error of taste' is a savage insult.

It isn't until I interview the fashion designer Inès de La Fressange that I truly understand Frédéric's abhorrence of tracksuit pants. A magazine has asked me to write an article on French style and it seems logical to speak to her—a former muse of Karl Lagerfeld, she is *bon goût* in living breathing colour. As the end of my second year in France approaches, increasingly journalism leads me into interesting areas of French life and culture that would otherwise be inaccessible. Some interviews turn out to be epiphanies, offering insights and helping solve mysteries. This is one of them.

When I arrive at her studio, the place is teeming with polished PR people, models and dressmakers, but Inès is easy to spot. From her name-brand sunglasses pushed on top of her head, down to her leather moccasins, she oozes casual chic. Although in her early forties her creamy skin is incredibly youthful. Sliding cheekbones conjure up images of Coco; the dark pixie crop is reminiscent of Audrey Hepburn. She epitomises the look French women aspire to: a mix of aristocratic beauty spiced with a dash of modern mum. Magazines run photo spreads of Inès in her covetable classics—white shirts with trailing cuffs teamed with tailored jackets; slim trouser suits worn with snug turtlenecks. Cradling a cigarette and a tar-black espresso, today she is wearing camel-coloured suede pants. Her long legs coil neatly under her chair. Five minutes later, in one illuminating breath, she has inadvertently highlighted the three guiding principles of the Gallic dress code.

'I think it's really bad taste to be too obsessed with looking wealthy,' she tells me. 'And totally good taste is too conventional. It puts your husband to sleep—you know, you're like a nun. You need accessories, different things. I try to make women elegant, but not boring.'

Discrétion. Séduction. Elégance.

Later, I come to the question which most baffles me.

'Do you find that it's, you know, an *effort* trying to look good all the time?'

Inès inhales on her cigarette (the secret to her thinness?) before replying. She speaks English perfectly, but with a French accent that's so cute you can't help wondering whether it's put on. Charmingly, she tells me that of course she has good days and bad days just like everybody else. Then she says:

'To stay the whole day neat and impeccable is much more comfortable than looking like you're in your pyjamas. You see, these women with tight leggings and huge sweaters, they imagine that because they are a little round it's better if they wear something big. But they just look worse. It is much more comfortable to wear a jacket that is well cut in a nice fabric than it is to look awful.'

She pronounces this last word 'offal'. And suddenly it's quite clear to me that I've spent a good part of my life looking offal. Fifteen minutes with Inès and I've mentally chucked out all my baggy jumpers for those nights in front of the telly.

When she coolly announces you don't need a lot of clothes, you need the *right* clothes it's obvious I have to start my wardrobe from scratch. Buy less, pay more, she advises, and so I vow to spend hugely, extravagantly. Never wear shorts in Paris, they're only for tourists, she declares. I cringe, recalling how I'd arrived at the airport for that first summer holiday wearing shorts. What was I thinking? 'When it's very 'ot, it's better to wear long pants in linen or cotton. You would feel more 'appy, and we would be more 'appy too.'

And there it is—the explanation for Frédéric's pathological aversion to tracksuit pants. The simple statement that instantly elucidates why in hotel rooms he'll remove any paintings from the wall that don't meet his approval. The first time he did it I couldn't believe it. Coming out of the bathroom, I blinked at the bare walls where less than five minutes ago there'd been three or four paintings, I was sure. And then I saw them, judiciously stacked in a corner on the floor.

'Why'd you do that?' I enquired, astounded. He'd pulled a face straight off some toffee-nosed aristocratic.

'They're ugly. I didn't feel well.'

If my tracksuit pants had practically given Frédéric a seizure, now it was my turn to be aghast. Admittedly the paintings *were* bad—insipid watercolours of flowers that looked like they'd been cut from a free calendar. But surely he could put up with them for a night? I mean who appointed *him* the hotel's arbiter of taste and art? This business of feeling 'unwell' struck me as utterly precious. But my objections didn't make the slightest difference: the paintings stayed on the floor.

'We're so much better now,' he'd declared royally, waving his hand at the unblemished walls. The look of queasy discomfort had cleared from his face; he'd perked up. In his mind he'd done nothing wrong. In fact he'd done us—the entire hotel, really—a huge favour. It was clear I would have to get used to this foible.

He can't help it, you see. The thing is, the French are highly sensitive to aesthetics. Anything unattractive—even something as insignificant as an under-dressed tourist—can make them uncomfortable. It spoils the lovely scenery. They become irritable. Unwell, as Frédéric put it. You might think this is ridiculous. But I have witnessed this bizarre phenomenon many times.

One weekend when we go to see Frédéric's father in northern France we end up stopping at the local Auchan hypermarket to buy a few groceries. It is Saturday morning and the carpark is packed with British coaches which have unloaded their cargo of eager day-shoppers from across the Channel. Compared to England, everything in France is cheap—most notably alcohol. We have to circle several times to find a car space, Frédéric grumbling ungraciously about the 'invasion' and how you'd think two centuries of British occupation in northern France were quite enough.

Inside, squadrons of English shoppers choke the aisles, wheeling trolleys piled with wine, spirits and enough beer to sink the ferry on the way home. As they pass in shorts and singlets, thongs and tracksuit pants—*PANTALONS DE JOGGING?!*—Frédéric's mood sours by the second. Never mind that the Auchan hypermarket in economically depressed Boulogne-sur-Mer is hardly a summit of style (more like a crevasse). Their sloppy dress standards are 'polluting' his hometown.

Revolted, Frédéric glares at an Englishman who is bending for more beer, causing his shorts to slide south and reveal a substantial expanse of pink bottom. We are standing behind him, waiting to get near the shelves, when he farts. Emphatically. Explosively.

It is not the most gracious of gestures, to be sure, but you've got to admit the timing is exquisite. What a succinct response to Frédéric's Brit-bashing! It's as though the shopper took aim—Frédéric (gassed and stunned) is just centimetres from the firing line. I practically fall on the floor laughing.

But someone experiences a serious sense of humour failure. Frédéric is truly, genuinely livid. The fart is not funny. It is—and these are his exact words—'a declaration of war! A lack of respect for French standards! AN OUT-RAGEOUS PROVOCATION!'. And France retreats in a petulant fury, abandoning the trolley and leaving the alcohol aisles to the enemy English.

If fashion in the provinces can be erratic, in Paris the pressure to look the part is unrelenting. Some streets are especially intimidating. Take Rue du Faubourg St-Honoré in the 8th *arrondissement*, for example, which is famous for the Elysée presidential palace and designer shops and fashion houses. This is where you go for skimpy scraps of luscious lingerie, €220 Hermès dog collars or to add your name to the waiting list for the latest fashion cult handbag. The street is seductive: before you know it you've fallen headlong in love with luxury.

Quite unintentionally, I end up there one day with Mum and Dad. It is their second trip to Paris and we've decided to go for a walk with no particular destination in mind. Straight off the plane from Sydney, before leaving the apartment Mum had hurriedly changed into a clean pair of faded jeans and a bottle-green jumper which stretches rather unflatteringly over her bottom. We walk to Opéra and Place Vendôme and then finally we're amid the mix of old-world gloss and up-to-date glamour along Rue du Faubourg St-Honoré.

The pavements are crowded with beautiful shoppers wearing dark glasses and affluent tans. Transfixed by each passer-by, Mum admires the slim cut of women's trousers, the exquisitely tailored jackets, the way shoes perfectly match violet or pistachio handbags. Usually someone who looks well-dressed and stylish, she is kicking herself for her carelessness. With each metre she becomes more self-conscious, all too aware that she is hopelessly out of place among the strutting glamour.

'I look like a tourist,' she says finally. Dad and I giggle. Then, remembering my interview with Inès de La Fressange, she adds, 'Really offal.' Dad and I laugh more. Mum ignores us, busily planning her wardrobe for future trips to Paris. 'Next time I'm only bringing my best clothes,' she announces. And sure enough, on subsequent visits she'll arrive with a suitcase stuffed with dressy little skirts, smart jackets and high heels which will be perfect for Rue du Faubourg St-Honoré but conspicuously inappropriate for tripping through French country markets.

Such is the power of Paris. It inspires me now to dress up too. The trouble is I'm inconsistent. The meticulous grooming which comes so naturally to many continental Europeans still eludes me. Try though I have to follow the advice of Inès de La Fressange, looking good all the time *is* an effort. And frankly sometimes I can't be bothered. Which means that on the Paris style barometer, I'm an unpredictable rollercoaster of peaks and troughs. Catch me on a good day and I can look *soignée* and stylish. But on a bad day, racing through the streets with wild hair and flying laces, I must leave a trail of 'unwell' Parisians in my wake.

Eleven

Our different attitudes to dress are by no means the most important cultural clash Frédéric and I have to face. There is one subject which creates a chasm between us every time it is raised. Often, our cultural differences are a source of jokes and teasing, but not this one. Incomprehension snowballs into conflict until eventually just pronouncing the odd-sounding name risks igniting an argument. *Baincthun.*

French people unfamiliar with place names in the country's far north trip over the curious combination of consonants, the clumsy phonetics, which colour the region as a result of several centuries of English occupation and the close proximity of Flanders. 'Bunktung', you say, clipping the invisible 'g' so that it's barely pronounced. It is an un-picturesque village about six kilometres inland from Boulogne-sur-Mer, and even if you have driven through it— which I sincerely doubt—you wouldn't remember it. Cars whip past the mud-grey concrete façades bordering the road, not paying the respect of slowing down. There is a run-down café, one rather bad *boulangerie*, a church which could be lovely if some money were spent on it—nothing, in other words, to distinguish Baincthun from hundreds of villages in northern France.

Except that this is where Frédéric comes from.

His family home is a lovely farmhouse overlooking an expansive, cobbled courtyard, enclosed by the long, low barns which are typical of the region. The first time I came here was during my month-long summer holiday. Frédéric's father, Alain, was away. Cottonball clouds bobbed in a luminous sky. The white shutters dazzled in the sunlight. The garden, which covers one hectare, was ripe with fruit and flowers. Roses and lavender sprayed the weathered stone walls. I marvelled at the perfect curves of a yew sculpted into a topiary ball—so different from the stringy gums and rambling shrubs you might find in an Australian country property.

Frédéric had wanted to show me the house where his father lives because he loves it with all his heart. For him it is not merely mortar and stone but somehow part of him—a living thing he and his family rescued from ruin, carefully restoring it in a way that respected history but also allowed air and light to flood the previously dark, closed rooms. He'd indicated the date engraved in stone beneath the eaves: 1619. To me, growing up in a four-hundred-year-old farmhouse seemed wonderfully romantic, straight out of an old-fashioned story book. Inside, there are massive exposed beams and period fireplaces big enough to sit in. Every centimetre of wall space is covered in paintings, every polished wooden surface strewn with objects: family heirlooms, primitive sculptures from Mexico, silver boxes from India. Each room is a testimony to the French habit of collecting things not for their material value but simply for their beauty.

But when I settled in France, Bainbthun took on an entirely new meaning. According to the French social code, this is where I'm expected to spend weekends at least once a month. Before meeting Frédéric I'd never even contemplated what lay north of Paris. Privately I'd curse my bad luck: why couldn't he have come from Arles, Aix-en-Provence or Avignon?

Roots are everything in this country. The French are incredibly attached to their *pays*, which in this context refers to the region where they grew up. Despite France's modernity—the TGV and the Concorde, the exemplary autoroutes—its people often proclaim they are *paysans*. While being called a 'peasant' is an insult if it refers to taste or manners, when the label is used to emphasise a person's links to a particular part of the countryside it is worn proudly. Throughout history, French writers have drawn inspiration from their rural provinces: Balzac from his native Loire Valley, Flaubert from Normandy, Pagnol from Provence. Radical urbanisation has really only occurred in the last forty years and practically every adult Parisian has cherished memories of growing up in a village or small town—or at least spending summer holidays there.

On weekends, Parisians are united in wanting to recapture their idyllic childhoods, recreate them for their own children. They return en masse to their *maisons de familles*. (According to the weekly news magazine, *L'Express*, the French have more secondary homes per head of population than any other Europeans.) Parisians who hail from far away regions buy *maisons de weekend* in Normandy or northern Burgundy. The countryside carries mythical importance: this is the real France, the French tell you, believing their own myth-making.

And so despite fifteen years in Paris, for Frédéric what's real is the Boulonnais, as the *pays* around Boulogne-sur-Mer is known. The region represents his roots, his identity, a sense of belonging. His family is part of the north's *grande bourgeoisie* which once earned its wealth from fine-quality woven textiles until recession hit in the seventies and the company was sold. It is a conservative, Catholic world of large families where three or four generations still gather round the table for Sunday lunch.

It's also a world that is totally foreign to me. For starters I can't get over this awesome proliferation. Frédéric's grandmother had ten siblings, his mother had seven, Léon who helped us move apartments is one of eight, his lovely wife Caroline one of nine children and his friend Thibault has five kids. Frédéric, with only one sibling and no children is an exception. And if *he* is an exception in this environment, then I am utterly alien. Not only am I not from one of the region's *bonnes familles* but I'm not even French. Worse, I'm getting on for thirty and I don't have any children! 'How many do you want?' the women ask anxiously, barely able to stop themselves from saying, 'You better get on with it.' One day, when yet another person asks, I decide to put an end to their fretting.

'Two,' I say, thinking this is realistic, although Frédéric and I have barely discussed kids.

'Two? Is that all?' She is dismayed. '*Seulement deux*? Oh that's sad.'

Separated by distance from relatives in New Zealand, my notion of family had been limited to a nucleus comprising a brother, sister and parents. But Frédéric grew up surrounded by stern grandfathers and eccentric great aunts, hundreds of cousins and second cousins. Imbued in each generation is a sense of continuity. He is the first chink in his immediate family chain to leave northern France, and even though Baincthun is only three hours' drive from Paris, he feels this distance almost as much as I feel the separation from Australia.

He likes to return for weekends as often as possible. To see his father, to be with old friends like Jean-Michel, mostly just to *be* there.

Usually, we leave Paris after work on Friday nights. Heading in any other direction we'd be trapped in the trail of cars crawling out of the capital but on the northbound A16 traffic is rolling nicely. After almost two hours' driving, the scent of cow manure seeps into the car. This is Frédéric's cue. Even in the middle of winter, he winds his window right down and sticks out his head, high on the pleasure of inhaling the countryside. The smell of cow dung reminds him of school holidays on his great aunt's farm near Ardres. *Not far now.* In the dark his eyes are like diamonds.

By the time we pull up outside the house it's usually around midnight and his father has gone to bed. Quietly, Frédéric carries out his ritual: a proprietorial pee in the garden, followed by a perusal of the grounds, straining in the darkness to see how each tree has grown. Inside the house, he straightens a portrait of his great great grandfather to whom he bears a remarkable resemblance, feels the weight of an old, handmade *boule* for French bowls, its nail-studded sphere not quite perfectly round, carefully examining objects as though seeing them for the first time.

He knows the Boulonnais by heart, knows all the tiny picturesque routes, the lovely manors and châteaux hidden from the main roads, he can even describe the paintings above their fireplaces because some of them belong to childhood friends. His face falls as we drive past run-down farmhouses with crumbling walls and collapsed roofs. He wants to restore every one of them, to be the saviour of all that is local and beautiful. He rails against local mayors, whom he blames for allowing development and industry to spoil the region's patrimony. '*C'est scandaleux*,' he'll fume, pointing to an ugly new factory that has shot up next to a small château or farming hamlet. 'Couldn't they have built it somewhere else?'

Frédéric could write poetic pages about the melancholy skies, the sensuousness of ribbed fields of charcoal earth, the coastal cliffs which overlook the English Channel from where on clear days you can see the chalky contour of Dover. These are the scenes he loves to paint time and time again with his old friend Olivier, a homeopath in Boulogne. Invariably Frédéric's efforts end in frustration: he can't render a brilliant shaft of light spilling through the clouds to illuminate a green hill, can't capture the force of the wind whipping the figures walking along the cliff nor the dampness of the ploughed soil. In his eyes, his watercolour paintings can never do justice to the reality.

Lunch is the central focus of our weekends in northern France. Even though there's usually just the three of us, Alain, Frédéric and I (Frédéric's sister and her husband live in Lille), a certain ceremony applies, beginning with the apéritif and ending with dessert. Having discovered the joys of cooking late in life, Alain has mastered an impressive repertoire of dishes ranging from home-made pâté de foie gras to delicious fruit tarts. His cooking is traditional: the crowning component is always a master sauce. '*Je suis un saucier extraordinaire*,' he boasts, without a trace of irony. To him, a sauce must have substance—it is not an aside, not an optional extra. To make him happy, you have to take lots of it.

He is a meticulous man, Frédéric's father, always impeccably dressed in well co-ordinated berets and tobacco toned jackets. Spills on his tablecloths send him racing for a stain remover that bubbles and pops around your plate. When a lovely whole sole stuck to his brand new barbecue grill and had to be scraped off in delicious, flaky pieces, there was no consoling him. '*C'est la cata complète!*' he fumed furiously, '*cata*' being short for '*catastrophe*'. He rails often against the English—France's 'historical enemies'—who, not content with Waterloo and mad cow's disease, have now invaded the local golf club.

Together, he and his son make a pair of mad militants, the sort of fanatics who'd attend Defence of the Boulonnais meetings, if only such a group existed. They'd like to be mayor of Baincthun—mayor of all the villages in northern France, actually—such is their abiding love for the region. They are convinced that the rest of France and probably the whole world have conspired to tarnish the image of their adored homeland. 'Did you see all that bad weather they forecast for us on the news?' Alain will grumble. 'Just trying to scare away tourists.' Never mind the howling wind outside, the rain hammering the window panes. Also in on the scare-mongering are journalists who write about the region's social problems such as the high levels of alcoholism and unemployment. In August, when half of Europe invades the Côte d'Azur and the evening news shows packed beaches and traffic jams, they gloat. 'Ha, look at those poor sardines! We don't have crowds like that in the north!' It doesn't seem to occur to them there might be a good reason for this.

In my opinion their passion for their homeland is irrational. To me Frédéric's sentimentality is obsessive. As for his sense of propriety, I've come to the conclusion it is delusional.

One weekend at Baincthun, we decide to go for a walk in the woods. From the main road, a new paved route leads into an asphalt carpark but Monsieur Nostalgic North—ever-ready for a trip down memory lane—insists on going the *old* way, along several kilometres of dirt road which is now closed to the public. As he drives, Frédéric reminisces about his boyhood adventures with Jean-Michel and Olivier, how they used to ride their bicycles along this very same track. I listen absently, distracted by the signs flashing past the windows: 'Private Property', 'Keep Out', 'Go Back'.

'Don't you think we should turn around?'

'*Non, non, ça va.*'

'But what's wrong with going the proper way?'

'This way's much more scenic. The new road has spoiled everything.'

Another notice announces 'Trespassers will Be Prosecuted'. The surfeit of threats has made me nervous. 'Are you sure this is a good idea?'

'*Mais bien sûr!*' Frédéric sighs, exasperated by my lack of gumption. 'We won't be long.'

The reason for such vigilance is that this part of the woods belongs to one of the region's richest families which has made its fortune in crystal tableware. Their holiday houses peek through the oak and beech trees. In an effort to be discreet, we try to hide our car off the road behind a dark thicket. Frédéric knows the family, you see—as a teenager he used to play golf with some of its members and later during university holidays he worked at their factory. It would be terribly embarrassing for him to be caught trespassing on their property.

In the end, we're away about forty minutes. On our way back, we spot our car in the distance—and a powerfully-built bloke with a rifle over his shoulder peering through the windows.

'*Merde!* It's the guardian!'

In that split second of panic, of imagining being frog-marched to the main house, Frédéric masterminds a brilliant story to extricate us from impending embarrassment.

'Let's pretend we're Australian tourists!' His voice is low and urgent. In the distance, the guardian looks up, sees us, and like a heat-seeking missile which has found its target, charges in our direction. Suddenly the situation looks serious. 'You do all the talking,' whispers Frédéric. 'I'll pretend I don't speak any French. He'll just let us go.'

And before I can suggest we simply tell the truth, before I can point out the myriad reasons why this plan will backfire (the most glaring one being that no half-sane, semi-seeing person would ever believe Frédéric was anything other than French) the guardian is upon us. Dressed in military green, he looks like an SAS soldier who has sprouted a handlebar moustache. I smile weakly. He doesn't smile back. His eyes have narrowed to slits.

'What are you doing here? Didn't you see the private property signs?'

Glowering at Frédéric, I say, 'We're on holidays from Australia, we weren't sure what the signs said.' I exaggerate my accent, speaking French like a four-year-old so it doesn't seem as though I live here.

'What about you then?' The guardian nudges his rifle towards Frédéric.

'No speak French,' answers Frédéric, in absurd pidgin English. He rolls the 'r' in 'French' and gives an apologetic shrug. My eyeballs back-flip. He seems to have confused his part in this pitiful pantomime. He sounds like an English-speaker *pretending to be French*, Peter Sellers playing Inspector Clouseau. I notice he's taken his jumper from around his shoulders and tied it around his waist—something he observed from visiting Australian friends, he'll later explain, pleased to have remembered this detail. I'm torn between howling laughter and the desire to strangle him. You'd have to be a fool to fall for this performance.

The guardian stares at us. His face muscles relax a little, as though he no longer thinks we're a threat. For a moment it seems maybe Frédéric was right, he'll let us go.

But no. 'You come, we go in car,' he orders, gallantly attempting English for Frédéric's benefit. 'Big problem.' And we are frogmarched back to our car, captive prisoners of a humourless man brandishing a rifle at our backs.

As we round a corner on the memory lane we came in on, it's suddenly clear the guardian wasn't joking about there being a problem. Two police cars with flashing blue lights block the track. Five officers are talking to a couple who turn out to be gardeners for the estate. As we pull up, their conversation abruptly stops, as though someone has pushed a pause button. All eyes train on us. Any humour in the situation has evaporated. Frédéric has paled.

'YOU do the talking now,' I mutter.

As chance would have it, one of the houses was robbed while we were on the property. We are suspects—the only suspects so far, in fact. Our car is searched while the guardian relates our story to a no-nonsense officer who appears to be running the investigation. He examines Frédéric's driving licence, then fixes him with a don't-bull-shit-me-son stare.

'An Australian tourist, eh?' And with the exaggerated patience of a country cop who's got all the time in the world to solve his crime, he reads out our Paris address and Frédéric's full, unmistakably French name. His tone is so dry it crackles.

'Doesn't sound too Australian to me.'

Over the next hour, Frédéric explains the whole silly truth as best he can, smiling cheesily, his manner reduced to total genuflection. My eyeballs roll further and further up inside my head until by the time he's finished they're almost stuck there. Eventually, we're free to go. It's obvious to the officer we couldn't even contemplate a burglary, let alone pull one off. For one rather thrilling moment it had seemed Frédéric might be slapped in a cell. (Under French law you can be held in prison for up to twenty-four hours without charges being laid, even forty-eight in special circumstances.) The guardian—livid to have been duped—urges the officer to teach us a lesson. But although the prospect of locking up a lawyer is no doubt appealing—a journalist, too, what a double bonus!—the policeman doesn't want us cluttering up his station. He wants us out of his sight, out of his jurisdiction, back in Paris, where in his opinion idiots like us belong.

Naturally, this experience does nothing to arouse my enthusiasm for the place. I don't think that anything can. The problem is, Frédéric's passion for his *pays* is matched by the strength of my aversion to it. Perhaps unconsciously, the intensity of his feelings triggers a corollary of negativity in me. Mostly, though, it comes down to the fact I simply don't like the region much. Without childhood memories and generations of family attachment to enhance it, I find the landscape depressing. It reminds me of one of those tenebrous oil paintings at the Louvre. I'd prefer honey-coloured hilltop villages any day. The weather doesn't help (it always seems to be raining), nor does the fact that I'm unaccustomed to this notion of fleeing to family homes on weekends, of being holed up indoors over long lunches. My eyes don't see what Frédéric sees—or at least they see it differently.

The last one hundred years have delivered tidal waves of tragedy to northern France. Some cities such as Dunkerque have been twice devastated by world wars. Boulogne-sur-Mer escaped damage in the first but was less fortunate during the second. From 1940 it was occupied by the Germans and the subsequent Allied bombardments destroyed much of the city apart from an impressive cathedral and a small medieval quarter. The fishing industry is less vibrant; the Channel ferries from Dover and Folkstone increasingly call at Calais instead of Boulogne. Once a relatively wealthy town, these days Boulogne-sur-Mer is synonymous with soaring unemployment and social problems.

To me the lovely landscape has been spoiled by expanding industry and motorways. The villages and towns were no doubt once charming too—the proof lies in places like St-Omer and Montreuil and coastal Wimereux which escaped destruction. But the ubiquitous post-war buildings are grim. Beauty exists but only in snatches—no sooner have you found a lovely stretch of countryside than you arrive at a sprawling commercial centre or a new stretch of identical low-cost houses, painted a ghastly peach. The loss, the melancholy, the hard times, to me they hang over the Boulonnais as obstinately as the clouds.

Nowhere do our visions diverge more sharply than on the beaches.

'It's gloomy,' I'd declared the first time we went to Dannes, about twenty kilometres from Baincthun. The tide was way out, exposing an expanse of beach so wide it looked like an autoroute under construction, the concrete surface not yet dry. That's Hardelot, Frédéric had said, pointing in the distance to a cluster of grey high-rise holiday apartments stabbed into the sand. It had all the charm of the communist-built 'resorts' I'd seen along Romania's Black Sea coast, I thought. Tossed papers and empty drink bottles cartwheeled in the wind. Clouds were busily building a leaden continent overhead, the roiling ocean matched the grey-brown sand. 'Opal,' Frédéric had corrected me. 'It's called the Opal Coast because of the colour of the sea.' And although the gemstone does come in many colours, this claim seemed a bit rich; '*Un peu trop*,' I'd told him, smart-arsed and sceptical.

'*Danger: Engins de Guerre*', warned a welcoming sign. World War II relics littered the landscape. Because of the coastline's proximity to England, the Germans were convinced the Allies would try to land here and they built scores of blockhouses for defence. At Dannes several of the monolithic concrete structures loom over the sand, having been left intact to preserve this period of history, and also because it would simply cost too much to dismantle them. Rusted barbed wire reaches through the dunes; thick concrete pins poke through the sand having being laid to prevent enemy boats from landing. Gazing fondly around him, Frédéric had reminisced about playing war games here as a boy, how he and his mates would vie for the roles of Resistance heroes.

Suddenly, incredibly, the unmistakable sound of gun shots had then shattered the peace. All these remnants of war had made me twitchy and my instinct was to dive behind a dune. Three portly men in baggy trousers and gumboots ambled by, casually waving rifles. Their faces were half-hidden by chequered berets and bushy moustaches and I'd wanted to laugh—they looked like French farmers straight out of central casting. More shots rang out, aimed into the air. It's hunting season, Frédéric had explained, nonchalantly. They're shooting ducks.

I couldn't hold my tongue any longer. 'You call this a

beach?' I blurted.

I'd pitied him this place, this pallid substitute for surf and sand where any moment you might be whacked on the head by a dead duck. How poorly it compared with the golden coastline which fringes my own homeland, the dark blue Pacific, starry in the sunlight. I'd felt superior in the knowledge that no-one would really think Dannes was beautiful if they knew what beaches were supposed to look like. I was dumbfounded when Frédéric told me that several years ago during a storm, this exact landscape—this monochromatic gloom—had inspired him to write a poem. Fighting my prejudices, I'd squinted and concentrated, trying to summon up the scene as he saw it. Failing.

You'd think a compromise could be easily reached. But the conflict over Baincthun is emotionally charged. At heart, it isn't about scenery: it is about who we are, individually, and what we are willing to become. It highlights ingrained cultural differences. Unfamiliar with the tradition of retreating to family homes on weekends, I resent the routine of it, the expectation, whereas for Frédéric, returning regularly to his *pays* is the most natural thing in the world. He thinks we're lucky having access to a country home just a few hours from Paris. Besides, the Boulonnais is beautiful! I must be crazy not to see it!

Raising the subject only polarises us even more. The script is always pretty much the same:

Me: 'Why don't you go alone if you want to go this weekend.'

Frédéric (unhappily): 'But you never want to go.'

Me (indignant): 'We were there a couple of weeks ago!'

Frédéric: '*Four* weekends ago.'

Me: '*Three*. Anyway, I'd just rather stay in Paris.'

Frédéric: 'But weekends are for leaving Paris!'

Me (insistent): 'What's wrong with you going alone?'

Frédéric (tired voice): 'You know how it is in France. Going back to family homes is something French couples do together.'

Me (exploding with impatience): 'Yes, well, I'm not French!'

Frédéric (theatrical sigh): 'When are you going to give up trying to start a revolution? Can't you just accept some things the way they are?'

This is my cue to remind him of the litany of things I've already accepted in order to be with him. Changing the country where I live, my language, my job . . .

Invariably, the discussion ends in mutual pissed-off silence.

Something has to give and eventually it does.

I'm not sure exactly when compromise is reached. It is difficult to identify the beginning of gradual change, to isolate the reasons for it occurring. But sometime during my second year in France we both start to face facts. No matter how much I might dream of Avignon or Arles, the reality is I share my life with a man from northern France. *Baincthun is part of the package.* I may as well accept it. Frédéric grows more realistic too. He realises that I'm not going to go up there *every* month and stops applying pressure.

On a deeper level, I think compromise became possible because of an important realisation: *each of us is doing their best.* I say this with hindsight, because it's only once it has ended that the conflict acquires clarity. Frédéric begins to understand that I am struggling on many fronts. With the French language and people and myriad cultural differences that ensure life is never boring but which occasionally leave me feeling defeated. In the struggle to find my place in France I've discovered a million details that matter to me — details which define me as non-French. Much as I'd initially wanted to fully integrate, I knew now I never would, not completely, I couldn't, *I didn't want to*. This wasn't a choice, it simply wasn't possible. *I will never be French.* Frédéric, I think, understood this now.

It dawned on me in time that Frédéric couldn't dump his upbringing, his past, all those rich cultural references either. In a country which is suspicious of change, where traditions are clung to and life beats to a rhythm of unquestioned routines, something like spending a lot less time in his adored *pays* represents a private revolution. Perhaps the New World, with its roots in mobility, can never totally understand the Old in this way. In any event, what had appeared to me an insignificant concession was, in fact, something that cut to his core.

Once I begin to understand that, a gradual evolution takes place. First, I stop hating the region. Then, I actually discover things in its favour. Some beauty is bedazzling — its self-evidence steals your breath and practically knocks you off your feet. It is *fact*. Paris springs to mind. Prague. The natural wonder that is the south island of New Zealand. And in my perhaps biased opinion, Sydney. But appreciation of beauty can also creep up on you. It can be a taste acquired through experience, time, love and deepening knowledge. It can spring not from the grandeur of the big picture but affection for the small things and parts which give a place its heart.

The Saturday morning food market at Boulogne-sur-Mer is one such experience I grow to cherish. Now, on our once-every-couple-of-months visits to the north, we always go there. It is an example of how markets should be, how they used to be: a collection of stalls selling whatever people could pull that morning from their gardens. The characters are salty and rough. Women with thick legs and old-fashioned floral aprons stand behind tables displaying a few handfuls of beans, four dirty eggs and one or two punnets of potatoes and strawberries—or some other miscellany. The hands that serve you are ingrained with soil. Conversation is carried out in a patois that in its purest form is incomprehensible to outsiders. Spread around the base of a lovely old church, the market is next to a row of cafés which by the end of the morning has filled with shoppers. The people of northern France are big beer drinkers and before leaving we join the crowds enjoying a pre-lunch ale.

Then there are evenings at Wimereux, a seaside town where we go for *moules marinières* at one of the cafés along the dyke. The dish comes in a deep casserole and I love everything about it: the generous serving, the delicate mussels which aren't too meaty, the hands-on method of eating using a shell as a pincer and fingers to dip the crunchy *frites* into the winey sauce.

When we can, we go to see Jean-Michel who lives in a nearby village. I have always appreciated his warmth but lately his hospitality has reached new heights. As well as dogs and cats his house is now home to a pet chicken, a rabbit and several families of rats. None of the animals are kept in cages. 'They'll sort it out,' he growls, whenever an altercation occurs, usually between a rat and a cat. Dinners turn into surreal comedy sketches as Poulet (the pet chicken) pecks around our plates and a rat scurries across the table. Compared with the formality of many Paris dinner parties, these mad evenings are a gust of fresh air, sweeping away the cobwebs of social convention.

Even the 'gloomy' beach is not entirely without redeeming features now. Although in my mind it still doesn't compare to beaches in Australia, there is something invigorating about the scudding clouds, the sunbursts that spotlight a dune, the effect so sudden and fleeting you wonder if you've imagined it. At other times, the retreating tide leaves tiny lakes in the dimpled sand, making the beach gleam with millions of mirrors. On a sunny day, the milky Channel waters sparkle with glints of blue, green and yellow, and yes, I agree, the colours are opalescent.

Twelve

Given my confidence about the superiority of Australia's sand and surf, it comes as a rude shock to discover our visions of my homeland may diverge dramatically at times too. At the end of my second year in France, Frédéric comes to Australia with me for a holiday. This is the first time he'll see my country and I am terribly excited about taking him there. But almost from the moment we land the trip teaches me a lesson in perceptions and how much they are linked to our connection to a place.

My brother and sister pick us up from the airport and we head straight to my parents' home on Sydney's northern beaches. It's about eight in the morning and, although there are some clouds about, even at this hour the light makes us squint. As we curve around the Cahill Expressway I can't contain my exhilaration: 'Look, the Harbour Bridge!'.

But to my surprise Frédéric admires it only briefly; he seems preoccupied. 'The buildings are so dark, so *English*,' he exclaims, and I know coming from a Frenchman this is close to an insult. Having imagined Sydney as a city of pale Mediterranean colours, yawning windows and balconies, he is amazed by the severe, liver-brick façades rimming the lower north shore. Determined to draw his attention to the beauty of the harbour, I keep up my tourist guide gaiety.

'That's Circular Quay. Ooh look, a ferry!'

But Frédéric is too busy making aesthetic improvements. 'They'd look much better painted,' he mutters about the brick apartment blocks. 'Why such small windows in a sunny country?'

After spending a couple of hours catching up with my parents, we decide to walk to Whale Beach, only five minutes away. By now it is midday and the sun is drumming down. 'That'll wake us up,' I say, jetlagged but bursting with happiness at being reunited with my family, at being back home, anticipating how much Frédéric is going to enjoy this swim.

As the footpath curls around a corner, the gum trees part and we suddenly have a breathtaking view of the beach.

'Why is everyone swimming in exactly the same spot?' Frédéric stares in astonishment at the dark patch of bodies on an otherwise gloriously empty stretch of sand.

'You have to swim between the flags,' I explain, indicating the surf lifeguards. 'It makes it easier for them to survey the beach.' But the logic of this wasted space seems lost on Frédéric. His Gallic sense of pride in flouting regulations can't fathom such meek compliance. He teases me as we continue down the hill, 'You Australians are real wimps!'

As we near the water, passing the yellow warning signs signalling a blue-bottle deluge and a dangerous current, his cockiness wanes. Although from higher up they'd looked unthreatening, in reality the waves are wild, breaking so close to the shore that we are repeatedly knocked off our feet just trying to get in. 'Come out a bit deeper!' I call after he's been slammed into the sand several times. Frédéric doesn't reply. He glares at me darkly: no way is he going to risk getting strangled by alien jellyfish or sucked all the way to Auckland by a killer current. And so there he stays, right where the waves are exploding, in the mistaken belief that the shallow waters are safer. He's like a jack-in-the-box, constantly disappearing and then springing up in a knee-high swirl of foam, gasping for breath. 'It's too violent,' he shouts above the crashing water, getting out. Shaken, afterwards he challenges me:

'You call this a *beach*?'

Mum and Dad had already met Frédéric last year on a trip to France, where they'd all hit it off wonderfully. On this holiday he meets my brother and sister for the first time. Although they have their own places they join us frequently for dinner. We spend long evenings on the balcony overlooking the sea, drinking my parents' nascent wine cellar. Some nights Frédéric and I go into the city and stay with friends. Sue and her husband Andrew have now returned from London and we crash frequently at their apartment in Bronte.

After a few days, Frédéric's European sensibilities seem to adjust. By the end of the first week, he is relaxed and sunburned and feeling right at home. He's even getting used to the 'violent' sea although he remains wary, never venturing further than waist-deep. Next thing we know he is unpacking his brushes and watercolours: he's feeling inspired! His paintings of Australia capture details and scenes that surprise him: the brightly coloured rosellas which jig on our balcony, a hibiscus bloom, the beach and even Sydney Harbour, all rendered in singing colours which contrast starkly with his habitual, muted palette.

To Australians Sydney may be utterly urban, but to Frédéric it still signals adventure. One night as we're sitting on the balcony, he suddenly leaps out of his seat, pointing excitedly inside. 'I think I saw a big animal!'

We all look sceptically through the sliding glass doors into the lounge. Other than our old boxer, we don't keep 'animals' in the house. There is nothing there, not a creature in sight. Maybe he's just jittery, reacting to a reflection on the glass doors of some movement in the trees. 'Must have run away,' my brother teases him. 'Think you'd better have another drink.'

'There!' Frédéric is on his feet again and this time we see it: a rather well-fed possum scuttling towards the kitchen— back for seconds, no doubt. The scene descends into pantomime. A tea towel is thrust at Frédéric and he is pushed towards the kitchen, Dad yelling instructions, as together they try to shoo the creature outside. 'Careful it doesn't scratch the parquet!' cries Mum. From a safe distance I laugh, watching Frédéric, who is clearly more concerned about being clawed himself, as he faces what he imagines is a man-eating marsupial.

His second close encounter with Australian wildlife amuses me a little less. As usual, first thing in the morning, we decide to go to the beach for a swim. Mum and Dad have left for work. Picking up my towel from a chair outside, I sling it over my shoulder—and too late I glimpse a dark vague shape among the folds. But when I quickly shake the towel nothing falls out. Maybe I imagined it—or, alternatively, whatever it was might have crawled onto my back. I hurry inside to ask Frédéric if he can see anything.

'WHAAAAAOOOW!' he shrieks the second I turn around, sending me catapulting into the air. From his hysterical pitch it's obvious I am in unspeakable danger. Ohmigod, there must be a snake sliding up my back, maybe a funnel-web! Panicked, I tear at my T-shirt and swivel my head but I can't see anything.

'What is it?'

'DON'T MOVE! IT BITES!' screams my saviour, running away. He flies into the kitchen—I assume to get a knife to chop off its head.

'GET IT OFF ME!' I am hysterical now too.

The blow to my back momentarily winds me as almost two thousand white pages strike at full force. The fat Sydney phone book which Frédéric has just hurled—presumably at the predator—crashes to the floor. Beside himself, he grabs it, 'I missed!'

'Oh for god's sake, can't you just . . .'

A second blow cuts off my protest. The A to K tome falls with another dead thud.

'Got it!'

We peer at the spider spread on the floor. It is hideous and huge, that's for sure. About the size of a man's hand, with thick furry legs that are making a final, futile attempt to crawl. But . . .

'It's only a huntsman. They're harmless.'

Frédéric doesn't seem to have heard me. 'It's ee-nor-mous,' he says proudly, carefully pushing the spider onto a white notepad using a piece of paper. He arranges it on the kitchen bench like a class science display. 'To show the others,' he explains.

Unfortunately for Frédéric, Mum—who is entirely fearless when it comes to spiders—is the first home from work. Driven by some misguided male compulsion to prove himself as protector, Frédéric eagerly shows her his kill. In death, the huntsman's long limbs have retracted, of course. It lies shrivelled and pathetic, no bigger than a five-cent coin.

'Oh, they're all over the house,' says Mum, airily. As if that weren't injury enough, she adds, 'I usually just flick them away with my finger.'

I can't let it pass, not with my back still sore.

'Hear that,' I hiss. '*Finger*, not a bloody phone book.'

We get a lot of laughs out of this story, although the description of Frédéric's role in the affair differs according to who is retelling it. Our time in Sydney flies by in a blur of dinners and drinks and hours spent on the balcony reading, or cruising Pittwater in a boat my parents rented. Too quickly, it seems, Frédéric's two and a half weeks are up (he couldn't take more time off work). One week later I'm back at the airport for my departure, saying goodbye to a few friends who insisted on coming, and trying to be brave farewelling my family. Pretty soon, with a great roar and a shudder, the Qantas Boeing 747 takes off from Sydney's Mascot airport.

Almost immediately, we arc inland and the inky blue Pacific Ocean disappears behind us. This is the worst part of the whole trip. A full twenty-three hours of crushing boredom—lucky it's a direct flight—stretch between me and Paris, as challenging as any marathon. It will take four hours of flying just to reach overseas airspace—let alone nudge the northern hemisphere. The economy class movie screen illuminates to keep us from these dark thoughts. The images flash in quick succession. They're a mix of Australian landmarks and predictable clichés—Sydney Harbour, lifesavers with zinc noses wearing skullcaps which use more fabric than their itty-bitty bathers. The airline's signature tune, 'I Still Call Australia Home', hums in the background as kangaroos spring across blistered earth and Aboriginal children with traditional face-paint flash gleaming smiles. We've all seen these snapshots hundreds of times.

So what on earth is wrong with me? Although I'd managed not to cry saying goodbye at the airport, a lump of sadness is

now strangling me. Mortified, I turn away and stare determinedly through the window at the burning blue sky, trying
to swallow it. In my pocket are a few gum leaves that I picked
walking to the beach and I scrunch up one of them and
inhale the eucalyptus oil on my fingertips. The flight atten-
dant looks on sympathetically, which only makes things
worse. Can't she look at someone else? Out come my
sunglasses—not such a mad idea, really, given I'm next to
the window and the afternoon light is dazzling. Now I'm
invisible. Big, pathetic tears splash into my lap.

Is this a normal reaction to an airline video? Was it the
kangaroos? The soppy song about an expatriate Australian
missing Australia? None of the other passengers seem to be
donning sunglasses. What's more, I don't even know why I'm
crying. It was brilliant having almost one month to spend
with family and friends, even if it flew by at supernatural
speed. Although it was sad saying goodbye to my parents,
they look at my absence as an excuse for not-quite-annual
holidays in France and they'll be over later in the year, for
sure. And now I'm going back to Frédéric and my life in one
of the world's most wonderful cities. Our bustling *quartier*. I
should be excited, not sitting here sobbing.

But I guess the reason for my tears is no great mystery. I'm
crying about leaving home.

The old Greek on Samos island had warned me. *'It's a
bitter–sweet thing, knowing two cultures,'* he'd said. *'It's
a curse to love two countries.'* Well I certainly don't think of
living abroad as a curse—I don't think the Greek believed it
either. He was just dramatising his dilemma, the feeling of
being torn between two places. And this is something I now
understand. For an expatriate, the whole matter of 'home'
is an emotional conundrum riddled with ambiguities and

caprice. Paris is my actual home: it's where I live. It can pull at heartstrings with a mere walk down our market street in the morning. But Australia is the home of homesickness and my history—a powerful whirlpool of family and friends, memories and daily trivia that I used to take for granted but now seem somehow remarkable.

Although I understand the French better now, the reality is in France I'm still an outsider. There seem to be so many contradictions, so many social codes for different situations that make life interesting but also leave you feeling a bit vulnerable. Living in Paris requires constant effort: effort to make myself understood, effort to understand and to be alert for those cultural intricacies that can turn even going to the post office into a social adventure. Yet in Sydney everything had seemed so familiar, so easy. I can't even explain exactly why. It was more than the relaxing effects of sun and surf and being on holiday. It was as though back in my old environment I could finally drop the guard I didn't even know I'd been carrying.

Outside my window, the earth below is beginning to blush as we fly seamlessly towards the Centre. Going from one hemisphere to the other can be disorientating. If air travel is fantastically fast, the changes are also abrupt. There is no acclimatising en route, no gradual getting used to the weather conditions and landscape that await you at your destination. Simply, woolly coats and scarves one day, T-shirts and sarongs the next. Or vice versa. My holidays home are carefully timed to coincide with the southern hemisphere's summers and winter in the northern hemisphere. But after one month of Australia's blazing light, returning to Europe in January or February is a shock. It takes time to readapt to the pale palette, for your senses to make the journey from one extreme to the other. Having already made the trip, I know what to expect.

When the plane touches down in Paris indecently early in the morning, the city will be wrapped in darkness and a morning fog which may or may not lift later in the day. (Better to not get your hopes up.) Terminal One at Charles de Gaulle will seem drab and grubby for the simple reason it *is* drab and grubby. There's no point telling Frédéric not to come to the airport, that I'll just catch a taxi. He'll be there, waving energetically through the sliding glass doors. This is his self-appointed role: a one-man Official French Welcoming Committee whose sunny presence at this god-awful hour is designed to melt any post-Sydney blues.

Despite his efforts to cheer me, a week or two will pass in a jetlag-fuelled daze, marked by a total lack of enthusiasm for my strange–familiar environment. The apartment will seem too small (how could I not have noticed this before?) and what's more, we've no sea view (the fact that I couldn't possibly afford one in Sydney will not occur to me). Where's our garden, our balcony? Details will depress me. The ubiquitous Paris pigeons, for example, which occasionally have the indecency to die in our gutters. How woeful they are compared to the kookaburras which squat on the balcony rail at my parents' home, their big heads cocked intelligently as they wait for raw mince from the refrigerator.

As the plane's engines drum distantly, I comfort myself with the thought that we'll be back next year. Frédéric is keen to return. After he'd got over his initial shock at the beach and the colour of the bricks, he'd had a great time in Sydney. He loved the atmosphere, the energy, the exuberance. And now I realise why this trip had been so important to me. It wasn't just a matter of whether he liked Sydney or not, it was the fact that he'd been home—to *my* home, that is. For the first time, he'd seen me in the context of *my* country and culture. The roles had been reversed. There *I* was the guide, the one familiar with how things work, where places are, the one explaining jokes that he missed. And he'd seen for himself how different Australia is from France—not better or worse but just so fundamentally different. He could understand my bouts of homesickness now, my longing for light in winter. Aspects of my character made more sense too. My directness, for example, which he sometimes finds too blunt, too honest—and on occasions even harsh. But in Australia he observed a raw frankness in everything from the burning sun and unruly gum trees to the people. It had hit home that some of my idiosyncrasies might be cultural, not just personal.

A sense of reciprocity and compromise is vital in any relationship and even more so I'd say in a cross-cultural couple. And at heart, that's what this trip had been about. By embracing Australia, Frédéric was recognising the importance of my home to me and consequentially its importance—albeit to a lesser extent—to him. Just like Baincthun is for me, for Frédéric, *Australia is part of the package.*

Beyond my fish-bowl window dusk is falling and the sky has turned a deeper shade of blue. In just over eighteen hours I'll be back in Paris. Images of my beloved rituals flash through my mind: morning coffees on Rue Montorgueil, daily market shopping, walks through Palais Royal. I start to feel better. My tears have dried up. Although it might take me a week or two to settle back in Paris, I also know that my homesickness will eventually pass, shifting like a patch of bad weather to settle, no doubt, on someone else.

A message from the cockpit interrupts my thoughts and

the cabin hum. Our plane is about to head out over the Indian Ocean, leaving land behind. If we look out our windows we can have one last glimpse of Australia, the voice says in that practised this-is-your-captain-speaking tone.

Sure enough as I watch, my homeland slides out from beneath us. The change in background is abrupt, leaving little time for sentimentality. One second we're flying over what had seemed an incessant desert—such a funny pink in the evening light—then the space beneath us is a vastness of deep blue. Looking back over my shoulder, I watch the evanescence of Australia, transfixed. The coastline, with its white frill of surf, becomes smaller and smaller, until finally it disappears entirely as though I'd imagined it. A pang of nostalgia stabs my stomach and then I take off my sunglasses.

Thirteen

When I first arrived in Paris the women in the street seemed to confirm every cliché I'd ever read about *parisiennes*. In their little skirts and figure-hugging tops they appeared almost like cardboard cut-outs to me—so steeped in myth and mystique they weren't quite real. The sexy classicism of their look was proof of the French powers of seduction. Sophistication seemed to ooze from every gesture, their habit of drinking wine in tiny, unhurried sips, the nonchalant way they waved their cigarettes in the air. They were like smoky seductresses in films: unruffled, together, so self-assured.

It took me just a few dinners to get an idea that *les françaises* are in fact immeasurably complicated creatures. It has taken me much longer to begin to understand what lies beneath their polished, impenetrable exteriors. Although still trying to figure it out, I have reached a couple of conclusions. Peel back the layers (and there are invariably many) and what you find at the core of many French women is a well of insecurities. Add to them this country's cult of *séduction*, an age-old tradition of coquetry and femmes fatales, and the result is a pervasive rivalry among women. Which perhaps also explains why I have so few French girlfriends.

This fact is brought home to me after my trip to Australia. Once I'm settled back in Paris, I begin to understand why being in Sydney had seemed so easy. Why I'd felt as though I could drop my guard. I *did* drop my guard there—and especially with other women. My month in Sydney had been a series of wine-soaked sessions catching up with girlfriends. Several times our group swelled to four or five when friends brought along other friends whom I'd never met. These girls' lunches and dinners were great fun, a release, and back in France they suddenly have a greater resonance. Because in Paris you hardly ever see groups of just girls out together.

The fact is, in almost two and half years I haven't once gone out with a group of French women. That isn't to say my social success rate hasn't improved. It has. As well as meeting a new, cosmopolitan crowd in our inner-city *quartier*, relations with some people whom at first I didn't like have changed for the better too. For example, Marie—who made the 'how's your little girlfriend's French coming along?' comment—has turned out to be really nice. In the last six months she's made a special effort towards me, drawing me into conversation and persevering until I thawed. Either she realised she'd been rude or perhaps I've passed some test of time; I don't know which. The hosts of that lunch—who'd coolly ignored me—have turned out to be fun and gregarious. Several months after my return from Sydney, as the weather is beginning to improve, we go away together for a weekend in Burgundy. Chatting before dinner, something comes up about our first few meetings. Emboldened by a few rum and lime cocktails, I decide to ask what I have never really understood.

'Why were you so unfriendly at first?'

Arnaud contemplates my question, which doesn't seem to have offended or even surprised him. 'The problem is the French aren't very comfortable meeting new people,' he says.

'For us, friendships form over years, at school or university. And after that, we're not interested, we're no longer curious. We think we've got enough friends already.'

It's a simple, honest answer. But it is revealing and for me somehow healing because even though that lunch was more than two years ago now, the cool reception, those unreciprocated what-do-you-do's, my anger, the hurt, had all accumulated in a knot which needed untangling.

It wasn't me, I think. *It was nothing personal.*

But despite these positive changes, despite a strong sense of life falling into place, I don't seem to be able to bond with French women. So many books and chapters have been devoted to unravelling their mystique that I'm almost loath to write about them. Yet we *are* incredibly different—and by 'we' I don't just mean French women and Anglo-Saxons. I've spoken to women from Mexico, Malaysia and Iceland; my girlfriends in Paris come from countries ranging from Morocco and Denmark to Austria and England. And *without exception*, for all of us, in varying measures, *les françaises* represent an ongoing—and sometimes distressing—conundrum.

This was brought home to me one evening when we went to a dinner hosted by a lovely French couple, Anne and Serge, whom Frédéric has known for about ten years. They'd invited two other couples who we'd never met before. Although I had interesting chats with both guys, their wives remained unresponsive and cold. Far from the immediate complicity I felt with those girlfriends of girlfriends in Sydney, this was more like instant animosity, perfectly tangible even if it was unspoken. When Serge filled up my wine glass practically to the brim—a long-standing joke between us because someone told him that's how Australians drink—the two women remained stony-faced. I felt a wave of disapproval—*resentment* would not be too strong a word—as though my robust consumption was yet another black mark against me. After we left I couldn't hide my disappointment. I'd been looking forward to meeting Anne's friends.

'Did I imagine it or were those two girls really weird to me?' I asked Frédéric, half wondering whether I've become oversensitive. After all, he'd managed to have conversations with both of them.

'They *were* really weird to you,' he quickly confirmed. If in the past Frédéric used to get defensive when I raised a question that implicated his culture—or worse, his friends—now he has more distance.

'Why, though? What am I doing wrong?'

'You're not doing anything wrong,' Frédéric said. 'It's just, I think, women here . . .' He hesitated then said simply, 'In France, that's how it is between women.'

In the months following my Sydney holiday my lack of Gallic girlfriends bothers me. It seems like a personal failure. The idea of living in a foreign city where nearly all my close friends are also expats makes me uneasy. That is not what I'd envisaged. After all, I have an advantage over many foreigners—I have a French partner. Most of our socialising is with French people. I'm not leading a closeted expatriate life.

I do have a couple of French girlfriends. It's probably no coincidence that they tend to be less conventional, well-travelled types. Florence grew up in an unorthodox household outside Paris with a lion and chimpanzee brought home by her father, who was a circus vet. Patricia, who comes from a *grande famille* in northern France, felt compelled to break out of the buttoned-up, bourgeois world she was born into and with her husband spent many years living in various African countries. Sophie is married to an Australian and after several years in Melbourne they have moved back to Paris. One day I broach the subject of French women with her and straightaway she pinpoints the differences. *Les françaises*—particularly *parisiennes*, she stresses—perceive those of the same sex as rivals, not as potential friends.

'As soon as a French woman meets another woman, she'll look her up and down, check out her clothes, her makeup, her shoes. She'll be very critical of the other one,' Sophie tells me. 'She'll be thinking: well, she might have nice blue eyes but she's got a really big bum.' The competition is not limited to looks, though. According to Sophie, the fear is also that the other woman might appear more intelligent, more interesting to their husbands or boyfriends. Foreign females represent an even greater threat, apparently, because of their alluring accents and 'exotic' appeal.

Sophie's unequivocal words, which echo what countless people had already told me, bring home a troubling truth: while I've been looking at women as potential new friends, they've been sizing up my legs and bottom! Of course, not everyone is competitive and I've been to many dinners where girls have been very pleasant to me. But there is no sisterhood in France. The sort of complicity that hints at the possibility of sharing wardrobes and wine, tears and jokes is absent from every encounter.

My early, naive attempts at befriending French women nearly always backfired. I met Charlotte midway through my first year in France when she came over for dinner. Attractive and opinionated, with intelligent brown eyes, she is a friend of a friend of Frédéric's and studying in Paris to be a doctor. I was hoping we might get along well: only a few years younger than me, she was one of the first Frenchwomen I'd met then who didn't have children. I envisaged us meeting up in the future for a drink. But while Charlotte laughed frequently as she talked to Frédéric, I soon realised I'd made a serious misjudgment in thinking we might be like-minded. In an erroneous effort to engage her in conversation, I brought up the story I was working on at the time concerning the number of women in French politics. According to the press, on this score France lagged behind all but one of its European partners—behind even Kazakstan and Kyrgyzstan and on par with Albania. In raising the issue, I wasn't trying to be provocative. Rather I was interested in Charlotte's opinion (she had one on everything else).

But to my surprise, her brown eyes snapped with impatience.

'You know, in France there's no battle between men and women,' she replied tartly, shooting Frédéric a look of sympathy. Her expression hardened. 'Your Anglo-Saxon style feminism doesn't belong here.'

And I'd been hoping we might find some common ground! That we weren't so different, after all. Instead, an iron curtain of mistrust and misunderstanding had gone up between us. We could have been Brigitte Bardot and Germaine Greer, regarding each other with total incomprehension. Just pronouncing the words 'Anglo-Saxon' and 'feminism' in the same sentence had made her mouth pucker in disgust, like she was tasting one of those unsweetened *citron pressés* French cafés serve. To Charlotte, raising the topic was obviously akin to lighting a bonfire of bras. The look on her face—a mix of derision and horror—was to become all too familiar. Although at home my views were entirely normal among my friends, in France I have a new identity. I am a Radical Anglo-Saxon Feminist.

It is remarkably easy to become one. I haven't had to

attend protests, write ranting letters to newspapers or join any women's groups (there aren't any). All it took was voicing a few rather unradical ideas. For example, I'd always thought if I marry I'd like to keep my own surname instead of taking someone else's. Politely suggesting to the *sommelier* that in fact I might like to taste the wine (instead of Frédéric or some other bloke) since I'd chosen it. Other small signs gave me away. Drinking beer as an *apéro*. Drinking more than the usual half-filled flute of champagne that French women indulge in at dinner parties.

Foreigners tend to be forgiven for not conforming. Our idiosyncrasies and un-French opinions can be intriguing (at least to men)—up to a point. But you know what they're thinking, you can see it in their eyes. *You're not one of us.* Occasionally, such as the time with Charlotte, I sense sympathy for Frédéric (who, it should be pointed out, has no problem with any of the above). How does he cope, they wonder, living with a Radical Anglo-Saxon Feminist?

This is another unexpected cultural shock. France may be famous for feminists such as Jeanne d'Arc and Simone de Beauvoir but the notion of 'feminism' is scorned in this country by both sexes. Despite the French penchant for revolutions, reforms for women have occurred through slow evolution, and generally later than in other developed countries. Incredibly, French women didn't get the vote until 1944, more than forty years after laws were passed in Australia and New Zealand and almost three decades after Canada and Britain. Until the mid sixties they had to have their husbands' permission to obtain a passport or even open a bank account, and their property and family rights were severely restricted.

It's not that other countries don't have issues to resolve concerning women—take a look at Australia where paid maternity leave is almost non-existent and the number of women in senior management remains negligible. But the situation in France is intriguing. Why, except for the short-lived Mouvement de Libération de la Femme during the seventies, has there never been a strong women's movement here? And what was Charlotte's reaction all about?

Some answers begin to trickle through five months after our trip to Australia. In June 1997 when the Socialists stun everyone (including themselves) by winning the elections, Prime Minister Lionel Jospin puts women in key cabinet positions. One of them is Elisabeth Guigou, who is appointed Justice Minister. An attractive, elegant blonde, several months earlier she published a book, *Etre Femme en Politique (Being A Woman in Politics)* which attempts to explain the absence of women in French politics. Certain passages are particularly insightful. Grabbing a pen, I highlight her words:

'The very specific history of France, which excludes women from a political role while granting them a well-recognised place in society . . . has created a unique situation between the sexes,' she writes. 'If women have not felt totally inferior, it is because their right to speak out has been consistently recognised, bringing them a certain role and power.'

In other words, if French women haven't fought for their rights, it's because they have traditionally been treated with respect. If women haven't shown anger towards men, it's because in this country there is no simmering male anger towards women either. As a woman, walking into a pub full of blokes in Australia can be intimidating: the attention often has a discomforting edge. Yet in France the male vibes are totally different. Sure, you might be stared at and one of the zinc bar 'philosophers' will no doubt try to buy you a drink. But it's all done in an overt, light-hearted way as though it's a game and the men are just playing their part.

Whereas in Australia both men and women enjoy the occasional night out with the boys or the girls, in France the sexes would much rather be together. The tradition of men's clubs doesn't exist here. A conversation one day with Frédéric's father exposes deeply ingrained differences in our societies. An avid golfer, Alain has heard that in Australia golf clubs often have restrictive policies concerning women.

'In some clubs women can't be full members,' he tells me. 'And on weekends, some courses and competitions are only open to men.' If I was shocked to discover how belatedly France gave women the vote, Alain—who is the antithesis of a flag-waving feminist—is dumbfounded by this flagrant sexism in my country. He's not placated when I tell him the situation has probably improved.

'Why would men want to play on their own?' he persists. 'There'd be an outcry here. No-one would want it like that.'

But it's precisely this harmony between the sexes in France that Elisabeth Guigou claims has masked severe sexism and patent inequalities in areas like politics. There's another paradox too: while men and women might feel at ease together, *les françaises* seem to feel uneasy about themselves. When I asked Sophie the reason for the rivalry among women she answered with the French expression, 'Because they don't feel good in their shoes'. Roughly translated this means they don't feel happy or comfortable with themselves. I would go further and say they don't feel secure. And this insecurity has to come from somewhere; women aren't just born with it.

Discerning its origins is a bit like grappling with the chicken and the egg riddle: it's hard to separate cause from effect when you're talking about a vicious cycle. But I can think of several factors which might make France an ideal breeding ground for female insecurity. Take this country's cult of beauty, for example, which means women's appearances (and I do think it concerns women more than men) are subject to intense scrutiny and criticism. It's quite okay in France to admonish a girlfriend for putting on weight, for example. Add to that the incredible emphasis on *la séduction*, which encourages women to define themselves in relation to men. Then there's the great Gallic myth of extramarital affairs—I say 'myth' because a recent study revealed that adultery is only fractionally more common in France than in the supposedly puritanical United States. Regardless of whether the risk is real or imagined, *les françaises*, more than their husbands or boyfriends, seem to live with a deepseated fear of their partners being unfaithful.

French people might say it's precisely this element of uncertainty that adds spice and thrill to relations between the sexes here, which they're convinced are better than anywhere else in the world. We rejoice in our gender differences, I can hear them saying, and it's true they do. Just look at the gorgeous lacy lingerie shops that line every street. They've got something over us casual, careless Anglo-Saxons with our drawers of greying knickers, and they know it. In their eyes we often appear unappealingly masculine. *Pas très sexe*, is how a few French friends described women they've seen in places like England and Australia. Not very sexy.

And yet I can't help wishing French women would sometimes break out of this seduction-obsessed mould. Once, at a dinner at Alicia and Rupert's apartment, a French girl (a lawyer) left us speechless by revealing that she never tells jokes or tries to be funny in the company of her husband for fear he might think she's *trop mec* (too blokey). As we were trying to digest this extraordinary declaration, the other

French girl at the table (a psychologist) concurred, 'Being funny isn't very feminine.' They were her words. Their husbands nodded in tacit agreement. For a second or two, I was filled with the urge to shake those two girls, to make them knock back a few drinks, to crack their composure, to see them laugh noisily, spontaneously the way Mum does, the way plenty of women back home do. Instead, in a feat of self-control, I turned and joined the conversation taking place at the other end of the table. There was no point even trying to understand. I knew I never would.

It strikes me as one of this country's many puzzling contradictions that this absence of battle between the sexes exists within a general culture of confrontation. Charlotte might abhor the aggressive ways of Anglo-Saxon feminists, but in a different way she is formidably combative herself. Faced with her stinging rebuke and snapping eyes, I'd wanted to shrink under the dinner table. This is not the first time I've been taken aback by a sharp response in France: far from it. Often these confrontations occur with women but sometimes they are also with men. Although the French adore poetic, oblique language, in daily encounters they can be incredibly direct.

'DON'T TOUCH THAT!!' screams the guy at the local electronics store one day, making me jump. I have just taken a packet of batteries off the shelf to check their size but from his reaction, you'd think it was a priceless piece of sixteenth-century china. For ten minutes he'd been too busy admiring his friend's wedding photos to even acknowledge my existence. Not so much as an appeasing I'll-be-with-you-in-a-minute glance in my direction. Hurrying to an interview, I need batteries for my tape recorder. But after shouting, the shop assistant turns back to the wedding album, whispering something inaudible which makes his friend snigger.

'What's the matter?' I ask in a lolly voice laced with arsenic. 'Forgotten to take your Prozac today?'

The smart-arsed salesman loses some of his swagger. He wasn't expecting a retort. Obviously I looked like a pushover. Sensing my anger, he adopts a transparently insincere you-know-what-it's-like tone. 'Well, you know, it's just that I can't have every customer coming in and taking things off shelves.' To win my understanding, his face tries out a pathetic little smile.

But I'm not understanding—not after being ignored, screamed at, and then whispered about. Menace simmers from every pore. My voice is low, even, surprisingly nasty. The packet of AA-size batteries is in my hand and then suddenly it is spinning through the air, skidding across the glass shop counter where it smashes into the wedding album.

'And I can't wait fifteen minutes for you to serve me.'

This incident, which occurs not long after my holiday in Australia, highlights another cultural contrast with my time in Sydney, where the days had rolled by without discord or drama. No shop assistant snapped, no-one rolled their eyes in impatience or lost their temper for some reason I couldn't fathom. For an entire month, I didn't have one shop scene. Everything seemed possible. Yes, I could exchange the top I bought for my sister which is not the right size. Your latté isn't hot enough? Wait a sec, I'll get you another. Sure you can just have an entrée. No problem.

Service in France comes in extremes: it's either brilliant or bad. Some shopkeepers and staff are heroically helpful, as though their lives depended on finding the eyeglass frames that best suit your face or the Camembert that is perfectly ripe for your dinner party tonight. But often very little is accomplished unless you are willing and able to put up a fight. Even the most straightforward task may require a confrontation. Sorry, the public relations person explains. She is far too busy to fax the press release. Never mind that it will take two seconds—not to mention the fact that sending journalists press releases *is* her job. She is *à la bourre* (flat-out). *Pas aujourd'hui*. France Telecom cannot reconnect your telephone line which they cut without warning because some employee misfiled your cheque. Not this week anyway. *Ce n'est pas possible, Madame*. Contrary to appearances, this does not mean it isn't possible. Not at all. Roughly translated, it means 'I could help you but I can't be stuffed'.

'*Il faut râler,*' Frédéric tells me all the time, which basically means you've got to make a scene. 'If you're too nice no-one will respect you.'

This is a novel concept. Too nice. But he's right. The French are not impressed by anything as banal as niceness. Smile sweetly at a waiter as you sit down and chances are you'll be treated with contempt. On the other hand, an air of assured superiority—preferably enhanced by a smart suit—will usually be rewarded with professional deference and prompt service. In an interview, the entrepreneur Francis Holder who heads the hugely successful French bakery chain, Paul, tells me it boils down to *rapport de force*. 'France is a very hierarchical society,' he says. 'The whole question of service is linked to old ideas of power and class. The person serving feels inferior to the person being served so they try and show they are important by being rude.'

Being too nice only gives them the upper hand: it makes you an easy target.

In France, sharp exchanges aren't treated with the same degree of seriousness as they would be in English-speaking countries. It's more or less accepted for waiters to snap at clients they don't know or for someone to launch into a diatribe before you've even had time to apologise for bumping them. To the French—and most particularly Parisians— being combative is simply a normal means of communication and they take these daily spats in their stride. Their anger seems to surge and subside as effortlessly as sound levels on a stereo.

But not mine. Although the surging anger part is easy, it's the cooling down afterwards that I haven't worked out. If you're not used to it, this constant conflict can be stressful. Some foreigners actually enjoy it—they find these disputes a healthy release, a way of letting go without risk of lingering ill-feeling or fist fights. But instead of unravelling like a yo-yo, my stress only seems to coil tighter with every clash. Occasionally—like the time at the electrical store—my self-possession surprises me and the words magically connect like lines in a play. These moments are hugely satisfying. But they are also quite rare. Usually, I remain tongue-tied—a startled fish-face with popping eyes and a wide 'O' mouth.

Among foreign friends in Paris we pool experiences and workshop strategies, replaying our encounters like favourite videos, splicing in the clever, cutting replies which escaped us at the time. Should you ask to see the manager if someone is particularly unpleasant? (Yes.) Will the manager be sympathetic? (No.) Should you tell a rude waiter *'vous n'avez aucune éducation'*? Some books on France say this is a clever comeback—perfectly polite and at the same time deeply insulting. But to me, telling someone they're badly brought up sounds snobby and old-fashioned. On the other hand *'vous êtes vraiment con'* is nice and explicit. You're a real dickhead. (Extremely impolite but perfectly appropriate in the right circumstances). I wonder whether I'll ever be brave enough to say it.

Over the last couple of years I've sought counsel from my library of advice books for foreigners living in France. Treat confrontations like a game, advised one (which is all very well but I thought games were supposed to be fun). The challenge (the fun bit?) is finding a way of winning over the person so that she or he actually wants to help you. For once this is accomplished, people will go to extraordinary lengths to help you. You will encounter touching kindness. Rules will be bent for you and sometimes even broken. The trick is to find a way of breaking through that seemingly impervious barrier.

Halfway through my third year in France, around the time a team of talented women quietly but assuredly changes the face of the French government, I discover the answer—or at least an answer. The Common Enemy Strategy. In the right circumstances it works like a charm. This revelation occurs one day at the town hall of the 2nd *arrondissement*, where I go to obtain a document which is required by the social security department. I have already traipsed across town to numerous administrative buildings in pursuit of this piece of paper, only to be directed somewhere else. Finally, I am in the right place. This time I vow not to leave without getting what I came for.

On the stress factor scale, encounters with French bureaucrats send the needle soaring into the red. Living legally in France requires a breathtaking amount of paperwork, and getting it all in order requires inhuman reserves of patience, not to mention a second life of spare time for queuing at the dreaded Paris Préfecture de Police, supplying eleven copies of this document and nine of that one and most pointless of all, a compulsory trip to a medical centre east of Paris where I spent most of the morning standing in line holding a jar of my own pee.

Of course, every country has its bureaucratic idiosyncrasies. What makes France intriguing is the arbitrariness of the administration. Your life depends on the mood of whoever is manning the counter. Your future is in the hands of civil servants and they know it. You, on the other hand, are an insignificant *demandeur*. The enemy. You risk making them late for lunch, bringing in your annoying problems too close to closing and generally taking up valuable time that could be spent doing a million other more important things.

Squinting at my birth certificate, the civil servant at the *mairie* shakes her head in a way that can only be unpromising.

'*Non, non, non.*' She actually wags her forefinger at me, making me feel like a five-year-old caught eating chocolate before dinner. The problem is that although Australian by nationality, I was born in the United States where Dad had been posted for several years. Apparently, to issue the document, she requires a letter from the American Consulate in Paris confirming my birthplace.

'But my birth certificate says where I was born.'

'We need confirmation from the American authorities.'

'But the American authorities *issued* my birth certificate.'

'*Non, non, non.* We must have this letter.'

'But no-one mentioned the letter! It's not on the list!' and frantically I wave the official print-out that specifies all the documents you have to bring to obtain this document.

The civil servant's face is a mask of bored indifference. It isn't her problem. 'Don't forget it has to be in French,' and she looks to the next person in line. Dismissed.

Visions of more wasted weeks flash before me. Desperate, I run through my options. Begging? Bribing? Weeping? Instead, in a lightning stroke of inspiration, I lie.

'Actually, I did try to get this letter a few months ago but the American Consulate was really unhelpful.' And although I have never even set foot inside the building, I feign a little shrug which is supposed to convey my honest efforts to comply with the French bureaucracy.

What a difference these few words make! Suddenly the mask melts. She is sympathetic. She is on my side. I am no longer Madame Nobody—I am a poor, hapless individual battling the uncaring behemoth that is the United States administration. This is a problem she can relate to. We have a Common Enemy. '*Ah les Américains!* They are so difficult! We have so many problems with the consulate. *Ils sont toujours chiants! Toujours, toujours, toujours!*'

France has a love–hate relationship with the United States. Allies in war, rivals in peace, the friction stems from the fact both countries claim for themselves a world role. The US accuses France of being self-important and meddling. To the French, American dominance of the world stage is considered arrogant and perhaps dangerous. Like a squabbling couple, neither loses an opportunity to score points. The other *fonctionnaires* behind the counter join in the assault and somewhere amid the verbal volley, my piece of paper is signed and stamped.

Sweetly, the civil servant says, 'Next time you have to come here, Madame, just ask for me.'

Walking out of the *mairie*, the stamped document folded

in my bag, I'm filled with a sense of accomplishment. My words had worked like a magic wand back there. The sullen civil servant metamorphosed into a cartoon character of caring co-operation; a seemingly insurmountable obstacle disintegrated abruptly. I feel like skipping all the way home. There'll be plenty of other times when things don't go my way, I know. But at least now I know the key to small victories like this is hitting on the *right* response. I need to step out of my old rubric and embrace a new one. To forget how I did things in Australia and learn a way of communicating that works in France. It occurs to me once I've achieved this, anything might be possible.

Fourteen

The Givenchy invitation had said 5.00pm. I arrive with two minutes to spare. The Carrousel du Louvre, a vast mall-like complex beneath the museum, includes some large, characterless auditoriums where many fashion shows are held. But although the ready-to-wear parade should be about to start, the area outside Salle Le Nôtre is almost empty. Where is everybody?

In fact, they're all at the Chanel show (for which I couldn't get a ticket). Fashion shows, I will discover, never start on time. A thirty-minute wait is obligatory. This often doubles during the frantic ready-to-wear seasons when ninety shows are crammed into nine days. The packed program barely allows for travel time—fleets of taxis hurtle across the city, carrying editors, buyers and clients from venue to venue. Journalists stand on street corners screaming stories down mobile phones to meet overseas deadlines; photographers tear back to their computers to scan and send their images. By the end of each day, the schedule is running hopelessly over time.

I'd thought carefully about what to wear to my first Paris fashion show. This was one time I really wanted to make an effort. It's important to get it right. The very last thing I want is to attract attention by looking out of place. It is a delicate matter, one which requires a balance between dressing up enough but not overdoing it, I figured. My outfit should convey the casual confidence of a regular show-goer who doesn't feel obliged to try too hard. (Already my reasoning has run off the rails—at the shows *everyone* feels compelled to try hard.) In the end, I decided on camel-coloured trousers, a soft, turtleneck top the same colour and a long, burgundy jacket and brown boots. I stepped out our front door, pleased with myself.

But oh no, god no! My outfit is all wrong! As the fashion pack arrives en masse for the Givenchy show, flooding the cavernous space like an invading army, I want to run and hide. No-one warned me there was a uniform. Oh sure, there's the odd flash of individuality—Isabella Blow's mad hat with a climbing octopus tentacle that will obscure the view of all behind her; the signature hair-roll of Suzy Menkes, the fashion editor for the *International Herald Tribune* who, let's face it, is so influential she can do whatever she likes with her hair. But one thing doesn't change: the very people who for several seasons have been declaring brown the new *noir* and extolling the virtues of grey are a monochrome of immaculate black. In this perfect scene, uncluttered by colour, my subdued tones scream like a garish stain. The fashion pack is a private club with its own unspoken rules. It's clear to everyone I am an intruder.

Of course, this shouldn't matter, it doesn't matter. How silly and shallow to worry about my appearance! We're here to look at the clothes on the runway, not each other! But it's no good: the cheery voice in my head can't convince me. There is something intimidating about this ultra-sophisticated crowd, many of whom seem to have spent last month's pay cheque on buying their show wardrobes. (If only I had done the same!) Of course, the ruthlessly polished exterior is deceptive. Several show seasons from now I'll know that the international fashion crowd is a walking cauldron of insecurities so palpable you can almost seize them in your hands. This accounts for the frail, emaciated figures; the absurd personal rivalries which mean that such-and-such an editor can never, ever be seated next to so-and-so (imagine the fireworks); how one day a familiar face may say 'hi, how are you going' and then later in the week stare coolly straight through you.

Flushed with self-consciousness, I join the knot of people surging to get through the auditorium door. My gaffe will be less conspicuous when the corrupt colours are folded into a chair. Finally, it's my turn to wave my precious ticket at the dark suits on the door. It's a lovely invitation—textured, creamy cardboard with a dainty rope of gold along its spine. Inside, *Madame Sarah Turnbull* has been handwritten in silver by someone who knows how to write. Above my name is my seat place, ST. My initials. What a nice personal touch.

But to my amazement the doorman shoos me away.

'Not yet, Madame. You must wait.'

I have already been waiting forty-five minutes. All these latecomers are being directed to their seats. Why not me? Shoving my ticket under his nose again, I try to barge past.

'NON, Madame!' He yanks me back by the jacket. Sensing my confusion (perhaps he's just noticed I'm not in uniform?), his face registers pity. He points to the seat code on my invitation, the silvery ST. '*Standing* tickets go in last.'

I can feel my face collapsing. I don't have a seat. ST means standing! No-one had even mentioned this possibility—certainly not the Givenchy press office which I had to fax five times. And for what? An invitation to stand? I could do that anywhere.

In a state of shock, I wait on the sidelines with one

hundred or so other fashion nobodies. The sitting crowd takes their time, greeting, gossiping, laughing, oblivious to the pen of people waiting for them to find their places. Only when they are all through the door and seated are we allowed in. It's like opening the gate on impatient bulls—the standing crowd stampedes. Elbows are shoved in faces, heels spiked through toes in the fight for the best positions.

'How glamorous! You lucky thing!' This reaction from envious Sydney friends when I'd told them about covering the Paris shows suddenly seems grimly ironic. If only they could see me now. Rejected, trampled and now compressed into two square centimetres of standing space. I don't even have enough room to pull out my notepad and pen. Luckily, these are no longer necessary—not from my vantage point, anyway. Unable to compete with the athletic energy of more experienced standers, I've ended up with my nose squashed in the back of an especially tall Dutch journalist.

The lights dim, the auditorium erupts in ear-splitting, stomping music and an aurora of swivelling laser beams. Somewhere far in front of me the clothes I'm supposed to be writing about step onto a runway. Although it's incredibly hot and stuffy, I'm too tightly wedged in to even wriggle out of my jacket. The show drags on for twenty-five uncomfortable minutes; I don't see a scrap of silk, not a sleeve of one of Alexander McQueen's supposedly sharply tailored jackets. Perhaps I've just missed a moment in fashion history, who knows. There's a lot of clapping and then the lights come back on. I turn on the heels of my sturdy brown boots and flee.

Paris might be synonymous with fashion but I'd never expected to end up writing about the shows. It's not that I was oblivious to them—living in Paris you can't be. Everyone from taxi drivers to your newsagent will knowledgeably discuss the collections based on what they've seen on television or photos in the press. And you can hardly fail to notice it's show time, not with all these models mincing around the streets and the frail-but-fierce magazine editors who drink the city dry of bottled water and steal your taxis. But while it was one thing writing the odd fashion related story such as the piece on French style, judging clothes on a catwalk was so far out of my realm of experience I'd never even considered it. To be honest, I wasn't that fascinated by fashion. I guess I thought it was fluff.

Then one morning a few weeks ago a newspaper editor called from Sydney. He was 'desperate'—he needed a journalist to write a summary of the upcoming Paris ready-to-wear week for his news features section. And in the circumstances it seemed like a great opportunity. After all, the commission had just landed in my lap, without any effort on my part. It would be stupid to refuse. If nothing else I figured the shows would be an education. I started to get excited. This might even be fun.

In fact my first fashion week is an exercise in humiliation right from the first faxed request for an invitation. The short notice from the newspaper editor didn't allow time to get accreditation from the organisation that runs the Paris show weeks which goes by the unwieldy name of Chambre Syndicale du Prêt-à-Porter des Couturiers et des Créateurs de Mode. Such is the demand for invitations these days that journalists are reduced to begging PR people for the privilege of giving fashion houses what amounts to free publicity.

Of course, if the designer is little-known or not currently 'hot' then tickets are practically thrown at you. It also depends on who you are and what publication you work for. The powerful *Vogue* magazines get enough invitations to send private armies. If you're an influential name in the industry, the fashion houses will not only send a ticket but also an €80 bouquet from the smartest florist in town. It helps if your magazine or newspaper is published in a country where the label has lots of clients. But I don't meet any of these criteria. *Non, non, non.*

For extra emphasis, the French often repeat things three times. It's a sign of utter conviction. An excellent meal will be *vraiment, vraiment, vrai-ment bon.* A vicious dog will be described as *très, très, trèèès méchant.* This repetition means the statement is non-negotiable, ruling a firm black line through the possibility of disagreement and even discussion.

'*Non, non, non,*' the public relations person at Christian Dior says to me now. 'You can't have a ticket.'

She doesn't care that I write for Australia's national news-paper. She has received more than one thousand ticket requests from publications around the world and there are only two hundred seats at the show for press. '*Vous voyez, Madame,* we can only invite the most important journalists. We have to draw the line somewhere.' Having learnt to be more pushy in France, I babble about how readers from Bris-bane to Broome are gagging for news about the clothes soon to step onto the Paris runways (which because of the reverse seasons will not appear in Australia for another nine months, if they do at all). She would be doing my country a disserv-ice—her fashion house too—by excluding me. The gist of my bluster is: this publication is important; *I* am important.

There is silence at the other end of the line. The PR has hung up.

Two weeks of phoning, faxing, arguing and pleading

produces about thirty invitations, mostly from obscure designers I have never even heard of. Somehow, I manage to squeeze my bottom onto several sought-after seats. But even this is not the thrill I expected. Invariably, I am in row O of a configuration that stops at P, which means that, although I can make out what the models are wearing from the waist up, their lengthy lower halves are obscured by fourteen rows of heads. At Stella McCartney's show for Chloé, Kate Moss minces out in a dainty see-through camisole. But is she wearing trousers or a skirt with it? Are hemlines thigh or ankle length this season? I can only guess.

Alicia—who by now has realised her dream and is writing for some of the world's top fashion publications—fills me in on the bits of outfits I miss and the major shows for which I couldn't get tickets. But not actually seeing the clothes is not the only thing hampering my ability to write an informed summary of the ready-to-wear season. Although I fill note-books with careful descriptions and even the occasional mad, stick-figure sketch drawn in the dark, none of this helps me actually remember the outfits when I'm in front of my computer. The week-long parade of ready-to-wear clothes has become a blur.

On the world fashion map, London is innovative, Milan has style and New York is imbued with 7th Avenue savvy of the bottom line. The Paris shows have traditionally been about monumental beauty and extravagance. But recently, an influx of commercially orientated foreigners have taken over the design chairs at Louis Vuitton, Céline, Cerruti and Loewe. For the venerable fashion houses, they represent an exciting injection of youth and talent. Their clothes are casual and clean and immensely wearable.

The trouble is under my untrained fashion eye, one

beautifully cut, minimalist trouser suit looks a lot like the next. By the end of the week I've exhausted the adjectives wearable, easy, pared-down, slick, sleek, sporty, contemporary, no-fuss. I can no longer discern one designer from another. The truth is these expensive clothes didn't seem that special, really. They didn't make me pine. My first Paris show season ends in disappointment.

But if ready-to-wear leaves me nonplussed, the same can't be said of haute couture. In Paris, the fashion calendar is divided into four show seasons: ready-to-wear falls in March and October, haute couture is held in January and July. When the same editor asks me to cover the July collections, this time I know the ropes. I get accreditation from the Chambre Syndicale, which makes getting tickets less of a trial. You still have to fax each fashion house and push to be invited to the most prestigious shows but haute couture generates far less interest than ready-to-wear and the reduced demand for tickets makes securing a seat relatively easy. The couture calendar is far more leisurely too, with only about twenty shows. And this time I know not to stray from the dress code: head-to-toe black.

Made to measure haute couture is what sets Paris apart from the other fashion capitals. The industry doesn't exist anywhere else. Which is probably a good thing, I tell myself. For me, it conjures up arty, spectacular gowns that you might buy for a fancy dress party if they didn't come with telephone figure price tags. The number of couture clients has slipped to less than two thousand women world-wide—most of them Arabian princesses or Hollywood stars. What's the point in wildly creative clothes that almost no-one can afford? I head to my first show convinced that haute couture is an obsolete extravagance.

The Austerlitz train station in east Paris seems like an odd venue but that's the address on the Dior invitation. Designer John Galliano is renowned for staging epic extravaganzas based on historical themes. What's he up to this time? I check the ticket to make sure my seat number is not some sly code for 'standing'. Fb5. It sounds reassuring.

Stepping inside the train station, I blink in disbelief. The scene shimmers like a desert mirage, too glorious to be true. Palm trees sway above saffron-coloured sand; exotic carpets line luminous tents. Baskets of fresh dates, figs and fragrant tangerines are sprinkled between seats which snake between two train platforms. Flat silver dishes contain a painter's palette of silky spices—cinnamon, cumin, saffron, ginger, turmeric, paprika. Waiters in colonial white carry trays of Turkish delight. The air is redolent with rosewater and preserved lemons, reminding me of the Marrakech souk. And what's that over there? Champagne and long glasses of amber Pimms!

Flute in hand, I'm shown to my seat. More like a bench, really, it's actually an old-fashioned trunk, covered in a purple silk cushion. Unbelievably, it is in the front row. (In fact, there are only two very long rows of seats in this unusual venue.) The trouble is, someone is already occupying it. The intruder is wearing dark Gucci sunglasses and her hair is sculpted into a perfect bob which is dyed that mahogany colour French women adore. This is an ominous sign. In my experience these women usually have formidable temperaments to match.

The usher asks to see her ticket and with an irritated sigh she hands it over.

'Your place is over there, Madame,' he says politely, pointing to a seat in the row behind.

Instead of apologising for her mistake, she pushes the

Guccis on top of her head, revealing a frown. 'No,' she says emphatically. 'This is *my* place. The other usher,' her poppy nails wave vaguely westward, 'told me to sit here.'

The usher asks would she mind very much standing, please, because the name of each guest is written on their seat. This will clarify the 'misunderstanding'. But incredibly, she refuses to budge. Instead, the precious fashion princess eyes me with steely composure.

'I don't understand why you're making such a fuss, Madame. Every seat has a good view. Why don't you just take that one over there?' And she points to the vacant place behind. Her seat.

The usher is young and judging from his dismayed look, I'd say this is his first experience of a fashion show. He doesn't know what to do. Neither do I. Although furious, I'm loath to make a scene—especially when the distance between her seat and mine is a matter of centimetres. In the back of my mind is the doubt that maybe I wasn't meant to be in the front row at all, someone has made a mistake. I go and sit in her spot, where her name and publication are clearly written. The view is fine. But the incident irks me. This is my first lesson in show etiquette. *Don't be a pushover.* In future I will stand my ground.

To calm down, I take another flute of champagne and fill a paper napkin with exquisitely tender Turkish delight. Several seats along, an American voice loudly wonders how anyone could possibly contemplate alcohol on such a hot day. It would go straight to her head. (It's gone straight to mine, that's the whole point, isn't it?) Scanning the crowd, I realise I've broken another unwritten rule. Except for some errant Europeans, everyone else is sipping a different kind of bubbly—bottled water.

The temperature in the station hangar matches the desert setting. It must be even hotter inside the train parked on the platform opposite, apparently, where spectators sit frantically fanning themselves with their programs. Frazzled heads hang out the windows for fresh air. These stuffy carriages are the equivalent of standing tickets. (That could have been me!) Those stuck in the desert don't look happy, either. Clouds of the richly coloured sand have been kicked into the air and everywhere you look people are impatiently slapping stains from their clothing. The tension levels in Gare d'Austerlitz soar with the centigrade.

More than one hour after the show was supposed to start, the by now totally fed-up audience is silenced by the whine of a train whistle. All eyes turn to a shimmering orange curtain. Suddenly a steam locomotive bursts through it—the Diorient Express. Out tumbles a cargo of Indian braves and top models in a puff of steam. Wow—what an opening!

I don't think anyone understood the clothes that followed. Not even the man who made them (afterwards, when he tripped out of the train to take his bow, John Galliano looked a little spaced out as though he was as bewildered as the rest of us). As usual, the British designer based his theme on a central, historical character. This time it was Princess Pocahontas, played by Naomi Campbell. There were a lot of feathered headdresses, embroidered tribal blankets and most bizarre of all, Tudor court frock-coats which looked like they'd been borrowed from the BBC costume department.

The show gets hammered by the press. The front row Dior clients with gleaming gold jewellery and bouffant hairdos hated it. A bright, embroidered blanket is hardly the thing for a society wedding or celebrity ball. But for me every moment was spellbinding. I loved the thrill of seeing these mad–amazing clothes swish past my feet, the deliriously imaginative setting which made it seem like high theatre rather than a fashion show. I adored the champagne, the extravagance.

I loved it for all the reasons I expected to hate haute couture.

As the five-day season unfolds, I fall increasingly under the spell. I am a poor critic—too wide-eyed, too easily impressed. But at least when it comes to writing my summary I can recall the outfits. There is none of the confusing sameness of ready-to-wear: each show is dramatically different. I marvel at Valentino's gypsy blouses covered in airy cobwebs of embroidery. Jean-Paul Gaultier's liquid gowns which pour over perfect bodies. At the Chanel show, ethereal plumes flutter like snowflakes. And although those YSL blouses with floppy bows leave me cold, there is no denying the exquisite cut of the famous trouser suits. Some of the outfits represent hundreds of hours work—feathers have been hand-dyed, a corset hand stitched with thousands of tiny sequins. The urge to touch is overwhelming. This is not fashion. This is fairyland. Inspiring. Moving. Magical.

Of all the shows, the one that intrigues—no baffles—me most is Christian Lacroix. From the very first outfit, it's an explosion of colour. Tangerine is teamed with turquoise, a lime corset trimmed with mauve fox fur. A knitted mohair dress is a sunburst of red and fuchsia and electric orange. Although some of the outfits look contemporary, the puffy ball gowns and sweeping skirts seem straight out of a more romantic epoch. Everything is embellished, embroidered, adorned. These are clothes for women who like to make an entrance. There is too much trailing taffeta for my liking, too much clanging colour.

But when Christian Lacroix finally steps onto the runway to

take his bow, the crowd leaps to its feet in a chorus of '*Bravo!*'. Red and pink carnations—the flower is symbolic of the designer's native Provence—explode like fireworks in the air. The French spectators seem particularly enraptured. As the crowd spills into the foyer of the Grand Hôtel, the venue for the show, I overhear two male members of the pushy photographers' pack enthusing. '*Sublime*,' says one and his friend nods in agreement. '*Il est un poète.*'

I would have liked to have asked why: what is it about the clothes we've just seen that makes Lacroix a poet? But they are racing to the next show to fight for places in the crowded photographers' pen and I don't get a chance.

Walking home afterwards, I can't help feeling that I missed something. The rave reviews of the show in the French press the next day only confirm it. Why are they so hot and me so lukewarm? What did they see that I didn't? Determined to find answers for these questions, I decide to try to meet the man who created the clothes. A profile on the designer would provide the perfect excuse. A few weeks later after getting the okay from a magazine, I fax him requesting an interview. I'm not certain he'll agree—big-name fashion designers are inundated with media requests and some loathe giving interviews. On the other hand, on the international scene, Lacroix is no longer considered 'hot' so he might be eager for publicity. Within a few days—in other words, remarkably promptly—one of his public relations staff calls to fix a day and time.

From the outside, the Lacroix headquarters on Rue du Faubourg St-Honoré has a stately dignity. The lovely seventeenth-century *hôtel particulier* wraps around a cobbled courtyard. But stepping inside, you instinctively reach for your sunglasses. The house of Lacroix is bursting with tropical pinks, oranges and yellows. Vermilion carpets run into terracotta walls with a painted skirting of black shapes that resemble leaping flames. The place looks as though it could combust, such is the intensity of colour. The effect is stunning, exuberant and, like his frocks, simply too much for some tastes.

Someone from the PR office takes me to the couture studio upstairs, setting the table with a bottle of water and two mugs, in yellow and blue crystal which were designed by Lacroix for Christofle. He breezes in a few minutes later, shaking hands. His face is open and friendly, with large features that convey a certain sensitivity, so that it's no surprise later when he says he's an anxious person who needs friends that make him laugh. Although he often dresses like a dandy in snappy suits with silk scarves, on this day his look is low-key: baggy Ralph Lauren trousers he says he has owned for at least twenty years and a lime sweater.

Some interviews assume a life of their own, prompting you to ditch your list of prepared questions so as not to interrupt the flow. This is one of them. Lacroix has a magician's power to conjure up characters and images, a magnetic ability to draw you into his world. Arles, his birthplace in Provençe has long been his source of inspiration. His memories of his childhood are vivid and incredibly detailed: the mint perfume his mother dabbed on before going out, her handbag with the big clasp that made a snapping sound when she shut it. Elderly aunts in traditional black lace; glittering matador costumes at bullfights; gypsy women with babies at their breasts; Sunday mass with the flowing gold robes, dramatic music and lighting which Lacroix likens to a couture show. His father's side had the austere demeanour of their Protestant forebears, his mother's family were Catholic and unreservedly Latin, always talking and crying.

'It was an intriguing world of secrets and sensuality,' he says. 'Beneath the moral exterior my grandfathers had hidden mistresses.'

Christian Lacroix is the sort of cultivated Frenchman who can criticise his country and culture while remaining flagrantly French (although he calls his identity 'Mediterranean'). He is irreverent about his country's reputation for style, claiming that these days the French dress badly. According to Lacroix, *l'élégance française* has been lost.

'In the past the French had innate taste, refined and personal. Now style is much more *petit bourgeois*, with the petty rules and silly rivalries of this class.'

His views come as a shock. The French are famous for their heritage of elegance, after all. Sure, they have great taste, great style. But what Lacroix is lamenting is the loss of originality. Several months later in another interview, the French–American actor Leslie Caron echoes his words. This time the subject is décor not fashion: we're talking about the Burgundy inn she has restored. 'The French have no taste at all,' Caron tells me categorically. 'They just inherit nice things.'

But if Lacroix no longer considers Paris the world's style capital, for him it remains the centre of *savoir vivre*.

'Go to Fouquet with all the fine food and beautiful products. There are wonderful little artisan *parfumeurs*, beautiful fabric shops, specialist florists. It's all very refined—especially when you look at what's happening in America with those malls.'

The story of the house of Lacroix, which now belongs to the Moët Hennessy Louis Vuitton empire, is one of constant struggle. Listening to the designer you can't help thinking how tough it must be, dreaming up new looks and finding fresh inspiration for four different collections each year. Lacroix's first couture show in 1987 sparked rave reviews— the voluptuous ball gowns perfectly captured the spirit of excess during the 1980s. But the designer knew it wouldn't last—and it didn't. In the early nineties, fashion moved on to minimalism, labels like Prada and Calvin Klein became hot, and those big dresses became irrelevant and dated.

Lacroix is philosophical about the fickle nature of the business.

'Don't expect eternal happiness,' he says, quoting the French poet André Gide. 'I wasn't brought up to think every day would be beautiful. I was taught to just stay open every day to whatever may happen and eventually the positive will come back to you.'

But the pressure is on now to sell, sell, sell. Lacroix knows he needs a change of image. He says he wants to design dresses to hang in wardrobes, not costume museums. He's trying to put those historical, albeit poetic, images of the eighties behind him. To seek inspiration from somewhere other than Arles.

But at heart he is a creative, not a commercial man. His greatest love is haute couture, which is so labour intensive that fashion houses rarely sell enough dresses to break even. Instead, these extravagant shows are supposed to be a showcase for wild creativity and craftsmanship. The theory is they help build seductive brand images, inspiring consumers to splurge on the more affordable items like sunglasses and perfumes.

To Lacroix, haute couture is part of the tradition of *savoir faire* which is unique to Paris. 'There aren't very many areas left where France really shines. There's micro-technology. Perhaps cuisine.' He looks doubtful. 'But Paris remains the world specialist in haute couture. No other city does it.'

'But what's the point of it?'

He nods, ready for this.

'After every collection I receive literally hundreds of letters from women saying how they were touched by its beauty. And that never happens after a ready-to-wear show, even though they're the clothes that sell. I'm not a dreamer, I like things that are real.' He touches the table for emphasis. 'But I do think inspiring people is important.'

That's what the audience reaction at his show was all about, of course. People felt inspired. By the exquisite handiwork, because perhaps no other designer in the world relishes detailed workmanship as much as Lacroix. By his jubilant aesthetic. By his desire simply to make women look beautiful. Let's face it, when a rich girl wants to look like a princess she turns to Christian Lacroix. (Catherine Zeta-Jones married Michael Douglas in an ivory satin gown shimmering with tiny glass beads designed by Lacroix.) To the French, he is an artist, not a maker of clothes. You don't have to want every painting to appreciate the talent.

It says a lot about the designer's ability to cast a spell that by the end of the interview I am planning a trip to Arles (it's not the same anymore, he warns). I need to be more daring with colour, it occurs to me now. Suddenly all that ubiquitous minimalism seems pallid, unimaginative. I can almost picture myself tripping about in one of those trailing gowns. At his next show, I'll toss my carnation into the air. And one year from now I'll make my first, modest Lacroix purchase from the Bazaar boutique—his most casual, affordable line of clothing. It's a snug twin set in a singing weave of lime and purple.

When my story is published, I send a copy to the designer as promised. Several weeks later, on a wet Saturday morning,

Frédéric and I are hunting for lost umbrellas when there's a knock at the door. Standing on our grungy landing is a courier, whose entire upper body is concealed by the most spectacular roses I have ever seen. There are thirty of them, maybe more, in delicious, sorbet shades of vanilla, lemon, violet and silky pink. The fragrance is incredible.

'*Madame Turnbull?*'

'*Oui?*' I can't keep the question mark out of my voice. It's not my birthday. I haven't been sick. And judging by Frédéric's equally surprised expression, this is not a romantic gesture. The courier asks me to sign for receipt of the flowers. And perhaps because I just stand there dumbly as he trips back down the stairs, he says, 'There's a note.'

A slim white envelope is tucked among the buds and blooms. Inside, written in lovely, inky script, is a message from Christian Lacroix thanking me for my story. The flowers come from Au Nom de la Rose, one of those speciality shops he'd talked about. And although seasoned fashion writers would be blasé about this gesture, so many gifts do they receive, I am touched, delighted. Sure, it's clever PR. But it is also the measure of a gracious man. The truth is I feel privileged—not just to get the flowers but to have been allowed to glimpse this unique world. To have met one of its contemporary masters. If I'd thought fashion was just fluff, now I'm awed by the mastery of technique which underpins haute couture. Its importance goes far beyond providing Oscar night outfits to Hollywood stars. Rather haute couture is about history and tradition, passion and beauty, art and inspiration—everything that makes France a measure of civilised life.

For the next ten days our apartment smells like a rose garden.

Fifteen

A few years ago, after a trip to England, Alicia returned to Paris with a tiny Yorkshire terrier. Lou-Lou is highly strung, smart and—as I discover when dog-sitting while Alicia and Rupert are on holidays—great company. Ever since her arrival I've been mulling over the idea of getting a dog myself.

While some people thrive on the solitude of working at home, I'd just say I've adapted to it. Although I love my job, although I have plenty to do, an empty apartment can make for a lonely work environment. In many ways it's pointless complaining about it because I need the seclusion to write. But sometimes I'd kill for a bit of company in my office. Another presence.

Inspired by Lou-Lou, after a great deal of thought eventually I decide a dog is the perfect solution to my dilemma. She—because I've made up my mind it must be a girl— would fill my office with a playful presence. Her need for regular walks will force me to take fresh-air breaks from the apartment. And this being Paris, there'll be few constraints; I'll be able to take her with me everywhere.

'A dog will change your life,' Alicia enthuses (and only later will I notice the omission: she didn't say how).

Frédéric is markedly less excited. For a long time, he tries hard to dissuade me. Yes, he understands that a dog would be good company. But what about the disadvantages?

'Who's going to take her down six flights of stairs at midnight for her final pee?'

'I will.' (We both know this is a lie. This sorry task will be shared.)

'And what about when we go on holidays, what then?'

'She can come too.'

'To Australia?' He has me there. Six months' quarantine is a lot to endure for a four-week holiday.

'Alicia will take her.' (She'd already offered.) But Frédéric hasn't exhausted his objections. 'What about when we go off on the motorbike for weekends?'

In fact, this is his main worry. Frédéric had recently sold his ageing Honda and replaced it with a thundering Kawasaki 1100. The acquisition happened in the serendipitous manner that Frédéric does a lot of things. Stopped at the traffic lights on his old bike, he found himself next to a gleaming navy and chrome machine making a lovely throaty growl.

'That's exactly the model I'm looking to buy,' he told its driver. Was he interested in selling, by any chance? In fact, the fellow was and one week later Frédéric rode the bike home, nervously trying to control its 250-kilo frame and surging power. Thrilled with his purchase, he had grand plans of weekends away, speeding through the gentle hills of Normandy or Burgundy. As far as he could see, a dog would only tie us down.

Secretly, he hoped it would be another of my shooting stars—a bright streak of enthusiasm which rapidly burns itself out. He'd witnessed this phenomenon before. My art classes, for example, which I attended for about two months before facing up to my lack of talent. Fencing lessons fizzled in an even shorter space of time. But this idea is different.

Instead of losing interest, I become obsessive, studying dogs in the street like some broody would-be-mum. Every day, I stop outside the florist at the bottom of Rue Montorgueil to pat the Great Pyrenees with bloodshot eyes who occasionally gives the pretty pails of bouquets for sale a proprietorial squirt. The Louis Philippe café overlooking the Seine becomes my favourite restaurant—not because of the food but because of the owner's statuesque Great Dane, who frequently rests his wet jowls on diners' tables. We make the mistake of taking visiting friends there, an American fellow and his Finnish wife. They are scandalised. In most civilised countries such a creature wouldn't get one paw inside a restaurant without the health inspectors arriving, they cry, amazed that we are not scandalised ourselves. I find myself bristling, wishing their horror wasn't so apparent. Privately, I embrace the laid-back Latin approach to hygiene which doesn't equate canines with uncleanness. And although in other circumstances I would never admit it, I admire the owner's audacity: if you don't like his dog snoring beneath your table go eat elsewhere. This nonchalant take-it-or-leave-it attitude is infuriating at times. But there is, at least, something upfront and honest about the French lack of compulsion to please clients.

As the weeks pass, my obsession gathers momentum. Dog accessories take over entire shelves of our kitchen cupboards. A few months ago, on a trip to Australia, I bought a sheepskin bed mat, and when Sue comes to Paris for work she gives me a ceramic dog's bowl with 'All Gone' printed across the bottom. I've even decided on a name. Maddie is christened months before she tumbles into the world—before, in fact,

Maddie's mum has even clapped eyes on Maddie's dad. Frédéric finally has to admit the battle is lost.

And so we reach a compromise, something to bridge my bubbling enthusiasm and his doubts and fears. In a catalogue, we'd seen canine carry bags for motorbikes which fit over the petrol tank. 'We'll get a little dog, one small enough to go on the motorbike,' I reassure him.

The option of getting a dog from the pound or the French equivalent of the RSPCA barely enters my mind. In Paris, you practically only see pedigrees. The idea of walking down Rue du Faubourg St-Honoré with a mongrel mutt is too absurd to contemplate. In a city that is so hung up on appearances, it's perhaps not surprising that there are fashion trends when it comes to pedigrees. Breeds go in and out with hemlines and handbags. On weekends, Rue Montorgueil resembles a showground.

Trends build slowly then inexplicably explode. At first it was a case of a British bulldog here, one over there. Then suddenly their stocky silhouettes were everywhere and the market street was invaded by foaming, four-legged generals with names like Winston and Wallace. After, came the Jack Russell craze. For a while there were just a couple in the *quartier*, scampering on hyperactive little legs. Next thing it seemed there was one under every second café table, wriggling its puppy-fat to reach a fallen sugar cube or a piece of bread. At some stage poodles must have been in vogue, because their creaky legs stalk the streets in perfect mimicry of their elderly mistresses.

But the ones that really catch my eye are wiry-haired and white, with bossy tails that stick straight up in a self-important wag. For a small dog, West Highland terriers, or Westies as they're called, seem emotionally balanced and boisterous, their solid little bodies imbued with personality. Consulting a dog encyclopaedia, I'm won over by a barrage of upbeat adjectives: 'Friendly, feisty, plucky and confident, a West Highland terrier has the personality of a big dog in the body of a little one.' That sounds pretty perfect. Without reading another line, the business of selecting a breed is decided.

Maddie is born near the pretty coastal town Honfleur in Normandy, in a house with a large garden and lots of trees which will make our apartment seem a little disappointing to her. The dog breeder has promised us first pick of the four female pups. Eager to appear responsible, we'd decided to take our car instead of roaring up on the motorbike. On the way, Frédéric is perky. He seems to have come to terms with the idea—that is until he learns how much my precious pup is about to cost me.

'*Nine hundred and twenty euros?* I thought you said she was going to cost *five* hundred?'

I must have fibbed, I can't remember. 'Nine hundred and twenty is actually quite reasonable for a pedigree in France,' I argue defensively, pointing out that's what you pay for one of those sad, yappy, caged creatures from the pet shops along the Seine, whereas for the same price we're getting a happy dog from hardy country stock. For some bizarre reason I convert the sum into English pounds, as though the smaller number might fool him into believing it's a bargain.

'That's less than six hundred pounds.'

His eyes leave the road for a reckless length of time to stare at me.

'More than you make in a month.'

Actually, that isn't true. I earn more than six hundred pounds a month. But sometimes not a lot more. My annual income is a jagged line of wild dips and modest peaks. I know what he's thinking because the same thought is running through my mind. This dog better be worth it.

In the middle of a well-heated kitchen, a large, plastic basket is piled with pups sprawled so haphazardly it's difficult to connect bottoms with noses and legs. It's a wonder they can breathe. The slumbering tangle wriggles occasionally; beneath downy white fur their skin shines piglet-pink. They are incredibly cute. Frédéric's resistance begins to melt.

The litter is unusually large — there are eight pups — and several are especially small. While the others doze, one determinedly tries to scramble out of the basket. She has little currant eyes, a black button nose straight off a wind-up toy and ridiculous Dumbo ears which the breeder assures us she'll grow into. Her body is shaped like a wombat's, with a broad rump and narrow neck. Perfect Westie proportions, apparently. In Frédéric's hands she squirms impatiently, desperate to explore the world beyond her boring basket.

'That one's the liveliest,' the dog breeder says approvingly. 'She's the smallest of the litter.'

This last bit of information blows the remaining clouds from Frédéric's face. Lately he's become obsessed with the size of West Highland terriers, pointing out that some of them are quite big. He worries Maddie might outgrow the motorbike basket. When the dog breeder assures us this one will remain petite, he can't claim her quickly enough. '*Bon.* Let's take her then.'

A stack of paperwork and twinkling trophies certify Maddie's dazzling pedigree. The boughs of her family tree bend with prize winners and aristocratic surnames — there's even an imperial branch consisting of great uncle Napoléon and auntie Joséphine. The dog breeder tells us how to care for her — everything from toys to *toilettage*, the expensive dog grooming that in France is considered essential. As we prepare to leave she gives one last piece of advice.

'Be firm,' she says, with a warning look. 'Remember, Westies are very stubborn.'

ᘓᕽ

Where I grew up, dogs are dogs. Their lives consisted of modest pleasures like long walks, Pal and boisterous ball games. A night out meant guarding the house. But in Paris, a city of roughly two hundred thousand dogs (an incredible number when you consider there are no backyards and only pocket-sized parks) canines lead lives that are remarkably similar to their masters. They stay in châteaux-hotels and have expensive haircuts. A night out means dressing up and dining at fine restaurants. What makes this unrestrained spoiling even more bizarre is that it's totally at odds with the strict discipline the French mete out to their kids. While children are expected to sit rod-straight at restaurants, eating and conversing like little grown-ups, dogs are babied and indulged, perched on velvet stools and hand-fed from plates.

Maddie draws me into this weird, uniquely Parisian world. Owning a dog reveals another realm of cultural peculiarities which cause me to look at my adopted home in renewed wonder. Just when you think you've grasped its complexities and contradictions, something else sends you spinning back into unfamiliar air space. Although living in France has opened my eyes and even changed my opinion on some things—hunting, for example, which somehow seemed less callous and more comprehensible when I'd witnessed the ritual of Jean-Michel preparing his catch for the table—I am adamant in my opposition to this Parisian pampering. I want a real dog, not some prissy pup that has pedicures and hangs out at dog parlours.

Just as Alicia had promised, the much awaited Maddie changes my life. Working from home is altogether different with a little creative gambolling after my every step—to the toilet or into the kitchen to fill up my coffee cup. She's an excellent distraction from writing. At the moment she needs frequent pee-runs, which means a lot of running up and down our six flights of stairs. Together we invent games—hide-and-seek and a form of tag where one chases the other round and round the armchair. I never quite know whether I'm the one indulging Maddie or if it's Maddie who's indulging me.

In unexpected ways, she makes my life easier. By virtue of proximity and ownership, I bathe in Maddie's popularity. Sour civil servants soften at the sight of her. Usually the staff at the local social security office conscientiously ignore customers, feigning busyness to avoid serving anyone. But when I walk in with Maddie, two employees actually get up from behind their desks to congratulate me on my 'adorable dog'. The first time we take her to a restaurant, the waiters perform a pantomime of fussing and pampering. They can't do enough to please her. Out comes a little bowl of water—the same dish which will later contain someone's soup or chocolate mousse. A few minutes later they slip her a sliver of pork *terrine*. A saucer of fragrant rosemary lamb—cut into tiny bites—lands under the table, making my mouth water. Maddie has had apéritif, first course and main before Frédéric and I have even glimpsed a menu.

Suddenly I have an identity. To the local *commerçants*, I'm no longer an anonymous foreigner, I am the *maman de Maddie*. This title carries street cred. Shop assistants who had previously ignored me now smile as they surreptitiously slide her a corner of croissant. The *fromager* calls her in for a chunk of Gruyère; Pierre blows her boozy kisses from across the street. Napoléon—who has never once asked how *I* am— enquires after Maddie every time he cycles by. In a city where establishing contact with strangers is notoriously difficult, suddenly it seems everyone wants to talk to me because of my dog.

∽

'*Oooh, le petit bebéee!*' The voice behind me is irritatingly saccharine. Anyone who calls a dog a baby is best avoided, that much is obvious. Quickening my pace, I tug Maddie who is struggling to swivel and greet her latest admirer. But the cooing follows us along Rue Montorgueil.

'*Oooh, mon toutou, mon petit cœur!*' Maddie—an incorrigible attention seeker—splays her legs and showing great force for a little dog, brings us both to a stop. Showered with endearments, she licks and leaps all over her admirer, an elderly woman with one bulging eye that looks, quite literally, like it's about to pop out of her head. I brace myself for the usual questions: how old is she, what's her name (which I will invariably have to spell), and then the inevitable 'what does "Maddie" mean?' to which I will tersely reply 'nothing'. If she knows any English, she might make the 'mad' joke (did you call her Maddie because she's mad?), and I will try to pull my mouth into a tight smile.

But no. Madame has not stopped me for pleasantries. Her falling-out eye is fierce.

'She's cold.'

Taken aback, I try not to stare at the odd eye.

'*Vous voyez, Madame,*'—she points an authoritative finger at Maddie, '*elle tremble.*'

My dog is not shivering. She's not even especially cold, I protest. But grandma is apparently a mind reader of mutts.

'She should be wearing a jacket.'

Well that's bullshit. According to my vet, those silly coats only make the dogs colder because they rub the natural protective oil from their fur. But I don't get a chance to set her straight. Shaking an accusing finger at me, the know-all granny has the last word.

'*Mauvaise maman!*' You're a bad mother.

Unfortunately, this is not an isolated incident. The most startling aspect of owning a dog in Paris is the reams of unwanted advice delivered by total strangers. After just one month, I could fill a book. Such-and-such a dog grooming salon is very good; try Louis Vuitton for leads—they're strong and smart (not to mention ludicrously expensive). Scoldings are frequent. Your dog's hungry, Madame. Thirsty. Two butchers on Rue Montmartre order me to stop walking so fast: '*il est fatigué, le pauvre!*' The poor little thing's tired. Sometimes the messages are delivered indirectly, deliberately dropped within earshot. 'Look at that poor puppy,' says a voice behind me one day, which sounded like a mother addressing a child. 'She's far too young to be on a lead.'

Alicia had warned me. She'd experienced the same endless interruptions with Lou-Lou, whose theatrical shivering in public draws sympathy and accusations of maltreatment. But not for a moment had I imagined it would be this bad. In my books about France I'd read that dogs are a great way of meeting people in Paris. They hadn't mentioned anything about being chastised. After a few months, the regularity of these interruptions begins to wear me down.

Frédéric comes up with a line to silence the busy bodies. One crisp, authoritative phrase that somehow says she's my dog and I know exactly what's best, thank you very much, now get lost. *'Je suis vétérinaire.'*

So when two guys start hassling me one day, it's just a matter of pulling the verbal trigger. They're sitting on a bench in Palais Royal, obviously bored. Meanwhile, I am endeavouring to walk my six-month-old pup, except that she won't walk. Instead, Maddie is skiing behind me, rump reared and legs splayed, stirring up a wake of dust. This is her tiresome I-want-to-stop tantrum: her body goes rigid with indignation at not being allowed to snatch a baguette crust or sniff a fresh piddle. Gentle coaxing and encouraging tugs are futile; the wombat bottom anchors to the ground, the currant eyes blink insolently at me.

'Faut pas tirer!' Don't pull her, one of the boys shouts. Ignoring him, I plough on, refusing to bow to my lumpish pup. Dust clouds accumulate in the air; kids point and laugh. In different circumstances I might have joined in. But under the critical glare of the truculent youths, I'm just keen to get out of here. To avoid a confrontation.

'C'est cruel!'

This time the cry is louder, more aggressive. Curious heads turn towards cruel me. This is it. My cue.

'Look, I know what's cruel and what's not,' I yell angrily. *'Je suis vétrin . . . vétra . . . Je suis un vétiner . . . un vet.'*

Unlike in English, the French translation of vet can't be abbreviated to three letters. Still, it's a pretty simple word, not the sort you expect to stumble over. Vet-ay-reen-aire. But inexplicably, I have always struggled with words containing more than one 'r'. Just as I used to stumble over pronouncing 'Frédéric', this word trips me up too.

My moment of anticipated triumph disintegrates into farce. The yobs practically roll off the bench with mocking laughter as I splutter and choke on what is supposed to be my chosen profession. Pleased to be the centre of attention once again, Maddie wags and pulls on the lead, desperate to go and greet her protectors. Inside, I am seething. Snatching her up in my arms, I storm out of the gardens, red-faced and humiliated.

∽

Instead of improving, Maddie's behaviour only gets worse. Despite regular training sessions, at eight months she is still wilful and disobedient. Oh, she understands the commands, all right. She knows she's supposed to trot over at 'come', she understands 'sit', she can even do 'stay'. When she feels like it. The trouble is, the urge to obey doesn't strike very often. Toilet training hasn't been a stunning success either. Some nights we spend up to an hour outside while she sniffs and circles, apparently waiting for a comet to pass or the planets to align or some other sign from the gods. Inspiration invariably only strikes back at the apartment on Frédéric's favourite rug that he bought in Yemen. Her obstinacy is breathtaking. Sometimes in the street she performs a swift, 180-degree turn and starts walking in *exactly the opposite direction*. Fair master and faithful hound—the romantic relationship distorted in a vision of dysfunction—performing a ridiculous tug-of-war.

The local vet is sympathetic. She's a *petite femelle dominante*, he declares, too cheerfully for my liking. A real *tête de mule*, that's for sure. He could tell the second she sauntered through the door. West Highland terriers are blessed with a happy disposition and a stubborn temperament which makes them difficult to train, he explains. Not a breed that strives to please its master. Very independent. Had I read further in the dog encyclopaedia, I might have known the truth earlier. Westies should come with warning labels: Beware, this dog could break you.

What should I do? Call the breeder and ask for a refund? After all, €920 seems rather a lot to pay for a dominant dog (whatever that means). Maddie the mule-head. I've been had. The vet hands me a folded brochure. Beneath a name are the words: Professional Trainer, Dog Teacher. YOU'RE FEELING DESPERATE, YOU CAN'T GO ON? it asks in large green print. CALL US. I hurry home to phone.

The dog trainer comes to our apartment. She is a sensible-looking woman with a soft, understanding voice. Maddie whips herself into the usual tail-chasing welcome she reserves for total strangers but the trainer just pushes her away without even glancing down. No cries of *ma fille-fille* or *mon petit cœur*. I can't help feeling vindicated. Frankly, I'm fed up with all this spoiling, these nauseating endearments. We have already discussed my pup's problems at length over the phone and the dog trainer has brought along a list of techniques and tips, all of which are designed to show Maddie who's boss.

First, though, we have to deal with the crux of the problem. By this I assume she means Maddie's innate stubbornness. So her next words catch me totally unawares.

'The real problem,' the trainer says, 'is that your dog doesn't think she's a dog.'

She delivers this line—which is naturally a joke—with a deadpan expression. I giggle but the dog trainer maintains an air of calm patience that suggests she's waiting for her words to sink in. Slowly, I try to digest the news: Maddie's disobedience is symptomatic of a deeper malaise. Her syndrome sounds shocking, I've never heard of dogs not knowing they're dogs. (Surely even mule-headed Maddie was born with that much basic knowledge?) But my pup is apparently so maladjusted she doesn't even know what she is. Not even pubescent yet, she's already going through an identity crisis.

Sensing my panic, the *prof* quickly explains that actually this is very common in Paris. How can dogs know they're dogs if they don't lead doggie lives? If they eat in restaurants and lie on chaise longues? They think they're human (of course). Equal to their masters. They think they can do whatever you do and feel outraged when you say they can't. I stare at my pea-brained mutt, suddenly sorry for her. How should I break the bad news? With stick figure illustrations of four-legged and two-legged creatures? A lesson in Darwinism? According to the dog teacher, a few firm rules will force the penny floating in the dim void of Maddie's mind to drop. She starts scribbling on a pad of paper.

It goes without saying this is a very different sort of dog training lesson to the one I'd been expecting. The *prof* isn't at all interested in getting me to parade in circles with Maddie, teaching me to teach her to sit, walk and stay. The session has taken a surreal twist. The trainer has turned into a shrink. The question is, who's on the couch?

Initially it had appeared to be Maddie, which seems only fair. (After all, you have to be pretty screwed up not to even know your own species.) But now I'm not so sure. The *prof* questions me in the sort of careful, soothing manner which indicates my answers might be significant.

'How did you feel, Madame, when Maddie refused to obey you in front of all those people at Palais Royal?'

The answer is so obvious I feel like shouting it.

'Humiliated. Furious.'

'And do you think Maddie understood you were angry?'

It's difficult to believe this conversation is taking place in my lounge room. The urge to laugh is almost overwhelming but the *prof* is so kind, I don't wish to offend her.

'I guess.'

She nods knowingly. 'So you see, Madame, that's the problem. She knew she'd won.'

Two hours with the dog trainer turn out to be a lesson in canine psychology. Crazy though the whole session sounds, within a couple of weeks Maddie has undergone a metamorphosis. Although still stubborn, she seems to have accepted her place in the animal kingdom. All it takes is a few firm rules such as never allowing her up on the sofa, not making a fuss of her when I walk in the door and not showing my anger when she disobeys me. It's such a success I give the number to Alicia. Lou-Lou, the ultimate deluded Parisian dog (who probably thinks she's Coco Chanel reincarnated or the heir to the English throne), starts seeing the shrink.

In time, I grow skilful at avoiding busy bodies in the street. Maddie even begins to pay dividends as a catalyst for social encounters of a more positive kind. The terraced lawns at Les Halles are about the only area within walking distance from our apartment where dogs are allowed to run off the lead and gradually I get to know the local dog-owners. There's Guy, a fun English dancer with the famous Lido cabaret who walks Caspar, another Westie. Then there's the Chilean restaurateur with Otis, a silky Afghan with a leopard print scarf knotted around her head who does ads and has an agent. One woman has four French bulldogs; a gay couple has five meticulously brushed beige pugs. Probably half the dog-owners I see regularly are elderly women. Many of them are sweet, slightly mad old ladies who love chatting about the ailments of their *petit trésor* who's invariably got eczema or a funny tummy or is on anti-depressants. (My vet once suggested anti-depressants for Maddie when she sulked for days after we returned from two weeks in the country.)

These people represent an interesting cross-section of Parisian life and they also reveal something about Paris. Although to outsiders it can look as though dogs are merely fashion accessories here, the explanation for the high canine population is more elemental. According to a 1999 census carried out by France's bureau of statistics, Insee, more than half of Paris homes are single-person households. There is no culture of flat-sharing in this country. And now I understand why the dog trainer was so familiar with Maddie's syndrome, what lies behind all this silly pampering. Quite simply, many Parisians are lonely. They don't treat their dogs like dogs because they don't see them as mere pets. In a city where canines can accompany you to the hairdresser or even to the doctor, a dog is like family and it becomes a way of life.

෬๏

The Marie Poirier hair salon sits on a stately boulevard in the 17th *arrondissement*. I've come here to write a story about this renowned boutique, which also dabbles in fashion—and for an appointment. Inside, the walls are covered in photos of famous faces who've sought Poirier's scissor skills—everyone from Sophia Loren to Christophe Lambert. Marie Poirier shows me her latest winter collection. 'We're doing lots of leather this season,' she explains. She pulls out a wee coat in some fabulously soft fabric, trailing a price tag marked €465. 'Also more cashmere, and, of course, lots of hoods. Colours are muted—grey, beige and brown.'

Clients with beautifully buffed nails and perfect hairdos

swan about the boutique, lolling in low leather armchairs as they wait to be shampooed and snipped. One of them, Chanel, a glam young thing with fine features, trots over to model a two-toned reversible jacket. 'All my clothes fit close to the body,' explains Poirier, tying the hood under Chanel's chin.

The scene resembles many fashionable Paris boutiques except for one glaring distinction: the clients here are canine. Poirier is a *coiffeuse* and accessories designer for dogs, a *styliste pour chiens*. Chanel is a Shih tzu, a dainty breed hailing from China. It is Maddie who's the customer, not me.

For months, I'd refused to buckle to the pressure. I'd resolutely resisted indulging in any bizarre behaviour which might be construed as pampering. But Paris is a powerful force. Lately I've begun to feel ashamed. At ten months, my pup looks as though she's put her paw in an electrical socket. Her fur is filthy grey and greasy to touch. Increasingly, the first question asked by strangers is not 'what's her name?' but rather 'what breed is she?' (if indeed she is any at all, they imply). All that pedigree I paid for is wasted on me. Maintaining your dog's appearance is just as important as your own upkeep in this city and even the fishmonger on Rue Montorgueil—who keeps a photo of his Westie in his shirt pocket—despairs at me. '*Oh la-la!*' he exclaims looking at Maddie when I go to buy fish one morning. The situation must be dire, judging from the draconian measures he recommends: no less than a shampoo *bombe* to whiten her fur, followed by a full body *épilation*, which means waxing. (Later I discover that in this context *épilation* means plucking fur with a fine comb, which is the recommended method of grooming West Highland terriers.)

An attractive, charming blonde with not a wisp of dog hair soiling her black trouser suit, Marie Poirier hit national headlines in 1987 when she started snipping Yorkshire terriers. France's pedigree associations were outraged, arguing that the breed traditionally wears its hair long. But dog-owners were delighted with the clipped cut which meant at last their pets had eyes. The style made it into French fashion magazines, which dubbed it the New Look. Now, Poirier's five thousand clients span a wide range of breeds. Some of them jet all the way from Nice and St-Tropez for an appointment. The salon treats pooches like people, she explains. Individual characteristics such as being nervous of hair dryers, prone to biting or sensitive to certain products, are recorded on computer.

The appearance of Christine, an officious assistant with that artificial coppery hair, signals it's Maddie's turn on the beauty bench. I am shown a style book featuring photos of West Highland terriers with worryingly high hairdos. Beneath a close-up of a puffy head is the description 'chrysanthemum'; another shot indicates '*la robe*' meaning the coat, which is left long so that it forms a skirt beneath the body. Nervously, I declare a preference for a more unkempt look. No long skirts, no chrysanthemums. Just a regular canine cut, please. Christine, the specialist in West Highland terriers, eyes me pityingly.

'In that case, Madame, you might as well have bought a vulgar mongrel.'

I don't say another word. Maddie is shampooed, plucked, shaved, and powdered white. Her face fur is trimmed, gelled and teased. The whole process takes almost three hours and costs me €84. An extra €8 charge has been added, explains Christine, for the time spent untangling her knots. I pay up meekly, apologetically. I forget I'm supposed to tip.

In future, Maddie will come four or five times a year, turning up in tandem with Lou-Lou for their detested double booking. Livid to have been duped into coming yet again, the pair of them slide reluctantly through the door like samples of seventies shag carpets, prompting reprimands from the staff about the merits of brushing. Premium-priced *toilettage* isn't my only indulgence either. Thanks to a tip from the fishmonger, I start buying dried pigs ears—yes, the real revolting things—because in France they're sold in every pet store and dogs adore them. Maddie's instinct is to bury them and we find them half-chewed and glutinous under cushions and pillows on beds and sofas—anywhere she's strictly not allowed. Even crazier, one bleak autumn Saturday twelve months from now, Maddie and Lou-Lou will actually be blessed at the American Cathedral in Paris. Along with a Noah's Ark of creatures including a circus panther, a chimpanzee, a bald eagle, a couple of guinea pigs and about eighty cats and dogs. Down the aisles the animals go, two by two, until Lou-Lou and Maddie reach the altar where—to their immense displeasure—they will be splashed with water by beaming ministers.

Yes, I guess Paris has changed me.

Leaving the Marie Poirier parlour after this first appointment, I take a while to adjust to Maddie's New Look. Christine, it's glaringly obvious now, took absolutely no notice of my request for a more unkempt style. Maddie's transformation is radical: she is almost unrecognisable. For starters, the chrysanthemum face cut is actually more of a dandelion puff—an airy cloud of fur that looks like it might blow away at the slightest breeze. Her shocking new whiteness makes you squint—it's like looking at fresh snow in sunlight.

Instead of feeling heavy and greasy, her fur is soft and silky and smells like the perfume section of a department store. As a parting gift, a red silk scarf with Marie Poirier printed neatly across the corner is wrapped around her neck. On the metro home, I keep staring at her, smelling her, unsure whether the result is grotesque or glamorous. Should I feel embarrassed or proud? Eventually I decide she looks pretty. For one brief moment, one of us at least, looks Parisian.

Sixteen

The apartment had appeared empty when I returned with shopping bags spilling leeks and celery but muffled voices and stomping overhead led me upstairs to the mezzanine. Standing on the beam, I poked my head through the open skylight.

Frédéric and a huge man I have never met, whose centre of gravity is surely not right for heights, are sitting on the edge of our sloping roof, perilously close to a six-storey fall into the school playground. Iron rooftops roll all around them. The stranger is holding a skein of string, whose end point (anchored by a teaspoon) is dangling in the void beside our building.

'What are you doing?'

Although he seems to be observing, not actually doing anything, Frédéric gives me a busy, manly look. 'We're measuring where the window will go.'

For months we'd been talking about creating a new window in our apartment and through friends had found an apparently reliable builder who makes a living out of these sorts of jobs. The man holding the string between enormous sausage fingers must be Mio from Montenegro. My heart sinks. I'd expected tools and technical precision, not this string-and-spoon method of ascertaining something as crucial as where we will smash a hole in our stone wall.

'Er, don't you think that might be a bit approximate.'

Mio's eyeballs roll in exaggerated impatience. Clearly I don't have a clue. 'Ah les femmes,' he sighs, his powerful shoulders sagging under the weight of my female stupidity. Can't live with them, can't live without them, he says to Frédéric, or words to that effect. And although they only met this morning they chuckle like old mates, the weighted string suspended in the abyss as though the roof edge is a riverbank and the pair of them are fishing. I retreat, leaving the business of measuring to the men folk, not sure who is more dangerous—Frédéric with his history of dodgy DIY jobs or the swaggering, sexist builder.

If there was one thing we didn't like about our apartment, it was the fact that an entire length of its rectangular form is devoid of windows. All the openings are in the roof or on the northern façade, which looks onto the other wing of our building and a couple of domed roofs on Rue Réaumur. We have plenty of light but no view. Our blind wall becomes a source of frustration, a solid, sealed barrier between us and Beyond. It inspires curiosity. Climbing onto our roof (I am content to stick only my head out the skylight), we discover the wall without windows looks on to the Gothic silhouette of St-Eustache church, rising above the rooftops. Wouldn't it be amazing if we could see this from our lounge?

We dreamed and deliberated for a long time before finally deciding to go ahead with the window. You see, it's totally illegal. We haven't sought permission. In Paris, alterations to building exteriors require official approval, understandably. Trouble is, the process of getting permission is a long paper-trail involving numerous bureaucratic departments, public architects, every member of the building's *copropriété* or body corporate and any neighbours who might be able to glimpse the alteration by tiptoeing on their toilet seats. Usually it arrives at a dead end. Invariably someone objects—if not the authorities then a jealous neighbour who can't bear the thought that you might have something—a rooftop terrace or room with a view—that he or she doesn't.

Our illegal window provides an illuminating insight into the way things get done in France, revealing just how simple life can be, how limitless the possibilities, when you ignore the tangle of red tape altogether. Taken to an extreme, this rampant rule bending and breaking accounts for the breathtaking corruption scandals involving politicians, banks and big business in this country. But on a far smaller (and I like to kid myself, responsible) scale it can be rather efficient. It allows for a certain suppleness. *On va s'arranger*, someone will say, meaning they're willing to strike a deal. It might not strictly speaking be one hundred percent legal but—and this is what counts—an agreement will be reached that keeps all parties happy.

A couple of friends revealed how well the system can work over dinner one night. They had just finished stunning renovations in the 5th *arrondissement*, converting an entire top floor of poky *chambres de bonnes* (maids' rooms) into one big, airy loft. It was a huge job which dragged on for about a year and involved various teams of workmen—in other words not the sort of job that could be carried out secretly; the other apartment owners in the building had to be alerted. The problem was, at the outset several of them opposed their plans. But our friend, savvy in such matters, saw through their woolly objections. His neighbours weren't really against the work—they probably couldn't have cared less. What they wanted (without actually saying so) was something *in return for their approval*. One was planning daring renovations of her own, as it turned out, and wanted our friend's support at the next *copropriété* meeting. Another, a pensioner who lived directly beneath, settled for a small wad of cash—to compensate for the noise inconvenience. '*Et voilà*,' our friend concluded, as though discreetly handing out envelopes of money is as everyday as getting a suit dry-cleaned. 'Everybody's happy.'

Although the French seem to make sense of their system, for a foreigner the approach to rules and regulations in this country is difficult to grasp. Some are applied to the absolute letter while others are openly flouted as if everyone—including the law enforcers—agree that it was a silly idea in the first place. Perhaps it's because in so many ways, the French have surrendered their lives to the state, blindly conforming to the rigid order imposed on them because that is the price they pay for cradle-to-grave perks and protection. *L'Etat* employs more than one quarter of the country's workforce. Cumbersome and omnipresent it interferes with almost every aspect of its citizens' daily lives.

So the French are forced to express their legendary individualism, their recklessness, in a thousand small ways: refusing to pick up their dogs' droppings even though law requires it; hurtling motorbikes onto pavements to avoid three seconds of red light. Paying everyone from house cleaners to plumbers *au noir* is standard practice because it has the delightful double advantage of saving money and cheating the government out of income tax and the 'social contributions' required of any employers. The thrill of disobedience is part of the Gallic baggage. *Il faut oser*, our renovator friend told us. You've got to dare.

Two architects—friends of friends—dropped by to outline the possibilities for the planned window. Wearing ill-fitting jackets, loosely knotted ties and bad haircuts, they resembled ageing hippy-intellectuals who have made an effort to look businesslike. *Soixante-huitards*, for sure, Frédéric says afterwards, meaning they probably threw a few cobblestones in 1968. An ordinary window is not very *amusant*, said one. It's a question of imagination expanded the other, outlining some more adventurous options. 'We could do a rotating glass door, a sort of viewing pad . . . or even better, a terrace built like a drawbridge, something big enough for a small table and a couple of chairs. We've just installed one in the 11th *arrondissement* . . . very practical with those surveillance planes flying overhead, so when the inspectors come knocking on your door, *toc!*' He slapped both hands together, making a triumphant shutting sound. 'The drawbridge is pulled up, they see nothing!'

I laughed at the madness of the scheme, its ingenuity, the fact that architects who occasionally work for the government should take such delight in outwitting the authorities. Of course, we don't want anything so extravagant, we just want a window, I said, looking at Frédéric, my law-abiding lawyer. Little lights of anarchy glinted in his eyes. 'That sounds very practical,' he nodded, thoughtfully, and I knew he was already imagining dropping the drawbridge each morning for breakfast on our sunny terrace with a view over Paris.

When Mio and Frédéric descend from the roof, we all chat for a while over coffees. Just as concierges are invariably Portuguese and most bistros in the capital are owned by people from Auvergne or Aveyron, a good number of the city's masons and builders hail from one of the countries that used to make up Yugoslavia. A towering two metres with an assertive belly straining his shirts, Mio studied philosophy after school and somehow ended up as a builder in Paris. His conversation is an unstoppable meandering of proverbs, quotations and ruminations on life and poetry. He sighs often, great bottomless breaths of Balkan gravity that slowly inflate then shrink his enormous frame, usually in contemplation of a problem that he alone can solve.

Given the window is technically possible (in other words, the building won't fall down when we bash a hole in the wall), and it won't bother anyone (none of our neighbours will even be able to see it) the main problem is the placement. It is imperative we get the position right—and not just for aesthetic reasons. Rising halfway up the other side of our blind wall, stopping at the end of our lounge, is a convent. Developers have been dying to get their hands on it for years because of its prime location. Imagine a rectangle sliced in two by a diagonal line. The rectangle is our wall, the diagonal line the sloping path of the convent's roof. The problem is simple: our window has to be *above* the convent's roof line, otherwise we will bash a hole straight into a nun's room. Based on the findings of the string-and-spoon experiment— whose purpose was to measure the distance between the two roofs—the outline of a window is sketched in chalk on our wall. It is a modest size—110cm by 70cm—and later we will wish we had been more daring. Frédéric is excited, Mio full of bravado; he'll start with a small hole, a reconnaissance, and if the first attempt comes out in the convent, he'll just patch it up and aim higher. Nervously, I picture our wall riddled with misfires.

The business of drilling through the stone is bone-jarring work. The wall is much thicker than we'd expected. By midafternoon, Mio has tunnelled a narrow aperture fifty centimetres into the stone and still hasn't reached the other side.

Powder clouds soar to the ceiling, showering dust down on the plastic sheeting we thankfully spread over our furniture. Sweating and exhausted, Mio is starting to look worried and I realise that for all his blustering, this is a tricky job and he wasn't entirely joking about the risk of burrowing into the convent. Every burst of drilling brings me running out of my office, hoping for a glimmer of light. But each time the hole remains dark, like looking through a telescope with a lens cover, and I become increasingly anxious that we've miscalculated, that our illegal tunnel is going to land us in trouble.

'ÇA Y'EST!' At Mio's joyous whoop I tear into the lounge again, where his giant frame is bending, peering into the hole.

'What's the view like? What do you see?' He steps back, maintaining a triumphant silence. I line up my eye at the opening.

Light streams from the other side of the wall and for a second or two I am too bedazzled and blinded to see anything. Then, sky! Clouds! These ordinary things suddenly seem miraculous. Better still, straight in front of me I see St-Eustache church, like a massive full-stop at the end of Rue Montorgueil. Hundreds—no probably thousands—of orange chimney pots. Relief mixes with elation. Not only is the opening a respectable one metre above the convent roof, but we now have a view! Later, I will recall something magical about this moment, the first piercing of what was, until a few seconds ago, an entirely sealed wall; the anticipation of seeing what lay beyond it, as though this little opening on another world will somehow change our lives.

Significantly, the window comes at a time when I am increasingly preoccupied with light and space: two elements which have acquired new meaning during my four years in

France and particularly since our move to the inner city. This is brought home to me one Saturday morning in May on the sort of sunny spring day that radiates promise. While Mio works on our window, Frédéric and I escape to Palais Royal which is the closest thing to a park within walking distance from our apartment. Desperate to be outdoors after a long, wet winter, lately we've been coming here a lot. In the last few days the tulips have surged and bloomed, making the gardens sing in a chorus of contrasting colour. Sultry purples and reds are juxtaposed with luminous patches of white and canary yellow. The place buzzes with energy: toddlers busily topple and rebuild castles in the sand pit; a handful of joggers—a rare sight in Paris—trip gamely around the quadrangle; scatty swallows dive on the tulips in search of seeds. By eleven in the morning the chairs around the central pond are configured in an east-facing arc, jackets slung over the seat-backs as sleeves are rolled and skirts hitched thighward.

But although the gardens look gorgeous, on this morning I become reflective. Maddie, undaunted by the No Dogs sign on the gilt-tipped iron fence and overcome with excitement at being let off the lead, is racing in deranged circles. I feel like doing the same. Perhaps we have both gone stir-crazy with confinement. I gaze at the picture-perfect setting.

'I miss space,' I tell Frédéric as we search for a couple of green chairs to squeeze between those already positioned around the pond. 'I mean, the sort of space where trees don't grow in rows and nature isn't organised into perfect, manicured gardens.'

The things I miss about home make an eclectic list of obvious and obscure items. Spicy Asian food that's hot enough to make you sweat. The surf, or to be exact, the feeling of renewal after diving under a wave and emerging in a bubble bath of brine. Good television current affairs programs, because investigative journalism is practically non-existent in France, where news analysis is conducted through round-table discussions by journalists friendly with the politicians they're interviewing. Most of all, people, of course, because there's no cure for those sudden desires to be at the family breakfast table or out drinking with old friends.

And yes, I realise now, I miss space too.

Living in Australia I took it for granted. Now, though, when I return to Sydney I'm struck by the size of the parks, the vast swaths of bush land rimming parts of the coastline, the abundance of places where you can jog or picnic or kick a football. The way nature is in your backyard, you don't have to drive for kilometres to find it. In my mind now Sydney shimmers like a mirage, all liquid and light and spaciousness.

The charm of Paris, on the other hand, lies in its concentration of beautiful buildings. Although thrilled with our *quartier*, although I have absolutely no desire to return to Levallois (definitely not), the experience of living in a densely populated, stone-and-mortar landscape is new to me. It has enabled me to discover new pastimes and pleasures. In Sydney, weekends were spent on the beach or sometimes sailing or bush walking in the Blue Mountains. In Paris we spend a lot of time simply wandering through ancient streets, strolling to bustling Rue des Rosiers for falafel from one of the Jewish takeaways or across the river for a browse through the art galleries along Rue de Seine and a glass of chilled Brouilly at La Palette.

In winter, life is relentlessly interior. Let's go to a museum or an exhibition, I often say now—as much to my own surprise as Frédéric's. Mostly we stick to small collections in city manors which have been converted into museums. A few months ago though, we'd finally managed to see Claude Monet's painting of Rue Montorgueil at the Musée d'Orsay. The last time we went it had been out on loan to a foreign museum. I'd lingered in front of it for ages, drawing near then pulling back, marvelling how at close range the painting looks totally abstract, incoherent even, yet at a distance the seemingly random brushstrokes magically conspire to form a picture. It is unmistakably our street, aflutter with flags to celebrate the International Exhibition of 30 June 1878. Our lively street rendered with so much intensity and vigour that it seems Monet was thrilled by the flurry of life, just as I now am.

Whatever we decide to do on weekends, we nearly always walk there. Part of the appeal of Paris is its small size — travelling from one side of the city to the other is a mere thirty-minute metro ride. From our apartment, almost everything you could want is within walking distance: restaurants, museums, cinemas, theatres, doctors, vets, supermarkets. This quaint scale makes the city seem less intimidating — more humane somehow — than some other big capitals. It isn't grandeur nor the many monuments that makes Paris so special, I realise now. It is *intimacy*.

But the downside of this compactness is that there's no room for sprawling central parks of the kind you see in London, Sydney or New York; nowhere to kick off your shoes in summer and lie on the grass. Of course, in other cities you don't have the luxury of strolling through places like Palais Royal or the Luxembourg gardens. But ironically it's precisely this state of poetic perfection — so appealing to visitors — that can become oppressive when you live here. Every sprig of lavender, every blade of grass is there by design; nothing has been left to chance. Immaculately trimmed lawns are stabbed by signs warning *Pelouse interdite.*

Uniformed, whistle-blowing guardians vigilantly protect the gardens from anything which might disrupt the harmony of the scene such as picnics or footballs. (Real life, in other words.) At times it's like living in a gorgeous museum. Even the people don't look quite real—those perfect-looking parents with perfect children in spotless navy coats. I dream of pushing them into puddles.

After a while Paris can seem claustrophobic. Sooner or later you long to break out of this beautiful confinement.

And I guess that's why the window is so significant: this small opening is a way of breaking out. It takes Mio one week to turn the tunnel into a full-blown rectangular cavity and only then can we appreciate its full impact. I'm not saying it's a substitute for being outdoors, certainly not. Soon we'll begin a ritual of heading off on the motorbike into the countryside around Paris and these daytrips will help fulfil the longing to sit on grass and breathe fresh air. But somehow the window makes us feel less hemmed in. Sunbeams pour through its pane making the apartment a lot brighter than before. It gives us a view over Paris and the fact that this view is unobstructed by other apartment blocks increases our sense of space. Now we can stand at the window and gaze far into the distance instead of staring straight at the building façade across the courtyard.

It's like a painting, Frédéric says of our view when it is finally framed and sealed. It is too. From this level, there is a delightful randomness to Paris that you don't see from the street or higher vantage points with their pancake perspectives. The tangerine chimney pots look as though they've sprouted from carelessly scattered seeds; the tilting roofs and crooked windows make a medieval tangle of odd angles and asymmetrical shapes which belong in a cubist painting. At night, the rose window of St-Eustache lights from within, its flying buttresses stretch like golden wings. Rising behind it is the sixty-storey Montparnasse tower, an eyesore on the Paris skyline. Standing on tiptoes, we can see Notre Dame cathedral, craning our necks to the right the Eiffel Tower. It is not the most amazing view in town—far from it—but to us it will always seem extraordinary.

The window looks as though it's been there forever. The only telltale evidence of its short life is the pyramid of rubble and stones in our lounge, waiting to be hauled downstairs. We all admire their handsome size and biscuity colour. Wouldn't it be lovely if the whole wall was in stone, says Mio, adding that he could do it for us if we wanted. But chipping off the plasterboard and concrete is a big job, you have to chisel carefully, so as not to damage what lies beneath. Not now, we tell Mio. We don't have the money at the moment.

'Oof.' Mio purses his lips in a dismissive pout, which indicates this is no obstacle. 'On va s'arranger.'

Nothing more is said. The promise of a future deal is left lingering in the space between us, taking seed in my imagination. How? I'm dying to ask. How does he want us to pay if not with money? Perhaps with one of our paintings? Immediately I look at the dreary Flemish cows which Frédéric so adores. I'd trade that any day and for a lot less than a stone wall. But for the moment the subject seems closed, the conversation has switched to something else and because I know Mio won't discuss business with me, I keep quiet. He packs his tools, promising to drop by when he's next in the *quartier*.

For the next few weeks, we enjoy our window. Summer is almost upon us now and a contagion of merry madness sweeps Paris. Café terraces fill with chirrupping crowds, windows are thrown wide open, music is turned up loud. Our gay neighbours across the courtyard throw a party and late in the night we're woken by a barely clad bloke standing at their window, screaming, 'EVERYBODY NAKED!'. From our new window, we watch an illegal terrace being constructed next to the school. It stands on short, hopefully solid little pegs welded to the roof. Plants appear, an umbrella and a table. The sound of glasses chinking in a chorus of 'chin-chins!' tinkles through our window throughout summer.

Then one morning Mio returns, stopping off on his way to another job. Just enough time for one of his sugar-stoked espressos and a chat. By the time he leaves, a deal has been struck. Despite my most enthusiastic efforts as an art dealer (Flemish paintings are going up in value, think of it as an investment), we're stuck with the cows. Mio wants our car, not the painting. Frédéric can hardly hand over the keys quickly enough. We've been talking about selling it ever since we moved into the inner city. We hardly ever use it now—and when we do need it, invariably it won't start. Curiously, Mio doesn't seem to care about its condition, he doesn't even want to see it first.

Two weeks later, all the plaster has been chipped off and our wall with a view is now entirely in stone. Our car has to be towed away to some garage belonging to one of Mio's mates who apparently manages to repair it. Only later do we think to ask what became of it after that.

'It's in Montenegro,' says Mio, matter-of-fact.

We stare at him, not comprehending. 'Montenegro?'

It seems our car had emigrated. It now belongs to some fellow in Montenegro, who Mio had employed to renovate the farm he owns there, somewhere in the mountains. The car was a form of payment; Mio delivered it personally. My eyes widen: our old Volkswagen Golf actually made it across Europe! Somehow, this seems a fitting end to the illegal window story. *On va s'arranger.* Well, indeed we had, and the merry chain now stretched across the continent. Most importantly, everyone seems satisfied—we with our stone wall, Mio with having found a non-cash form of payment for his friend, which also provided an excuse to visit his homeland. As for the bloke in Montenegro who ended up with our car, we have never heard from him.

∽

The illegal window changes our lives in ways which we'd never imagined. Several months after its creation, the convent is finally sold to a developer: the nuns received an offer they couldn't refuse. The gracious, run-down building with its small, cobwebbed rooms is to be entirely renovated and converted into apartments. We are dismayed. Even though we rarely saw them, having nuns as neighbours seemed special. I'm not in any way a religious person but to me the convent was a reassuring, dignified presence. More importantly, the sale could have dire consequences for us. What if the developer decides to create another floor by raising the roof? We'd have to close up our new view. In theory, large-scale renovation projects in inner Paris are subject to sharp scrutiny by public authorities whose guidelines would almost certainly prohibit such a plan. But those mad architects who wanted to build us a trap-door terrace provided an eye-opener. In Paris, there is a way around almost every rule. Trying to prepare ourselves for the worst, we decide to enjoy our window while it lasts. For a few months, busy sounds of bashing down walls emanate from the convent. Anxiously, we watch through our window for ominous signs.

But after only a few months work stops. When it hasn't resumed weeks later, we enquire at a local real estate agency where we learn the developer has run into financial difficulties. Although we don't know it, incredibly the convent will remain empty for years. Its vacancy opens up new possibilities. Now, not having to worry about disturbing the inhabitants underneath, we climb easily through our new window onto the convent roof, whose incline is gentle enough to sit on.

Carrying books and sometimes breakfast, we prop our feet against the skylights for support, backs leaning against the vertical ledge at the top of the roof. Our building is among the tallest in the *quartier* and from here we can see much of Paris. Gilded domes glitter in the distance. The air seems fresher than at street level, perhaps only because at this height there is always a faint breeze. We become ridiculously proprietorial. The rooftop is a surrogate balcony, a garden, *la terrasse*, Frédéric grandly calls it.

Friends think we're mad and mostly decline invitations to join us—which is not altogether surprising given this particular terrace slides into thin air as abruptly as a cliff edge. But we are not the only Parisians driven to desperate lengths. On hot days the surrounding rooftops resemble the Riviera: towels are thrown over the hot iron slopes as all around us people sunbathe and read, women go topless.

My favourite time is in the evening, when the breeze has cooled. Cradling glasses of wine, we watch as the sun slips behind the Eiffel Tower. Lavender clouds streak the sky and the roofs glow flamingo pink in the fading light.

Seventeen

To Frédéric's great delight, one of the consequences of my new desire for space is that increasingly it's *me* who suggests going up to northern France for weekends. Maddie has made me more keen too. I love watching her elation at having room to run. As for the beach that took me two years to grudgingly appreciate, she adores it. The flat surface means her ball rolls far into the distance and she fills the sky with seagulls as her short legs scamper after it. The irony of my new enthusiasm is not lost on Frédéric, who relishes teasing me when I propose going to Baincthun. 'Oh no,' he says pulling a serious face, 'I'd rather stay in Paris.'

And so for Frédéric's fortieth birthday we decide to celebrate with a big party at his family home. Preparations were, as usual, last minute. No invitations were sent, people were simply phoned and names ticked off lists which were quickly lost. Wanting the celebration to be casual and carefree, Frédéric had invented an open *déjeuner–dîner* formula which meant guests could attend one or the other—or stay for both. A big Aussie barbie, he joked—all going well, the weather should be perfect for it in late June. Buffets would be laid out in the barn that serves as a garage, tables and chairs set up in the garden. In between meals we'd play *pétanque* or go swimming at the beach. In theory, it sounded like effortless entertaining.

In reality, there are a couple of *catas*, as Frédéric's father would say, waiting in the wings. About eighty people had said they were coming. But who planned to be there just for lunch, or just for dinner? (Frédéric thought it better to leave it open-ended, people could decide on the day.) What if all eighty stay for both? Although we'd intended to arrive at Baincthun at least one whole day before the party to prepare, work commitments prevent us from leaving until Friday afternoon. Reaching Boulogne-sur-Mer, we drive straight to the Auchan hypermarket, stressing about all that has to be done before the first guests walk through the stone gate posts tomorrow for lunch.

Naturally, Jean-Michel is in charge of the barbecue. Two twenty-kilo lambs—which he selected from a farm belonging to friends and slaughtered himself—are to be cooked on a spit, one for lunch, the other for dinner. I'm responsible for salads. In spite of our time constraints, I decide on a labour-intensive selection which involves cooking lentils, chick peas, Thai noodles and beetroots, peeling mandarins, grape-fruits and prawns, pitting a mountain of olives, roasting pine nuts and grilling goats' cheese. Precious time is wasted hunting for ingredients such as fresh basil and coriander in a provincial hypermarket where coconut milk and even red onions are considered wildly exotic. I plan nine different salads in all, each one with its own special dressing. Unable to contemplate buying vinaigrettes in a bottle now, I stay up late Friday night mixing them.

Even more ambitiously, to mark the occasion I've decided to overcome my loathing of making desserts and cook a couple of enormous pavlovas—something I would never have made in Sydney but which somehow seems patriotic in a cool kind of way on the other side of the world. In France, you buy cakes and tarts from patisseries instead of making them yourself (in the past serving home-made sweets to guests was considered unsophisticated, stingy), and these are to be practically my first desserts in four years. Pavlovas would be a novelty for the French, and more importantly, Mum's pavs had always seemed fail-proof. Hers would slide from the oven as thick clouds with crunchy, slightly cracked crusts which we'd eat with mounds of cream and passionfruit pulp.

Egg-whites, sugar, a few drops of vinegar and vanilla essence, a lot of whipping. What could possibly go wrong?

We wake just after six on the day of the party to find the garden bathed in buttery light. At least we won't have to worry about the weather. Even at this hour the sun has strength and we can tell it's going to be hot (thirty-three degrees, as it turns out, the hottest day of the year so far). I head straight into the kitchen to begin peeling and chopping. Jean-Michel is already outside—his rambunctious seven-year-old son Louis in tow—digging a shallow pit behind the house in which to build a fire for the spit. Frédéric goes into the garden to set up the tables, chairs and tablecloths, which were delivered yesterday by a local party-hire company.

His furious roar travels across the stone courtyard, through the arched front door, hurtling up the length of the house to ricochet around the four walls of the kitchen.

The ten white tablecloths, left overnight in the garage in a carefully folded pile on one of the tables, are strewn around the garden like scrunched paper napkins. My first thought is that they'd been blown about by a mysterious wind. But Frédéric is holding one up by its corners and now I see what the yelling was about. The immaculate white is marked by dirty smudges and paw prints. More devastating is the string of chewed holes in a perfectly straight line down the tablecloth's centre. It looks like one of those paper cut-outs children do at school, cutting the folded edges so that, unfurled, it becomes a perfectly symmetrical pattern. In a rare display of cunning, Oseille, the pup of Alain's other dog, Malik, had attacked the folded corners, ensuring maximum visual effect and costly damage. A total of six tablecloths have been chomped, three others are just covered in paw prints, only one is totally untouched.

'They'll be fine,' I tell Frédéric, unhelpfully, 'just fine, really.' And I race back to the kitchen, too preoccupied with my pavlovas to worry about aesthetics.

Help arrives at eleven in the form of four Australian friends. Sarah and Nathan happen to be over from Sydney on holiday; Kate and Graham live in London. Friends of mine from school and university, they arrived altogether from England last night and are staying at a B & B nearby. Although they don't speak French, about ten other native English-speakers are coming from Paris so I figure they'll still be able to mix and meet people. Earlier, when they called to see whether we needed a hand setting up I wanted to scream YES! but managed to say it calmly. And now here they are, ready for work, which is a great relief. Standing in the cobbled courtyard, I tell them the story of the tablecloths which is already starting to seem funny.

A shout suddenly pierces our chatter, this one travelling from the kitchen to the courtyard. Before there is even time to mutter 'what now?' Malik, a dopey Beauceron, charges out the front door, followed by Frédéric's brother-in-law, swatting her bum with a rolled-up magazine. '*Le dessert!*' he pants urgently. The dog gallops crazily around the courtyard as though high on something (sugar, as it turns out). From the look of her muzzle, it seems she's collided headlong with a snowdrift.

Thirty egg-whites whipped to airy perfection, carefully cooked until only the highest meringue peaks had faintly tanned, are smashed to pizza flatness on the kitchen floor. Although one appears to have survived the fall from the table intact, the other has shattered into tiny pieces which have rolled across the tiles. Its soft underside reveals cavernous depressions from Malik's long nose; much meringue seems to be missing. A crowd has followed me into the kitchen, and now registers my fallen face. 'They'll be fine, really,' says Kate, my exact words to Frédéric a few hours ago. Calmly, she collects the fragments, scoops up the sweet, snowy foam with a spatula and proceeds to reassemble the mixture into a massive, deformed cake shape. 'With the cream covering it, no-one will ever know the difference,' she says brightly.

We haven't even finished cleaning up the mess when disaster strikes again—only it'll be a little while before we know it. Outside Alain is locking up his two disgraced dogs, ensuring they don't cause any more trouble. As he steps into the barn, Jean-Michel's son races up behind him, seizing the opportunity to create mischief. Louis slams the door, sliding the heavy metal latch across on the outside. Already dapperly dressed for the party in polished shoes, a tie and silk handkerchief poking from his jacket pocket, Alain is shut in the dirty, windowless darkness with his dogs.

'I've locked up the boss! I've locked up the boss!' bugles Louis to anyone who'll listen (no-one, in other words). We're all too preoccupied with our preparations—Jean-Michel cooking the first lamb, the Australian boys rigging up the hired beer keg, Frédéric mixing punch for *l'apéro*, Sarah, Kate and I endlessly chopping and slicing to make enough salads for both lunch and dinner. Thrilled with his own daring, Louis races into the kitchen, batting a few roses off their stems on the way past a vase. *'J'ai enfermé le patron! J'ai enfermé le patron!'* I hardly hear his words, am only aware of his noisy, troublemaking presence. 'Get lost,' I say, not looking up from my chopping board. *'Casse-toi!'*

Consequently, it's a good twenty minutes before anyone actually listens to what Louis is saying. When Alain is finally released, he doesn't walk out, he catapults, charged by indignation and fury. Time is relative, after all, and 1,200 seconds had limped by in that rodent-infested, black barn. Frédéric's father is a proud man who doesn't suffer humiliation easily. He dusts down his still spotless jacket with rapid, furious slaps that are clearly meant for little Louis (who in a flash of prescience, has removed himself from sight).

Dog destroys tablecloths, dog eats desserts, naughty boy locks up stern *patron*, who is now very, very angry. It sounds like a farcical plot—sheer slapstick rather than the unembroidered reality. Judging from their bewildered expressions, my Aussie mates are having difficulty digesting the succession of mishaps. This is more pre-party drama than they'd bargained for. They must be wondering what on earth has happened to the legendary French *savoir faire*. Hurrying into the kitchen, I overhear Graham summing up my own sentiments with fitting eloquence.

'Fuuuck,' he says slowly to the others, the word weighted with a mixture of wonder and foreboding. 'And it's not even midday yet.'

Sixty people turn up for lunch and for a while everything goes smoothly. In the heat, the deceptively potent punch is cooling and later people will complain it slipped down too easily. There is plenty to nibble on—*saucisson*, tapenade and *anchoïade* on toasts, nuts, tubs of olives. People even seem to be mingling, more or less, which is always my greatest worry hosting the socially reticent French. The setting is picture-perfect. Frédéric has performed miracles with the table-cloths, sponging off most of the paw prints and strategically placing jars of flowers over all but a few of the chewed holes. The garden is radiant. Hydrangea blooms fill the air with billowy pink clouds, swollen pears quiver gently in the after-noon breeze and cows look on curiously from the next door paddock. It is all going so well, in fact, that I forget about the food for a while, the salads which have to be thrown together and dressed at the last minute. Suddenly, Jean-Michel corners me urgently: 'It's ready.'

Word travels that the lamb is *à point*, and within seconds, without waiting to be told, our guests surge to the tables, filling the seats. It all happens in one spectacularly swift migratory movement. Only a small island of English-speakers is left standing around the keg, oblivious to the vacuum which has just been created. It is a revealing moment, and later the contrast in cultures will seem comical. The English and Australian contingent is content to keep drinking, knowing that lunch will be served eventually. With plenty of practice standing around in bars and pubs, they're in no hurry to sit down. It probably wouldn't have mattered much to them if the lamb was burnt charcoal-black or still bleating in the field.

But judging by their panic, for the French the whole day will be a disaster if the *agneau* is overcooked. They're not used to having more than one drink before a meal and would much rather be *à table* than on their feet. 'It's ready, let's eat,' people murmur, knives and forks poised. Forty-eight pairs of eyes accuse me — it's my fault the salads aren't on the table, *I* risk ruining the lamb. Relaxed by the rum, I'm having difficulty rousing the frantic urgency which the moment seems to require. 'Lunch'll be a few minutes, go and have another drink!' I shout, causing brows to crinkle, a ripple of disapproval. They are unimpressed with my poor timing, annoyed by my cavalier attitude towards the *cuisson de l'agneau*. How typically Anglo-Saxon, how thoroughly un-French. *I am not one of them, for if I were, I would know that this is not incidental but a matter of great importance.*

I am angry too. To me their impatience seems rude, ungrateful. This is not a bloody restaurant, after all. Entertaining is not about everything going perfectly, it's always a little chaotic. Why not just have fun instead of getting all wound up? (Actually, I'm more wound up than anybody now.) And for what? A couple of slices of meat that might be a few minutes past perfection? I stomp inside where ingredients will be chucked together indiscriminately, the meticulously prepared vinaigrettes ending up on the wrong salads. Frédéric hurtles in to help.

But they are not being rude, they are simply being French. The passion for food is one of the most loveable, enjoyable aspects of France. It requires attention to detail and leaves little room for error. Culinary failures are not treated lightly in this country, not turned into jokes, no more than a barbecue without beer would amuse Australians. There is a culture of criticism in France which means people don't hold back from telling you something is bad. As a friend, François, once told me, here you don't have the right to make mistakes. No-one is admired for simply 'having a go' in France. Whatever your endeavour, you *have to succeed*. At French dinners, imperfect *plats* will be dissected by the table, each guest offering advice on how the recipe could be improved, where the host went wrong, how they would have cooked it differently. I am not a gracious recipient of such comments and on occasions have advised friends to shut up and eat, or words to that effect. To me their behaviour is offensive. But to the French it's no more than constructive criticism with the earnest aim of ensuring the dish is perfect next time.

In the end, lunch is a great success. Having been painstakingly basted with rosemary-flavoured olive oil throughout the cooking, Jean-Michel's lamb is fragrant and perfectly pink in spite of the extra cooking. The guests are enchanted by the salads which to them seem wildly innovative compared to traditional French staples such as Niçoise and Auvergnate. We arrange the bought tarts in a pretty line along the buffet but it's the pavlovas which are devoured first. Covered with cream and a topping of strawberries, raspberries and redcurrants they look straight off the cover of a glossy gourmet magazine. No-one in the know mentions the dog disaster. Everyone wants the recipe.

After, we play *pétanque* and the Australian boys try to teach the rules of rugby to Louis, who has been surreptitiously guzzling half-finished beers and can barely focus let alone kick straight. The ball thumps repeatedly into the pretty garden beds. Alain glowers from the sidelines. A few people drive to the beach. Jean-Michel crashes out under a plum tree for a siesta before rising heroically to cook the second lamb, cursing Frédéric and his grand plan to provide two meals (my sentiments precisely). Too little sleep the night before combined with the last-minute rush and all this running back and forth to the kitchen, a good three hundred metres from the garden, has left me exhausted. Frédéric and I have barely sat down all day. (Why didn't we get caterers or think to hire waiters?) I would dearly love to relinquish my role of Hostess

Lacking the Mostess—relinquish my boyfriend too, with his idiotic, ambitious ideas. To crawl to my bed under the beams.

But any minute now more people will arrive with the reasonable expectation of being fed. And there's not a lettuce leaf left over from lunch. The salads which were supposed to last two meals have been entirely consumed. There aren't even enough ingredients to make more. The giant wheels of Brie have been reduced to skinny triangles, the baguettes are a pile of untidy butts. I want to hide.

'What'll we eat?' asks Anne, a Belgian friend from Paris, as we stare in dismay at the avalanche of fruit peelings, olive pips and tomato seeds covering the kitchen benches.

I'm too tired to care. 'Lamb.'

Our guests seize control. Wonderful, life-saving Anne disappears then returns one hour later bearing plastic bags of groceries, having found her way to the supermarket. The kitchen transforms—chaos is replaced by order, my remote despair by quiet efficiency. A chain of sous-chefs chops and slices more salads. Arnaud (the host of the lunch near Lille during my first year in France) starts whipping up aïoli even though he's only just arrived. Sarah, Nathan and Kate make bruschetta. In a spirit of international co-operation, English-speakers try out a few French words and French friends practise the elegant English which they've masterfully managed to conceal from me for four years.

About fifty people come for dinner, half of whom have stayed on from lunch. Thanks to the initiative of our friends, the looming *cata complète* is averted and the menu consists of more than just meat. The only thing lacking is beer: the keg is empty. Unfazed, Vinnie—an Australian friend—heads back to the table, his fingers pinching three plastic cups of wine in each hand. A French group stares, apparently amazed and amused. They must think they're all for him. 'We'd better hurry,' mutters one. 'They've finished the beer, now they're starting on the wine.'

After dinner, Léon sets up a CD player and loudspeakers and the garage turns into a dance floor. Madonna starts singing 'Holiday' and the English-speakers are the first on their feet, shuffling and wiggling in the inexpert, abstract way that for us constitutes moving to music. The song is interrupted, the CD changed and the booming voice of Gallic rocker Eddy Mitchell bounces off the stone walls. The French flood the floor.

And suddenly the garage looks like a choreographed scene from an old rock'n'roll movie. Dancing in pairs, joined at the hands, they spin, bop and step in neat, measured movements which have obviously been learned. They appear to be able to anticipate what their partners will do next, both pulling back at precisely the same moment, hands releasing and rejoining in rhythmic unison. Alain is on his feet too, looking practised and polished and significantly more relaxed than earlier in the day. When the French do something, they like to be good at it—in fact they like to be excellent. The last thing they want is to look funny or foolish. There is no fumbling, no clowning around on this dance floor. Each move is deliberate.

Surrounded by such professionalism, the non-French contingent loses confidence. Impressed but intimidated, they retreat to the sidelines where I am giggling, having experienced this humiliation many times myself. Best leave the rock'n'roll numbers to the experts. Although French youth are increasingly into contemporary, freestyle dancing, most people over thirty learnt *le rock*, and at weddings, parties—

sometimes even dinners—delight in taking to the floor in pairs.

In the northern countryside, the air usually dampens and cools after dark but tonight feels almost tropical. A couple of guitars appear and the remaining crowd settles on the cobbled step which curls around the courtyard. It's almost impossible to find songs that some of us know the words to and that our musical duo, Rupert (who's English) and Paul (French) can also play. We end up singing to a limited repertoire of old Beatles and Simon & Garfunkel numbers. Someone decides we need percussion (we need something) and so we pour Alain's packets of rice and pasta into jars, passing around the improvised maracas.

Without street lights and neon glare bleeding it of blackness, the sky is brightly sequinned. An owl hoots overhead. It's not a haunting cry but a slow, whimsical sound that could be a laugh, as though the day's absurdities have been keenly observed. Frédéric and I know this bird, which is often busily hunting when we arrive at Baincthun late on Friday nights. Once we surprised it in the garden during the day and were bewitched by its wide, human eyes. Its pale wings glow in the dark. We watch it floating above us. Then, as though it has just checked the time and seen a new day is about to dawn, the owl performs a sudden seamless arc and vanishes through an opening in the roof of the barn.

Eighteen

'What's *that*?' Frédéric stared suspiciously at the *plat du jour* which a waiter had just set down in front of me.

'Cod,' I said, although I was no longer completely certain. We'd decided to eat out at a new restaurant in our *quartier* but on first sight our meal didn't look too promising. My main dish swam in a thick sea of butter and cream which artfully disguised what lay underneath. Taking a mouthful didn't provide many clues either: the sauce had overwhelmed all other flavours so that it was difficult to tell whether I was eating fish or chicken, although according to the menu it was the former. It wasn't that it tasted bad, only that it didn't really taste of anything except richness. The potatoes were too oily and the beans had been cooked to a grey mush.

This decidedly average dinner isn't an isolated experience either. Curiously, while the French may be formidable food critics and perfectionist about details such as the *cuisson de l'agneau*, eating out in Paris can be disappointing. Attacking French restaurants has become something of a sport in English-speaking countries and some of what has been written is unjustified, in my opinion. Even London—long regarded as a culinary joke in France—has claimed it serves better food than Paris, an assertion which invariably prompts

Gallic gasps of disbelief. Despite the undisputed revolution in English gastronomy in the last decade, not for a second do I believe that vertiginously expensive London offers better value for your food money than Paris. Often, French restaurants seem to be criticised for little more than their ongoing Frenchness: for not embracing 'fusion food' and fads.

The last thing I want is country cooking with a creative sprinkling of coriander. I'm not offended by menus that haven't changed in thirty years. Why change something that's good? You can still eat very well and cheaply in France. I've had memorable meals at country inns where you can taste *le terroir* (the region) in every mouthful. In Paris, I love having lunch at La Cloche des Halles, a smoky wine bar with a huge ham on the counter and sturdy wines by the glass. To me this simple fare is soul food.

My criticism of traditional Parisian bistros and brasseries concerns quality. Standards do seem to have slipped—or maybe it's just that the rest of the world has caught up, as many people claim. Whatever the explanation, all too frequently the food is not as good as you'd expect. Although French cuisine is actually incredibly varied, heavy sauces have become its trademark. Surprisingly often, pre-prepared meals are delivered straight from the microwave. Even salads are no guarantee of freshness—the lettuce leaves drown in too much dressing and the tuna or corn or beans come straight from a can. In Paris, French restaurants are now outnumbered by foreign restaurants, which are an increasingly popular option in terms of price and quality. When Frédéric and I go out it's usually to eat Italian, Moroccan, Chinese or Thai.

Which is why I'm so excited about my next assignment. For a story on Alain Ducasse—only the second person in the one-hundred-year history of the Michelin Guide to gain six-star status—I've been invited to dine at his eponymous Paris restaurant in the fancy 16th *arrondissement*. It will be my first taste of haute cuisine; I've never been to a Michelin three-star restaurant before. It's also an opportunity to see what lies behind France's reputation as the country that elevated eating to an art form. This is the sort of job journalists dream of: an afternoon of de luxe dining in the name of research. An invitation to play pampered guest at a place where I couldn't even afford the hors d'oeuvres. I can't wait.

Succulent ingredients are considered the mark of the master chef and Ducasse's press attaché had advised me to come early to see the raw produce. At seven in the morning, the second chef François Piège is instructing the twenty other cooks in crisp whites to move and weigh the deliveries of live *langoustines*, prawns and Périgord truffles. The air crackles with urgency. Every order is answered with a barked chorus: *OUI CHEF!* Close your eyes and you might think it's a military training camp.

For the next four hours, the chefs are preoccupied with minutiae. (Curiously they are all men—the world of high cooking in France remains resolutely male.) Perfect-looking asparagus spears are trimmed of their tiny pointy knuckles which will later be used to flavour sauces. Another chef carefully shaves the black truffles into thin discs, measuring and weighing each slice to ensure exactly the right thickness. Although this twenty-kilo box is worth the price of a new car, they look deceptively ordinary—like clumps of dirt. Someone else selects only the inner, baby leaves from healthy bunches of herbs. Parsley is being reduced to a paste, pushed and repushed through a superfine sieve, and I wonder why it couldn't be zapped in a mixer. At the Alain Ducasse shortcuts are apparently out of the question.

When the main man finally tears into the kitchen just before lunch, it's not to stir and slice. Trailed by a French film crew, Ducasse consults urgently with Piège, tastes a sauce, all the while staring intently at a bank of television screens which monitor the restaurant. Tiny beads of sweat bud on the brows of the young cooks as their boss scans the gleaming benches for stray olive oil dribbles or splashes of stock. (There aren't any.) In France, celebrity chefs enjoy the sort of hero worship that in Australia is reserved for sports stars. Like Paul Bocuse and Joël Robuchon, Ducasse has become a travelling ambassador for French cuisine—and something of a media darling.

But more than any of his contemporaries, Ducasse has redefined what it means to be a grand French chef. With a growing list of restaurants—one in Paris, another in New York plus the three-Michelin-star Louis XV in Monte Carlo—there is an increasing demand for him to consult, give interviews and take on new business projects. Ducasse is more likely to be caught leaping into Lear jets than standing at the stove. He's a *provocateur* and you sense his business savvy and global outlook might irritate the more traditional members of the French culinary establishment. But despite his designer suits and jet-setting, up until 2001 the chef manages to maintain his six-star status.

Although he's friendly and unpretentious, interviewing Ducasse is difficult. He crams more into sixty seconds than most of us fit into one hour which means you can't hold his attention for longer than a five-minute stretch. His office telephone rings often and we are frequently interrupted by assistants and staff bearing messages and papers to sign. At one point he has receivers to both ears while he checks the computer for bookings at the Louis XV. Everything is done at sprint speed—the way he ricochets his chair to reach an article from the stack of international magazines which have recently interviewed him; his rapid-fire way of talking. He says his dream is to steal forty-eight hours from a day of twenty-four.

Asked to define what makes high French cooking so special, Ducasse doesn't talk about luxury ingredients but the enigmatic *touche française*, which I'd witnessed earlier in the kitchen. 'It's a bit like in haute couture,' he explains. 'We're not the makers of the rarest silks, there are beautiful silks and materials everywhere in the world but there is a French signature. And I think our cuisine—before the produce—comes down to a *savoir faire*, an incredible heritage.'

This know-how means that Paris is home to some first-rate restaurants which elevate eating to gastronomic experiences. But Ducasse admits that lower down the price scale there is less magic. Finding simple, fresh affordable food in Paris is difficult, he says, adding it's not possible for under €30 a head. There's a gap in the market. Judging from the entrepreneurial gleam in his eyes, Ducasse would like to fill it.

But for the moment at least, his name is not synonymous with cheap eats. By 1.30pm, the Alain Ducasse dining room has filled with the sort of sleek suits you'd expect at a restaurant where lunch may cost anywhere between €200 and €300 per person. Our table—I am accompanied by a photographer who is taking pictures for the story—is in the corner, a perfect vantage point from which to survey the room. Dark wood panelling, a *trompe l'œil* library and sombre green walls give it the feel of a stuffy gentlemen's club. (The restaurant has since moved to the Hôtel Plaza Athénée where the décor is fresher.) Waiters glide around the dining room, almost outnumbering the guests. They are charming and unfailingly attentive. A wee footstool magically materialises on which to rest my bag—a bulky black vinyl thing deformed by pockets and zips for notepads, leaky pens and god knows what which looks totally incongruous atop the plush velvet pelt. Across the dining room, perched on another footstool is a chic beige handbag (probably a Kelly bag with a price tag of about €3,500) which belongs to a handsome woman whose tanned skin shines like polished wood. I vow to upgrade—if not to Hermès then at least to leather.

Would Madame like sparkling or plain water, our waiter enquires. Small bubbles, medium-sized bubbles or fat bubbles? Butter with or without salt? This pampering doesn't seem pretentious or the slightest bit intimidating. *Au contraire*, I'd like to move in.

'You'll eat quite a lot of black truffles today,' the waiter announces, outlining the set menu of seven courses which consists of an avalanche of priceless delicacies. I think of my usual home-made lunches: boiled potatoes topped with grilled cheese or instant Asian noodles swimming in soy sauce. A rivulet of vintage champagne tickles my throat. I have to stifle an overexcited giggle.

First up are the *langoustines* (looking a little less active than they were this morning) served with Iranian caviar with greenish egg-bubbles so fat and glossy that it seems totally unrelated to the gaudy red and black stuff sold in supermarkets. The next four courses all come with truffles: truffle-flavoured ravioli stuffed with duck foie gras; *coquilles* Jacques with more black truffles; fattened young chicken with a creamy truffle sauce followed by a frilly salad topped with truffle shavings to cleanse the palate before cheese and dessert.

It must have taken some poor dog weeks to snuffle out the fortune of fungi I wolf down in less than two hours. For someone who has never tasted truffles, this is quite an initiation. Truthfully, at first they leave me rather indifferent. I can't discern a distinct, to-die-for flavour. Every dish is delicious but might it have been just as great without the truffles? It takes the simple salad where there is little competition from other ingredients to win me over. The texture is sort of crunchy and biting into a slice releases a warm earthy aroma. It's difficult to describe the taste, maybe it's more fragrance than flavour. Certainly it bears no resemblance to ordinary mushrooms. *Like tree bark*, I scribble finally in my notepad, an incongruous comparison (given I've never actually eaten tree bark) which would no doubt send the boys in the kitchen into a collective swoon.

The food at the Alain Ducasse is 'bourgeois', in the words of the chef. At his Monaco restaurant the culinary style is Mediterranean and you sense fresh fish and olive oil flavours are his personal preference. He recognises that traditional French cuisine has an image problem—'it's considered old and heavy'—and says that his job is to give it a modern spin. Although rich, the sauces at lunch are not heavy. They are subtle yet intense, brewed from those *bouillons* I saw bubbling earlier. Each dish exudes delicacy and depth. By the end of our meal both the photographer and I are feeling faintly sick.

Still—and this is telling—I struggle on to the end. When the post-dessert trolley of patisseries arrives, each creation so exquisite they look like collectors' items, I even summon the stamina for a slim coffee éclair. Admittedly, when it's time to leave it requires a heroic effort just to get up from the table. Our charming waiter presents us both with the customary gifts: a personalised menu detailing the wine and courses we'd had and a round loaf of bread baked in the Alain Ducasse kitchen—a handy snack for the trip home. I stumble into the fading afternoon light, bloated but also utterly content.

It was a memorable lunch. Unlike any restaurant I've ever been to and, of course, it should be pretty special given the prices. More than anything, though, it is the image of those sous-chefs which will stay with me. Watching them toil over each dish, sauce and garnish, their every move carried out with concentrated dedication, the scene struck me as wonderfully French. The obsession with only the finest produce, the almost absurd attention to detail, the *savoir faire* which elevates even the simplest task to art. Haute cuisine might well involve a touch of magic—genius even—but viewed from the kitchen it just appeared terribly hard work.

The fact that I'd managed to eat my way through that Ducasse feast is proof in itself of my amazing progress. Before arriving in France, I hardly ever had more than two courses at restaurants and was totally unaccustomed to rich flavours. In a not so distant life in Australia, I had a refrigerator full of soya and skim milks and low-fat yoghurts alive with apparently desirable cultures. My cupboards contained costly health food shop items such as bee pollen granules and lecithin. Every day started with a fresh juice made from oranges, carrots and celery and a bowl of unsweetened, untoasted cereal. For snacks, I ate carob chocolate and yoghurt bars, convinced that these were better for me than Bountys or Kit Kats. The meat I cooked was cut into little pieces for curries or Asian stir fry dishes, where its meatiness was diminished by spices and vegetables. Mostly I stuck with fish and chicken. I could quite easily have turned vegetarian.

But France took care of all that.

These days, breakfast is a *café crème* with a croissant or a *pain au chocolat*, which I guess is a bit like starting the day with coffee and cake. When Frédéric has time he prepares a fresh fruit salad — served with snowdrifts of full-fat *fromage blanc*, sold straight from the farm at our local cheese shop. As a treat, sometimes I add a dollop of *confiture de lait* — a delicious creamy spread which tastes like caramelised condensed milk, only better. I can no longer tolerate skimmed anything, and studiously avoid low-salt products — the butter I buy is packed with crunchy crystals from Brittany. On his first trip to Australia, Frédéric was appalled by the presence of margarine in every refrigerator. It's supposed to be better for you, I'd said, thinking this was an adequate explanation. 'But it's tasteless!' he'd retorted, astounded by the notion of replacing something that tastes good with something that has no taste at all just because the latest, soon-to-be superseded medical opinion says it's better for you. (Don't try explaining health food fads to a Frenchman.)

France has this effect on foreigners. It turns your eating habits and food principles upside down so that before long you're rhapsodising about the delicate silkiness of *foie gras entier*, without a thought for the fat content, let alone the poor goose or duck who was force-fed through a tube down its throat. The damage is irreparable — there's no turning back to muesli after flaky pastries filled with ribbons of dark chocolate. (Incredibly, most people I know who live in Paris don't put on weight, which just goes to show there must be some truth to the red wine theory — or that there are benefits to living without lifts.)

Some foreigners undergo a metamorphosis. Alicia was vegetarian and totally uninterested in cooking when she arrived in Paris. Within weeks she'd developed a taste for *saucisson*, slicing sausage, which is about as carnivorous as you can get given the contents—anything from pig parts to wild boar, deer and donkey. After six months of endless *chèvre chaud* salads in restaurants she decided avoiding meat was just too dull in France—take away the lump of protein and there's precious little on the menu. Now she whips up four-course dinners, stews *bœuf bourguignon* and pulls sizzling legs of pink lamb from the oven.

The radical transformation many of us undergo in France is partly a natural response to the incredible range and quality of food available. For if restaurants can fall short of expectations, the produce is inspiring. Anyone who has ever walked through a Paris food market—better still a regional one—knows what I mean. Stalls spill with thirty different sorts of *saucissons*, olives marinated dozens of different ways in herbs and spices, more varieties of chestnuts than I ever knew existed. These markets are uplifting; there is no other word for them.

Social pressure also plays a part. Dinner parties are the main way of entertaining and let's face it, vege lasagne is hardly likely to be a hit in a country of carnivores. In France, food is rooted in ritual and diverging from it can be hazardous. At one of our early dinner parties in Levallois, I served a main course of fresh ravioli with a tomato, basil and pancetta sauce. A friend of Frédéric's took me aside in the kitchen. 'Just so you know,' he said not unkindly, 'in France we *never* serve pasta as a main dish.' His voice was hushed and grave as he explained the facts of French life to me. 'People expect meat or fish.'

Even the promise of something casual doesn't mean the same thing in France as it did in Australia. When Frédéric's cousin invited us to a last-minute Sunday lunch of takeaway chicken, I went expecting to help set the table and prepare the salad. But despite the short notice, no detail had been overlooked. The champagne was chilled, the red was already breathing, and Normandy cider was waiting to accompany the almond-paste *galette*. Swathed in perfectly ironed white linen, the table was laid with beautiful glasses and silver cutlery. The takeaway chicken was no ordinary chook either: it was a golden fat, farm variety prepared by the butcher.

Surrounded by this culinary and aesthetic perfection, it's easy to feel intimidated. Many foreigners at first feel nervous about hosting dinner parties in Paris. To avoid making mistakes, some friends religiously obey the guide books written by fellow English-speakers for expatriates in France. According to these, my life here has been a series of unforgivable faux pas. For example, if you're a guest it is not polite to ask to use the host's toilet, apparently: they might feel embarrassed because it isn't presentable for guests. And as a host, don't whatever you do, pass the cheese platter more than once. It's considered ill-mannered, I read, after I'd done precisely that at least five hundred times. Skipping courses is another big no-no. Follow the French example and serve entrée, main, salad, cheese and dessert. This advice is also routinely ignored in our household. Unless Frédéric feels inspired, we never do first courses because I can't be bothered.

You might ask how I was allowed to commit such terrible trespasses without a warning from my very own (apparently negligent) Frenchman. 'Did you know that?' I asked Frédéric, after reading the toilet and cheese rules. He said he did. And he admitted that at first he'd felt uncomfortable about not serving entrées because he knew most French people would expect one. But when I asked why he never said anything, he'd shrugged. 'These things don't matter so much anymore,' he said.

His remark reflects change on a personal level. Frédéric has had to adapt, to relax his standards in some ways, living with an errant foreigner who isn't familiar with his country's customs. But it's also an indication of broader change. 'We're too uptight,' the French complain in their hypercritical manner. *On est trop coincé.* This has been said to me countless, countless times by friends and even virtual strangers. When I first came to France I was amazed by the formality of dinners and drinks parties. I assumed they must always be like that and the thought depressed me. Although a lot of social occasions *are* very formal by Australian standards, there is also evidence of an easing up, a deliberate breaking away from traditions. This became apparent over time as I met different groups of Frédéric's friends and our circle widened to include a number of cross-cultural couples.

And so our social life can sometimes seem schizophrenic. In a typical week, one night we're eating pasta with people who have relinquished this pursuit of perfection, the next we're at a dinner which is stiflingly *comme il faut.* Frédéric used to warn me beforehand so I could prepare for what was in store: 'this dinner might be a bit *coincé*' or 'tonight should be fun'. For several years our social life didn't make sense to me. It only accentuated the feeling of being in cultural quicksand. I didn't feel part of the scene—and the 'scene' was constantly changing. And then it clicked. *Stop trying to fit in.* Now, whether the scene is restrained or relaxed I'm content to just be myself.

It is probably something I've learnt in France, this being less anxious to please. While there's a great deal of wisdom in the 'When in Rome . . .' maxim, I don't think respecting a different culture means you have to follow all the rules. Some, yes, but not all. True, non-French behaviour can raise eyebrows. Even something as harmless as laughing loudly can mark you out as different because women here tend to laugh delicately, discreetly. On occasions I have roared delightedly at a sarcastic or ironic remark (which in fact was probably totally lacking in intended sarcasm or irony) only to meet surprised silence, edged with disapproval. These sorts of reactions used to make me feel embarrassed, alienated. Now I don't care—or at least I care a lot less. In any country, you select your friends. If someone is offended by loud laughing, then they're not a person I want to see again anyway.

∽

In Sydney, dinner parties used to mean a quick trip to Woollies after work where I'd race around filling the trolley with little foam trays of meat and vegetables hygienically encased in cling-wrap. In Paris, it's a tactile task that calls for all five senses as you taste and sniff cheeses and squeeze the *saucisson* to make sure it's *sec* and not too fatty. Dinners now involve a ten-stop shop.

Tonight we've invited six French friends over. The menu is pretty simple but also, I hope, good. Although fun and relaxed, this group takes food seriously. We're having *anchoïade* on croutons with the apéritif, then duck breasts in an orange and ginger sauce served with beans and new potatoes; green salad; a selection of five cheeses. Usually I buy a tart for dessert but the red berry fruits are beautiful at the moment so we'll serve them with *fromage blanc* and *crème de marrons*—a sweetened purée of Ardèche chestnuts which you buy at supermarkets.

Although there are four butchers' shops along Rue Montorgueil, there is only one place I'd dream of buying meat. Run by several men and one woman—sturdy country types from Auvergne and Brittany who are passionate about their produce—it's the sort of shop where customers discuss their back problems, weight loss, their baby granddaughter's allergies. There's always an atmosphere of quivering excitement, as though the presence of so much fresh, fine meat has set Gallic mouths watering, minds wandering to the moment when it's sitting on their plates.

At first, I only ever bought chicken breasts. How many would you like today? the butcher would ask as soon as it was my turn. Thai chicken curry was my dinner party staple (although the quantity of curry paste had to be halved for French guests). But the enthusiasm in the shop proved infectious.

'*Ooooh, c'est beau!*' The cry echoed down the line of customers as the butcher appeared from the back of the shop one day dragging a vivid-red flank that looked like it had come straight off some bovine beast. The country might be in the grip of mad cow panic but no-one in the queue was passing on the *bavette*. Swept up in the rush, I ordered a couple of slices too, completely ignorant of what cut I was buying. The woman behind told me to fry it in butter with chopped shallots, prompting a rapturous murmuring about *bavette à l'échalote*.

Nodding at the sliced flank the butcher assured me, 'You're going to have the time of your life with that.'

Gradually I started buying solid cylinders of beef to oven roast, chestnut-fed pork filets, beef chunks for *bœuf bourguignon*, and during the hunting season even pheasant and hare. Duck breasts are my latest discovery. My increasing daring draws interest and occasional encouragement. 'Madame's very into duck at the moment,' the butcher observes approvingly when I order them for tonight's dinner party. He sounds like a teacher pleased with the progress of a student, reminding me to leave on the thick white layers of fat which will infuse the breasts as they cook. As we're leaving, a missile of raw meat flies from behind the counter, skimming a customer's nose and landing with a wet splat on the floor. For Maddie.

The queue at the cheese shop stretches out the door. I'll be here for a while. I put down my shopping, which now includes two heavy bags of fruit and vegetables and four big bottles of Badoit water from the supermarket. The *fromagerie* is owned by a charming couple with two handsome sons who give each customer patient, personalised attention, helping decide on dinner menus, wine lists, refusing to hurry even as the queue grows longer by the minute. It used to drive me mad. *For god's sake, make up your mind!* I'd privately implode, when someone had sampled at least ten different cheeses and still couldn't decide. But Parisians are admirably serene in such situations, knowing that when it's their turn, they'll take their time too. I have learnt to do the same.

'What's good at the moment?' I ask at last. Like the butcher, the *fromagerie* has also been an education for me. Before, I never realised cheeses were seasonal. Now I know the taste depends on whether the cows are grazing on young spring grass or a winter diet of straw and silage and that the goats' cheese season finishes around October, November, when the milk is fed to newborn kids.

'*Le Brie est magnifique*,' the younger son tells me, pointing to its oozing, custardy centre, which appears to be making a bid for freedom. He cuts me a sliver to taste from the massive, thirty-five-kilo wheel of *vieux comté* which arrived this morning. Having been aged for two years, it's full of flavour. I choose three others: creamy St-Félicien which is so ripe it quivers at the slightest movement; *brebis corse*, a Corsican speciality made from sheep's milk and rolled in rosemary and thyme; a *chèvre*—not too dry but tasty, I specify. A lot of the *sec* goats' cheeses have a powdery texture which I dislike whereas the younger *chèvres* can be milky and a bit tasteless. He recommends the small discs of *Picodon* from the Drôme region.

There might be six bakeries on Rue Montorgueil but I'm also particular about where I go for bread. Contrary to popular belief, not every baguette in France is brilliant. In fact, good ones are getting harder to find as increasingly poorly trained bakers resort to shortcuts like buying pre-made frozen dough. In an interview years ago an award-winning *boulanger* in the 18th *arrondissement* told me how to pick a good one. It should be creamy, not white, Thierry Meunier had told me. Sturdy as opposed to being airy and the surface should be imperfect-looking, not smooth. The final test, he said, is to scratch the inside with your thumb and if crumbs fall away then it's no good. (The thought of some crotchety Parisian shopkeeper placidly standing by while you tear open a baguette is too incongruous to contemplate.)

Any Parisian polish I might have possessed is obliterated by the three *baguettes traditionnelles* I buy. Even though it might mean doubling back down the street, I always make the *boulangerie* the last stop because baguettes are awkward to carry when your hands are full. Squeezed into one of my shopping bags, they bump against my legs, covering my jeans with flour which bakers dust on bread to give it an authentic, *artisanal* appearance. After an hour-long crawl up the street, my fingertips look like raspberries from the bouquets of plastic bags slicing into each hand. Frédéric will come down later for flowers and wine and the *saucisson* I forgot. People pass pulling those smart little shopping trolleys, which would be a sensible investment if it weren't for the fact we'd have to lug ours up the stairs along with everything else. I puff up the six flights, sweating, reflecting that it's no bloody wonder Parisians don't entertain spontaneously with all the effort that's involved.

Frédéric sets the table as I'm cooking. Even when I try to do it like him, with the crystal knife rests, two glasses for each place, the linen napkins, the sprinkling of candles and flowers, it never looks as good. If we're having people over midweek, he'll set the table before going to work. To Frédéric a beautifully dressed table is as fundamental to a dinner party as food. Now his sensibilities are much appreciated but in the past I saw this painterly perfection as a sign of formality. I used to sabotage his work, replacing silver cutlery with bent forks and unfolding his carefully folded napkins in the misguided belief that the appearance of carelessness would create the casualness I cherished.

We'd said eight thirty to our friends, safe in the knowledge that no-one will turn up before nine. Lateness is institutionalised in Paris to the extent that if you arrive for dinner on time your hosts might not be terribly pleased to see you. Tonight's group is made up of friends Frédéric met as a student in Paris. Two of the guys went to *grandes écoles*, France's elite administrative finishing schools which fill the country's ranks of top civil servants and engineers. Their wives are full-time mothers. The other couple—both lawyers—arrive at 9.20pm.

A Parisian hostess has to be a contortionist. To appreciate her skills—'her' because I know few French men who venture into the kitchen—try preparing a perfect four-course meal for eight on top of your washing machine. That's exactly what we used to do at Levallois where the only bench space was the washing machine surface with its awkward hip-height that caused a lot of back-ache. Thanks to Mio's renovations, in this apartment we now have a luxurious metre and a half—not bad by Paris standards. Like many Parisians our 'oven' is a dodgy portable thing no bigger than a microwave. It sits on top of the refrigerator (that is the only spare spot) where it defrosts the freezer every time we use it.

I stick the duck breasts under the grill. Soon their fat is popping and spitting, occasionally igniting the orange ropes of heat. My impersonation of a perfect Parisian hostess is interrupted by mad dashes into the kitchen to extinguish the flames. Sometime after ten we move to the table, where our friends now visibly relax, comforted by the knowledge that the duck is not burnt and that at least three hours of unhurried eating and drinking stretches before them.

As I now well know, the French are bad at small talk with people they've just met (which is why drinks parties are often so awkward). In a country where discretion is a highly valued virtue, asking personal questions—including what someone does for a living or whether they have children—may be considered inappropriate and sometimes rude. Even at dinners with good friends, the conversation remains remarkably impersonal. And if a one-on-one chat does veer into private territory, it often has an abstract quality. This can be both liberating and limiting. While it allows much to be said without revealing too much about yourself, it also precludes the sort of open, intimate exchanges that, in my culture at least, help form close friendships. Mostly, the entire table takes part in the one discussion. Between them tonight's crowd seems to have read every French classic, all the latest political tomes. They blithely refer to France's transport minister in 1959 or the cultural minister in 1971 as though the names of every government minister from the last century were something they learned by rote in first grade. The guys from the *grandes écoles* talk a lot, delivering intelligent opinions in an eloquent flow that is devoid of the stumbles and grammatical faults which are inherent in the way most people speak. The conversation is lithe, lively, skipping from serious to silly subjects in a breath.

Dinners like this used to be hard work, intimidating even. It was a struggle to get a word in edgeways. The *grandes écoles* guys seemed terribly confident. (Now I know they're not: countless French people who have attended one of these prestigious institutions have since told me the highly competitive education system has left them with a lingering sense of never being good enough.) The conversation was too fast, people too quick to interrupt. Nobody ever asked me anything about myself. They seemed far more interested in airing their own views than listening to anyone else's.

At first I didn't get it. Then in my second year in France I saw *Ridicule*.

Bubbling with tightly bodiced bosoms and wicked banter, the film portrays the decadent court of Louis XVI—a world where wit is a powerful weapon. The story centres on the good Baron of Malavoys who goes to Versailles to win support for his project to drain a swampland that is spreading mosquitoes and disease throughout his province. But dying peasants make for dull court conversation. The baron is befriended by a kindly aristocrat who advises there's only one thing that will get him an audience with the fickle King: a fine wit.

And so the young baron with his provincial ways sets about trying to gain the King's attention. The aristocrat instructs him how to dance, powder his face and most importantly the art of verbal jousting using *les jeux de mots*—play on words. Conversation is a game; the courtiers are cruelly competitive, delivering sharp epigrams designed to belittle their opponents. When someone fails to deliver a clever comeback or misquotes Voltaire the others smirk behind their fancy Flemish fans. Everyone lives in fear of humiliation. Anyone who fails to entertain is banished from the court.

Louis XVI might have ended up on the guillotine, but the Revolution didn't change French society as radically as is often believed. *Ridicule* speaks volumes about France today. It is still an incredibly hierarchical country. Dependence on the monarchy was simply replaced by an unhealthy veneration of the state. You only need switch on television and watch the satirical puppet show 'Les Guignols' to see the French can be ruthlessly cynical about their politicians. But belying this irreverence is a deep fascination and awe for power. In interviews, French journalists are astonishingly deferential to politicians and rarely ask probing questions. A *Conseiller d'Etat* or an *Inspecteur des Finances* inspires the sort of hushed reverence that would be unthinkable for even the most erudite ministerial advisor in many English-speaking countries.

Many of the prejudices portrayed in the film persist: the Parisian view that *les provinciaux* are unsophisticated; the view in the provinces that Parisians are snobby, superficial and rude; the fact that style counts just as much as what's actually said. One scene in *Ridicule* made me laugh out loud. It captured so beautifully the French emphasis on refinement and sophistication. In it, the kind aristocrat congratulates the country baron on his witty remark which had caused the court to titter admiringly. 'Shame you laughed, though,' he scolds, referring to the hearty way in which the baron had enjoyed his own joke. 'You'll have to lose that manner of laughing with all your teeth. *C'est infiniment rustique.*'

These days in France no-one gets expelled from the dinner table for being dim-witted. But in educated circles conversation can still be played like a game, dominated by those possessing an elegant command of the language and an awesome general knowledge, or *grande culture*. The French still adore wordplay. People still fear being made to look stupid ('appearing ridiculous kills you,' goes the French saying) which is why the less confident say nothing at all.

To me *Ridicule* was a revelation. I finally understood French dinner party conversation. It isn't about getting to know anyone better or trying to include everyone in the discussion. No-one really cares about guests establishing a rapport with each other, not even the host. Quite simply, it's about being brilliant. *Everyone wants to shine, to impress.* The film forced me to face facts—my style of communicating doesn't work in France. It had to change.

And gradually it did. These days, I don't feel compelled to fill silences. It has sunk in: there's no obligation to make small talk in France. I've learnt to control my Anglo-Saxon impulse to persevere with questions. Now, faced with an indifferent neighbour, I can maintain stoic silence throughout entire weddings and long dinners. It may not sound exactly like progress but it beats heading home with a sense of being diminished by wasted effort. In the same way, faced with an unfriendly French woman, now I quickly stop making an effort. I've even learned how to deliver the odd cutting riposte.

The day of our dinner party, walking into the patisserie to buy a quick snack, I passed a smartly dressed elderly gentleman with a superior sneer. He looked like he lived on some stodgy avenue in the 16th *arrondissement*. I was loaded with my shopping bags and Maddie trailed behind me on her lead. He'd glanced at Maddie then stared at me with cold contempt.

'*Tiens,*' he said to his wife, his accusing eyes not leaving mine, '*un chien dans un pâtisserie.*' Fancy that—a dog in a patisserie.

Now, either this fellow was in a foul mood and wanting to take it out on someone or else I'd happened on the only Frenchman in the world who objects to dogs in food shops. At this particular patisserie, my regular, Maddie is a favoured client. But what riled me much more than his message— which might have been reasonable had it been delivered differently—was his supercilious manner. For once surprise didn't render me speechless. I didn't miss a beat.

'*Tiens,*' I mimicked, my eyes beaming back murderously, '*un con dans une pâtisserie.*' Fancy that—a dickhead in a patisserie. I added an icy smile for effect.

As replies go, it was very rude—and very effective. Mr Smart 16th looked disbelieving, then outraged. He stormed out of the shop, his shocked wife tripping after him. I continued nonchalantly to the counter where the *serveur* was giggling and looking impressed. My anger at the man quickly subsided. By the time our friends arrived for dinner that night, I'd almost forgotten the incident.

Frédéric makes me repeat the story to the table. Everyone laughs. Serge congratulates me on my *mot juste*, '*con*' (dickhead). But it is Frédéric who is most delighted by my exchange at the patisserie. 'Perfect! *Impeccable!*' he'd cried earlier when I told him my reply. Now he beams proudly. He is relieved, I realise. Because this time I didn't come home full of anger and frustration at my inability to immediately respond. There was no need for a postmortem, going over all the things I should have said if only I'd been quicker. This time I'd had the last word.

Five years ago when I first arrived in France such casual rudeness would have been beyond me. Warmed by the compliments and Frédéric's pride, I suddenly see the incident for what it is: a glorious sign of my progress. Surveying our dinner party, it strikes me that I have evolved on other fronts too. The food ritual and conversation, two sides of a coin elemental to French life, used to seem baffling and terribly foreign. I found it weird that hosts would go to so much trouble to ensure everything was perfect—the many courses, the wine, the table settings—and yet not bother asking guests about themselves or try to get to know them better. The effort seemed misdirected, contradictory.

But I've grown to love the civilised attitudes to wine and food in this country. And I guesss I've adapted to the way French people interact and converse. Perhaps I'm wrong and the sides of the coin aren't contradictory at all. Maybe it all has some kind of sublime logic.

Nineteen

During my first few years in Paris, there was one underlying theme to virtually every news story coming out of France. The terrible strikes, the rise of the far-right National Front party, the alarming unemployment—not to mention acute Gallic depression—these were all merely symptoms of the same problem. Simply put, France was a mess, a social and economic basket case about as stable as a hexagonal boulder poised to roll off a cliff edge. Even its dreamy capital was in peril: dull, dull, dull, declared every international magazine that counts. Compared to hip London with its new restaurants and budding bars, Paris was a stage cast in stone— gilded and glorious but dead nonetheless.

At the time I wasn't sure what to make of these reports. On the one hand it was discomforting to know that in the eyes of the world the French capital was *dépassé*. It created a vague impression of being in the wrong place at the wrong time. But I didn't know Paris any other way. My new home was alien to me and the process of figuring it out made life far from dull. And so when the French themselves began lamenting *le mal français* and *la crise* I thought maybe they were just jumping on the bandwagon. Maybe they were constantly claiming crises and nationwide depressions. It wasn't until years later when the city came to life that

I could appreciate how downcast Paris had been.

Many people claimed the catalyst for change was *l'effet mondial*—a reference to France's stunning World Cup victory in 1998. Frédéric and I watched the match at a bar along Rue Montmartre. Like everyone else, we thought it'd be an early night; of course, France didn't stand a chance against Brazil. After Emmanuel Petit scored the final goal for the French team, giving them a decisive 3–0 victory, the city turned inside out. Parisians poured from buildings, whooping and waving flags, surging along Rue de Rivoli towards the Champs Elysées. Paris hadn't experienced such euphoria since Marshal Leclerc marched down the same famous avenue to symbolically end the German Occupation.

To appreciate the significance of the World Cup celebrations, you have to understand this is a country where cerebral skills have traditionally caused more excitement than sporting prowess. Switch on French television and chances are you'll catch not a rugby replay or the tennis but a group of *intellos* pontificating about what's wrong with France or the world. They have weekly columns in news magazines, where they opine about the violence in Algeria, the formation of a new 'European culture' and even their own role in society (which has diminished, although they remain influential). Often I get to the end of these articles still unsure of the writer's position on his or her subject. 'What's their point, exactly?' I'll ask Frédéric, perplexed, because I can't help feeling it's all a bit abstract. Exasperated by my Anglo-Saxon simplicity, he reminds me the point is to explore the range of possibilities.

But the celebrations over France's World Cup win took place far from the slick television studios and articulate intellectuals. It is a night I'll never forget. Who would have predicted such incredible emotion from the French over a soccer game? And at a time when more and more people were voting for the anti-immigration National Front party, who would have imagined this kaleidoscope of black, white and brown faces painted the colours of the French flag? Like the winning team itself, the revellers were of varied ethnic origin. The subsequent mad celebrations seemed to go beyond a sporting victory to embrace France's diversity.

In contrast with Australia where our multicultural society has become a source of pride, in France 'multiculturalism' is pretty much a dirty word. I'm not saying that Australia is a bastion of tolerance—racism can flare in any ethnically mixed society, causing it to fracture and even combust. But outwardly at least, many Australians champion diversity whereas the French cling stubbornly to the idea that theirs is a white nation. To me culture is fluid and constantly evolving. Yet in France—an old country with a strong sense of its own identity—culture is viewed as an established entity that must be preserved and protected from foreign influences.

As with any society, there is racism, although it's different from racism in Australia. At dinner parties with educated, urbane Parisians I've been appalled by comments that just wouldn't be permissible in the equivalent crowd in Sydney. 'They were Arabs, *of course*' said one friend-of-a-friend about a gang who'd robbed a service station. In the street, police regularly harass blacks and North Africans for their visas and papers whereas in all the time I've been here I haven't been stopped once.

Having pondered the issue, though, I've come to the conclusion that the French are no more racist than any other people. Perhaps they're just more upfront about it because there's no culture of political correctness in this country. Besides, it's also true that the French—far more readily than

Australians—will take to the streets in defence of principles, like the massive demonstrations that occurred in Paris when the previous government tried to introduce a system of informing on illegal foreigners.

This heightened sense of responsibility stems partly from a heritage of defending human rights which dates back to the French Revolution. So the reality in France is multi-layered. Yes, I've heard many racial slurs here. Yet when Gallic cultivation is mixed with kindness and curiosity, the result is an enlightened worldview and an uncommon openness.

But compared to say America, England and Australia, immigrants in France are startingly absent from high-profile, public life. Despite the great wave of migration during the fifties and sixties, there are no North African or black news readers on television, for example. A French journalist who worked for one of the national networks told me a colleague of Algerian origin was 'encouraged not to show his face in news reports' because viewers wouldn't like it. Perhaps, having worked in TV, I'm overestimating its power but I do think television should be a mirror of society. It seems to me vital that the children of immigrants see French people of their own ethnic origin presenting the news or other highly-watched programs so they feel accepted in mainstream society.

Youth anger and resentment is already rising. For one story I went to Montfermeil, a poor suburb east of Paris, to speak to young people, mostly children of migrants from northern and sub-Saharan Africa. I was stunned by the deep hatred they expressed for France, their country of birth. Their feeling that it had betrayed them. 'When they needed people to do the hard jobs the French didn't want they welcomed us,' one twenty-year-old boy said, referring to how after the war France brought out North Africans to help rebuild the country. 'But as soon as things go badly they want us out.'

Bitter about their living conditions and job prospects, and often poorly educated, a minority resorts to violent crime which during my years in France has soared to record levels. In the grim suburbs surrounding many French towns, celebrations such as Bastille Day and New Year's Eve turn into violent rampages as youth smash shop windows and torch cars. We've felt the impact of the crime leap too. At Les Halles, where gangs from the suburbs sell drugs and occasionally steal mobile phones and wallets from tourists, aggression simmers in the air. I've been spat at. A girlfriend of mine was punched in the eye in broad daylight. Many Parisians I know avoid the area altogether. The situation at Les Halles is confronting: it challenges your liberal beliefs. On one level I think the anger of these guys is justified. But then I don't want it taken out on me. I'm as guilty as anyone of wanting a police crackdown, of wanting them shifted somewhere else, out of my backyard, so I can walk my dog in peace.

But the night of the World Cup victory, the streets pulsated with positive energy and the summer air was charged with feel-good vibes. When the photo of Zinedine Zidane, France's two-goal hero who is a second-generation Algerian, was suddenly projected on the Arc de Triomphe, his image on the most pompous of Napoleonic monuments prompted a rush of goose bumps. It was hard to believe it was actually happening. At that moment I felt ridiculously proud; wholly French, suddenly part of this melting-pot nation. And although I know we're talking about ninety minutes of soccer here, although with hindsight it's easy to be circumspect, there's no question that every one of us in the crowd felt this was a history-making moment. Nothing would be as it was before. France had entered a new era.

French Renaissance! French Revolution! French Recovery! Publications ranging from *Time* magazine to British *Vogue* trumpeted the transformation which by the middle of 2000 was confirmed by hard facts and figures. France *had* entered a new era. Although the problems in the suburbs didn't disappear (in fact they were getting worse) a new dynamism and vigour were tangible. Unemployment in France was falling, the economy was surging, inefficient state-owned behemoths were being privatised at an unprecedented rate. Ambitious young entrepreneurs were showing new daring — and some of them were actually staying in their birthplace instead of fleeing to more business-friendly shores. Wary international analysts warned there were still serious sticking points: the country's bloated public sector and the government's plan to reduce the working week to 35 hours, which has been widely mocked in the market-driven English-speaking world. Even so, the Socialist prime minister Lionel Jospin — austere, Protestant and professorial — inspired confidence. The national mood swung from depression to optimism.

Sleeping Beauty woke from her slumber. Bars and new restaurants sprouted like spring grass across eastern Paris. Although a lot of the Left Bank remains gentrified, on the Right Bank previously unfashionable working-class neighbourhoods such as Belleville, Oberkampf and the canals of the 10th *arrondissement* now draw lively cosmopolitan crowds. The new self-confidence has also triggered less tangible changes which can only be supported by anecdotal evidence. The old insularity seemed to be giving way to a new openness. Visiting friends have said the capital seems friendlier. On their last trip, my parents observed that when their French ran out, Parisians were more willing to try English than ever before.

Our *quartier* is changing, too.

The first sign that something is up occurs in our very own building. Walking down the stairs one day, I stumble into a blockade of sewing machines leaking oil onto the oak steps. The third-floor clothing sweat shop is moving to the heart of the Sentier where the owners won't be bothered by live-in residents complaining about their noise. A few weeks later the garment maker on the second floor packs up too. For several months the apartments remain empty while the walls are repainted, the grubby carpets peeled back so the parquet floors can be sanded and polished. The new tenants obviously require smarter premises than their predecessors.

'Silicon Sentier'. That's the name coined by the French press to describe the influx of internet start-ups drawn to our *quartier* by the relatively low commercial rents and fast access provided by the network of fibre-optic cables which had been installed for the nearby stock exchange. Our new neighbours on the second and third floors of our building are ambitious, global-minded twenty-somethings who greet me in English even though they know I speak French. No more thumps from crashing fabric rolls, no more delivery men spitting on the stairs. Our concierge no longer has to sweep up cigarette butts and sequins.

The dot com crowd with their scooters and short shelf lives is hardly going to force out the Sentier seamstresses. But their arrival is part of a general smartening up that has swept much of the inner city. Everywhere you look buildings are shrouded in scaffolding, façades are being stripped of the cement which was once considered chic to reveal the lovely biscuity stone beneath. Run-down *hôtels particuliers* are being restored and divided into sought-after apartments. Next to the fruit market, the modest Besançon hotel reopens as the stylish Hôtel Victoire Opéra, with mauve orchids quivering in the windows and pillowy velvet couches. Room prices don't just go up, they double overnight and the hotel takes a flood of bookings from fashionable travellers.

Property prices have soared too, driving many long-time residents and businesses to sell up while the going is good. And each new departure creates another chink in the character of the *quartier*. Clothes are replacing food as the district's chief commerce. Rue Etienne Marcel has become a stretch of designer fashion boutiques, each one glossier than the last. Gone is the pork wholesaler with hams and dried sausages swinging from the ceiling. In its place the Costes brothers (who own Hôtel Costes, Café Marly at the Louvre and Georges, the restaurant on top of the Pompidou Centre just to name a few) are planning a restaurant which will no doubt be another super-hip spot with apathetic waiters, where the interior design takes precedence over the food.

On Rue Montorgueil, one of the big fruit and vegetable shops has shut; the large butcher's at the top of the street has been replaced by a shoe shop and a bland home design shop has opened, assuming its prime position with such authority that I can no longer recall what was there before it. Le Commerce, where I often used to go for my morning coffee, has been sold too. Although still a café, the new owners have polished up the bar and put candles on the tables and raised the price of a *café crème* by €1.50. The band of old-timers who used to spend the morning leaning on the bar with their beers have left in disgust, of course. This was the idea, apparently. 'The new owners want a more chic clientele,' whispers René the barman, who misses the morning visits from his mates. He tells me they've dispersed to different cafés in the area.

The new proprietors aren't spearheading change, they're just trying to keep up with it. The fact is the regulars—the very people who make our *quartier* a real *quartier*—won't be around for much longer. They're all pensioners living in apartments they or their parents bought for next to nothing twenty or thirty years ago when the area was considered run-down and rough. And when they die they won't be replaced by a younger working-class population. The rents are way too high.

A new law passed by France's Socialist government in December 2000 requires every sizeable town to allocate at least twenty percent of its public housing to low-income earners or face penalty fines in the far future. By setting a minimum quota for rent-controlled flats, this regulation will obviously go some way towards maintaining a social diversity in cities. But in Paris, 'social housing' as it's called is not spread evenly, it's concentrated in the east, not in central districts like ours. Although the new mayor of the 2nd *arrondissement*—the only Green party mayor in Paris—is trying to create more, the loss of the *quartier*'s working-class character is a *fait accompli*.

Inner cities all over the world are becoming gentrified, I know—Frédéric and I are part of this change, after all. But prominent Parisians are now sounding the alarm: the centre of Paris risks losing its authenticity, its charm. The problem is not just the shifting population. Poor planning decisions by the authorities have exacerbated the situation, they say, pointing to the fact that the food market at Les Halles could have just been scaled down—or converted into a flower market—instead of moved out altogether. According to the radio broadcaster and writer, Philippe Meyer, Paris risks ending up like Venice: a city so geared towards tourists that its soul has been destroyed.

Although not pessimistic, I believe Parisians are right to sound the alarm. The wondrous preservation of Paris—the palaces and buildings and old-fashioned shops—creates an impression of immutability. Yet the inner city has changed quite dramatically even in the few years since we bought our apartment. In many ways it has been improved. Change is vital, of course; it gives a city energy, a heartbeat—qualities that in retrospect were lacking when I moved here. But steps should be taken to ensure that it doesn't come at the cost of character, that the entire inner city doesn't become a glamorous, vacuous showcase. For centuries Rue Montorgueil has specialised in food and produce and it would be a terrible shame if that tradition is allowed to die. Virtually every time I pass, I check to see the horse meat shop is still there. *How long can it hold out,* I wonder? French people these days are more likely to indulge in fast food than a slice of horse. And what about the funny, dishevelled little boutiques which line the side streets of our *quartier,* the dated barbers' shops and the Turkish tea rooms full of men who work in Sentier sweat shops? I might not frequent these places but I hope with all my heart they don't disappear.

For a while it seemed as though even the rats had packed up in protest at the gentrification of their stamping ground. Curiously, they have never repeated their audacious, all-ensemble appearance on our front doorstop which so horrified me that night we moved in our first belongings. It was, it seems, an impeccably timed one-off performance orchestrated for maximum shock and effect. Then, one night last year, we saw them again: six or seven huge rats gorging on something in the gutter. The sight of them was oddly heartening. The rats are not ready to relinquish the belly of Paris yet.

Other traditions remain immune to change too. The trail of lime trees outside our building is still a public loo. I'd rather it wasn't: I'll never get used to people peeing openly in the streets. But seeing them no longer surprises me. Some of the culprits are homeless and where are they supposed to go to the toilet in a city where public toilets are about as common as UFO sightings? (What's more, you have to pay to use them.) The sight of drunks sleeping outside our entrance doesn't shock me anymore either. These days the space next to our front door attracts quite a crowd on cold nights. A new supermarket has opened below and its refrigeration system pumps hot air into the street. This winter the step in front of the vents is occupied by an amiable, elderly Hungarian called Stan who cheerfully greets me each time I walk out the door. There is a reassuring regularity to our morning exchanges which always begin with an assessment of the weather. 'You should have brought an umbrella,' he'll tell me, waggling his hand to indicate the probability of rain. Sometimes he compliments me on my clothes, 'Hey, nice boots!' The other day he stared at me intently then declared, 'You're looking better today. Not so tired.' I thanked him, smiling at the incongruity of the exchange: that this man who has nowhere to sleep at night, this man whose life is immeasurably harder than mine, might notice something as trivial as my tiredness.

Pierre is still swaggering around too, yelling drunken abuse at anyone he doesn't know, acting for all the world as if he owns the place. At the moment he's squatting in the building next to ours which is empty because of renovation work. He still has his rotten red scooter which he parks near Frédéric's motorbike and the two of them often discuss what they'd like to do with the youths who occasionally siphon their petrol at night (Pierre's punishments being only slightly more draconian than Frédéric's).

According to the French charity Emmaüs, there are about ten thousand permanent *clochards* like Pierre in Paris, while each year a further thirty thousand people are rendered temporarily homeless through circumstance and spend a period living on the street. The word *clochard*, literally means 'tramp'. But while the English translation has a pejorative edge in French the word conveys a certain status. Pierre quite proudly describes himself as a *clochard* whereas it would be difficult to imagine someone importantly claiming to be a 'bum' or a 'tramp'. The word originated at the old Les Halles market where a bell or *cloche* used to toll at the end of every day when it was time to close the stalls. (The bell still hangs above the wine bar, A la Cloche des Halles.) It became tradition that when the ringing had stopped, any leftovers and overripe produce were given to the homeless and the hungry.

The bell no longer tolls but *clochards* still come to the same spot for food at the end of the day. They gather on the steps of the St-Eustache church, where a soup kitchen serves hot meals throughout winter. Beneath the massive neo-classical columns, their breath ignites pale steam clouds in the dark. I'd watched the scene hundreds of times before volunteering to work one night a week.

I'd never been drawn to any kind of charity work in Australia. But then I'd never seen people sleeping on cold concrete outside my apartment before either; never lived in a place where homeless people were so woven into community life. Sometimes it's unsettling, privilege and poverty so closely mixed. The disparity is sharpest in winter, when each year a few *clochards* die of cold in Paris. Meanwhile, the shops along Rue Montorgueil fill with the traditional pre-Christmas luxuries. The seafood stalls spill over with *langoustines*, smoked salmon and prawns, piled like swollen, pink commas. The specialist delicatessens at the bottom of nearby Rue Montmartre do a roaring trade in pâté de foie gras. The bottle shops' windows fill with champagne. One day in late November I'd just bought some oysters from Philippe, the charming oyster vendor from Ile de Ré who has returned for his twenty-fifth year of selling on Rue Montorgueil. I'd also bought a bottle of champagne. It was bitterly cold and I was hurrying back to our heated apartment. And then I passed the old Hungarian, huddled in front of the supermarket's warm air vents. He was holding his crackly transistor radio to his ear, one of his few possessions, nodding gravely at some piece of news, too absorbed to notice me. All the same it was jarring, me with my luxuries, him with next to nothing.

But this close proximity also has a humanising effect. It lessens the 'them and us' distance. Sure, some locals can't stand Pierre and their attitude is not entirely unjustified. He can be noisy and aggressive and downright dangerous on his scooter. But many people give him clothes, money and blankets. The shopkeepers are remarkably tolerant too, given that Pierre spends much of his time slurring over their counters, asking for food or peeing on their windows after closing. Anywhere else they might group together to try to drive him away. But when I asked the *fromager* if he minded Pierre's presence, he just shrugged and said: 'He's been here longer than I have.' His reply seemed a typically French blend of resignation and humanity.

At the St-Eustache soup kitchen, meals are prepared near the front entrance of the church in a small space shielded from the street by an iron gate reinforced with wooden panels. When I arrive for my first evening's work, people are already queuing in front of it even though it will be more than an hour before they are served. Behind the gate, two massive cauldrons simmer in the corner and I quickly discover that 'soup kitchen' is a misnomer. In fact the charity provides a four-course meal: soup, a main meal, salad and cake and coffee. About ten volunteers are chopping tomatoes and cucumbers and putting yoghurts, bread and biscuits into little bags which will be handed out as ration packs to each person. Several others are doing the rounds of local bakeries which donate bread and leftover cakes for dessert. I'm in charge of cutting up baguettes to make croutons for the soup.

'What are we having tonight?' A pair of eyes peers through the rectangular gap between the gate panels.

'Ravioli in tomato sauce,' I say.

The fellow makes a clicking sound in disgust. 'Well it's not worth queuing then . . .'

A few minutes later another set of eyes fills the hole. The exchange is repeated.

'What kind of ravioli?' she insists.

I call to the kitchen and relay the answer: 'Beef.' I've tasted it myself and it's really not bad, I tell her.

'Where's the beef from?'

'Um, I don't know,' I say, taken aback and also reluctant to pester the cooks with a question they surely can't answer. My ignorance makes her angry.

'You can't just give us any old beef without telling us where it's from, you know. I'm not going to eat beef if it doesn't come with a proper veterinary certificate . . .'

There is a shuffling sound as she moves away, muttering where I could stick my mad cow ravioli.

Xavier, who manages the different teams of volunteers, had warned me. 'Don't expect gratitude,' he'd said. 'Being demanding is a way for them to maintain their dignity: they'll accept the meal if you insist, but it better be good because they're not begging.' But still I'm taken aback by the constant complaints and criticisms. These people might sleep in metro stations but that doesn't mean they're less discerning about food than any other French person. 'The soup's not salty enough.' 'Mine's not hot.' 'I've told you before, I hate couscous.'

Standing outside with a twenty-something woman who's offering extra salt and a retired school teacher brandishing pepper, I sprinkle handfuls of croutons over soup for whoever wants them. Most people are polite, appreciative. Some are astonishingly exact about quantity. 'More, more, more, more, stop, I said STOP,' one guy cries, upset that an extra crouton slipped through my fingers. Certain characters seem to confirm Xavier's assertion that a large proportion of people on the street are mentally ill. One young fellow sticks his face right in mine and flashes me a lovely smile. '*Salut* Lady Di,' he says in an oddly bright way. 'Nine. I want nine croutons, please.'

A biting wind whips across the exposed plain of Les Halles. The cold has brought nearly two hundred people tonight. Most come because they're hungry but some of the elderly also seek the comfort of company. A few years ago the St-Eustache volunteers regularly fed about three hundred people each night. The drop in numbers is partly due to the introduction of the RMI, a minimum guaranteed income which buys street people food and basic shelter—a cramped *chambre de bonne* or perhaps an underground parking space that they share with others.

The traditional Parisian *clochard*—the old, shabby charac-ter on a street corner—is gradually being replaced by a new type of needy. At least half the people in the queue are recently arrived immigrants, a number of whom are surpris-ingly well-dressed. It's rumoured that some of those from Eastern Europe are ex-prisoners, released on the condition they clear out of their countries. Whether this is true or not I don't know but certainly some in the crowd look like charac-ter actors playing Russian gangsters. Tension occasionally flares between different nationalities. A few years ago, fights used to break out almost every night, often sparked by local crack dealers of African or Antilles origin who'd arrive coked-up to their eyeballs. Eventually the police clamped down on the trade, although Les Halles remains one of the easiest places in Paris to buy drugs.

The mood on the steps of St-Eustache church can still be volatile. When four strapping Polish blokes arrive and attempt to jump the queue there is a volley of furious protest from the line. Within a split second, a group of Kosovars materialises, their smaller frames offset by the menace on their faces. Fortunately no punches or knives are pulled and eventually the Poles leave in disgust.

Curiously, none of the local street people I know turn up. Later, Pierre explains he doesn't come to the soup kitchen anymore because he always ends up in fights. Then, just as we're beginning to pack up, a familiar silhouette lumbers through the darkness with an authority that sends one volun-teer flying to the stove to reheat some ravioli. I recognise the wobbly gait, can soon make out the clumpy boots with their loose tongues. Napoléon. Bossy and bellicose, he orders the small cluster of people milling for leftovers to get lost. It's obvious he considers himself King of the *Clochards*. He turns to me, his eyes bubbling with trouble. Brightly, I explain that actually we've stopped serving but—lucky him!—someone is kindly heating up . . .

Napoléon's roar ricochets off the neo-classical columns. 'I want caviar! IMMEDIATELY!'

Up close he resembles a bear, with hair sprouting from ears and nostrils. If you didn't know him you might be scared. But Napoléon is all bark and no bite.

'Caviar's finished,' I say. 'How about ravioli?'

He refuses. I suspect he's not even hungry. He just wanted to show off, to throw his considerable bulk around. Instead he begrudgingly accepts one of the little plastic bags containing yoghurt, biscuits and bread. Watching him lumber off into the night, the orange street lights giving the scene a filmic glow, it occurs to me that perhaps Paris is not such a bad place for people like him, the less fortunate, the crazy or the homeless. I don't mean to put a rosy tint on the lives of those living in the street because at the best of times it's grim and in winter it is insufferable. But the way the city is structured, the way it is broken down into 'villages' means that at least people like Pierre and Stan are not anonymous. Neither is Napoléon, who, although he has his own apartment, clearly has no money. They belong to a *quartier*.

That's why the shopkeepers put up with Pierre's trouble-making and why Frédéric gives him the clothes he no longer wears. It also explains why each morning I stop to chat with the Hungarian and frequently slip him a few coins. It is not that we are especially charitable. But familiarity breeds compassion and even affection. Quite simply, living side by side you can't pretend they're not there.

Twenty

When people ask how long I've been in France now I can scarcely believe my own reply. Six years. Has it really been that long? In many ways the time seems to have passed at lightning speed; it's a kaleidoscopic blur. Yet when I think back to arriving in Paris in my camel-coloured shorts, my mind plays another trick and that day seems more like twenty years ago than six. It's like a snapshot from a past life although in reality it was the beginning of a new one. Remembering makes me wonder whether the girl in the image is really me. How much has France changed me?

For a brief moment the other day I thought I'd changed radically—at least in appearance. Walking down Rue Montorgueil an American tourist startled me by taking my photo. 'She's so Pareesyanne,' he exclaimed to his wife, loudly, apparently assuming I couldn't understand English. And then, click! Immortalised in someone's holiday album as the ultimate *parisienne*! I imagined his family in the Midwest cooing over my French style. I couldn't wait to tell Frédéric. I felt ecstatic. 'Such a cuuute dog-gie!' added the tourist, and with dismay I realised the lens pointed at the street, that it was Maddie who was immortalised, not me, Maddie who after three hours of de luxe dog grooming looked so picture-perfect Parisian.

Apart from the obvious irritation at being upstaged by my dog (yet again), why should this have mattered? Why should I have been so delighted by the idea of looking quintessentially Parisian in the first place? It's not as though I'm hung up on wanting to look French. Yet believing for one brief moment that the tourist was talking about me was an undeniable thrill. No-one has ever said I looked French before. In France I'm used to standing out as foreign. The worst is when a shopkeeper or passer-by addresses me in English *even before I've opened my mouth.* Quite apart from my accent, my appearance seems to give me away.

Of course, looking foreign gives you exotic appeal and sometimes the attention is very nice. 'Are you English? American?' a handsome man enquired as I waited for friends in Juveniles wine bar. He offered me some of his Château Margaux, causing me to mentally cancel the modest Pays d'Oc red I'd been about to order. When my friends arrived he shook my hand and filled my glass with the remaining expensive Bordeaux. 'A Parisian welcome,' he said charmingly, and was gone.

'How do people know I'm not French if I haven't even said anything?' I quiz Frédéric later.

'Because you look Anglo-Saxon.'

I frown. Living in France you're constantly reading and hearing about the Enemy Anglo-Saxons who have conspired to globalise planet Earth and destroy the French culture and language. It's as though we're one massive army of insidious insects, invading France with our fast food and foreign words such as *le weekend* and *un break* and expressions like *surfer sur le net.*

'What do you mean?' I ask. He considers me for a second, choosing his words.

'Well, er, it's just that you could never be mistaken for French. I mean, you look less Anglo-Saxon than before. But you don't *look* French.'

'Why, though? Is it my clothes? My walk? My hair?'

'It's everything.'

His nebulous answer doesn't satisfy me but later, mulling it over, I discern some meaning in what he'd said. Although sometimes I'd like to be able to switch off the neon sign beaming 'Anglo-Saxon' from my unaccountably Anglo-Saxon forehead, you can't pretend to be something you're not. I am an Australian living in France and the reality is my foreign status is almost permanent. I could stay here thirty years, even take on French nationality, but that won't change how people perceive me. My identity in my new homeland is defined by my country of origin. *'C'est la petite demoiselle australienne au téléphone,'* the lady at the butcher shop told one of the butchers when I called to place an order. It wasn't said in a patronising manner, simply by way of identification.

In some ways, living in France has made me feel more Australian. Separation heightens your sentimentality. I sat in my office and cried watching the opening ceremony of the Sydney Olympics. Lately I've taken to buying big bunches of gum leaves from the florist. Occasionally, I'll pick off a leaf and scrunch it up to smell the eucalyptus oil, just like I used to do passing trees back home. Sometimes I fear turning into a ridiculous parody of my old self, still using expressions like 'daggy' and 'unreal!' because they were part of everyday speech when I left.

But the girl who got off the plane from Bucharest all those years ago *has* changed. I might not look the archetypal *parisienne* but living in France with a Frenchman, osmosis has occurred without even noticing it. That fight with Frédéric over what to wear to the bakery was more than four years ago. And I haven't worn tracksuit pants since.

They've been chucked out along with my shapeless T-shirts and baggy woolly jumpers, which were donated to a local homeless couple who to my knowledge have never worn them. The scuffed, beloved Doc Marten's haven't stepped outside in years—in France, their clumpy form screams 'Anglo-Saxon!'. Just as my mother started bringing only her best clothes to Paris, I have been influenced by the city too. I no longer race outside with washed, wet hair—a major concession for someone who hates blow-drying. Comfort is still my priority and pants my preference, but for the first time in my life I now have one or two flirty skirts, some delicate, strappy sandals, lots of close-fitting tops and even a couple of pairs of (practically unworn) heels. I've followed the advice of Inès de La Fressange too, and now buy fewer clothes but pay more. As for shorts, the only time I wear them is on holiday in Sydney.

The style victories haven't been totally one-sided, though. Frédéric's silk neckscarves have been banished. I don't care that they belonged to his arty grandfather. 'They make you look like a walking Gallic cliché,' I'd grumble, which only made him retort, '*Et alors*? What's wrong with that?' At last I'd said meanly, 'They're ageing,' which had the desired effect. The scarves now stay in his wardrobe. A curious swap has even occurred. While I buy all my clothes in Paris, Frédéric saves up his shopping for annual trips to Sydney, where he prefers the slightly looser cuts and the wide selection of casual men's wear, that is partly a product of our climate. His wardrobe now includes R.M. William stock boots (which he maintains in a state of polished perfection), bright board shorts for the beach and Country Road shirts.

But it isn't just my clothes that have changed: the way I think has been influenced too. For example, I've become used to the Latin approach to rules and regulations. The wonderful words *'on peut s'arranger'* (we can do a deal) which contain so many possibilities. In comparison, Australia sometimes seems a bit over-regulated. On one holiday in Sydney, Frédéric had lunch in the city centre with Sue's husband, Andrew, and came back railing that my country is 'not a democracy'. He'd been at an outdoor café smoking a slim cigar when a woman sitting nearby had demanded he put it out. 'I was outside,' he'd repeated, scandalised. I thought her reaction was scandalous too.

On another trip home a policeman pulled me over for turning left onto Military Road at an intersection where you're only allowed to make the turn between certain hours. I was twenty minutes too late. I stepped confidently from my car, believing that for such a minor mistake he would simply reprimand me. (What's a few minutes? The truth was I hadn't seen the sign until it was too late.) But he was already writing out my ticket before he'd even heard my excuse. I thought of the times in France I've been pulled over for committing similar traffic offences in hire cars, the numerous occasions I've been caught on trains without the required dog ticket for Maddie. And not one fine. You just smile and invent some unlikely excuse and invariably the conductor or police officer lets you off. It's not flirting, exactly, because although police officers are mainly men I've seen guys let off too. It's more a matter of using charm to appeal to their good natures. As the unflappable Aussie cop wrote out the ticket my indignation rose. Oh to be in Paris where I would receive a wink and a warning.

Back in Australia I find myself arguing why French should

remain one of the official Olympic languages even though hardly anyone speaks it; why champagne only comes from Champagne, earnestly championing the cause of José Bové, the cheese-making French activist with a handlebar moustache who smashed up a McDonald's outlet in protest against globalisation. At least the French are making a stand against American imperialism, I spout, surprising friends with my jargon. The irony of these situations doesn't escape me: in France I may stand out as foreign yet in Australia I feel a bit foreign too.

Such is the nature of expatriate life. 'Betwixt and between' was how one Paris-based American writer described having two homelands at a literary evening I attended. Stripped of romance, perhaps that's what being an expat is all about: a sense of not wholly belonging. After six years in France I feel like an insider. Having a French partner is a huge help, of course. But at the same time I'm still an outsider. And not just because of my accent or Anglo-Saxon appearance. To be a true insider you need that historical superglue spun from things like French childhood friends and memories of school holidays on the grandparents' farm and centuries of accumulated culture and complications.

This insider–outsider dichotomy gives life a degree of tension. Not of a needling, negative variety but rather a keep-you-on-your-toes sort of tension that can plunge or peak with sudden rushes of love or anger. Learning to recognise and interpret cultural behaviour is a vital step forward for expats anywhere, but it doesn't mean you grow to appreciate *all* the differences. One moment, living here makes my spirits soar; I adore these cultivated people with their intriguing idiosyncrasies. The next, I'm swearing and thinking terrible thoughts about how Paris would be perfect if it weren't for Parisians. Some days the city appears cold and stony; at other times it is lit by sunbeams of gold.

Everyday incidences elevate into moments of clarity simply because they would never, ever happen in your old home. I have accumulated hundreds of these vignettes which would seem random to anyone else, but to me are precious for their intrinsic Frenchness.

Being stopped in the street by a terribly chic blonde who advises me to use eye-makeup remover on Maddie's leaky eyes (any old brand will do but her dog likes Lancôme), and I'm so captured by her charm that the absurdity of the conversation escapes me. The sunny Sunday afternoon we went to see an exhibition of wartime photographs of Nazi concentration camps, expecting it to be empty—who wants to look at morbid images on a lovely spring day?—only to find half the city queuing to get through the door, the museum overflowing with Parisians silently examining each picture. Places like La Palette, where the owner François will treat you precisely as it pleases him, so that one day it's all kisses and handshakes and the next you're snapped at to wait over there until he feels like showing you to a table. The interview with actor Kristin Scott Thomas who described being stopped outside her Left Bank apartment by a fan, whose words took her totally by surprise. Not, 'can I have your autograph?' or 'I really liked *The English Patient*', but a message of tender grace: 'Thank you for the emotion.' Touched by the memory, she'd looked at me and shrugged and I understood exactly what she meant. Where else in the world would someone actually say that?

There is a certain comfort—serenity even—which comes from being able to see my experiences in this country as a whole: the good with the bad, the bitter with the sweet. Having emerged from the fog of the early difficulties—trying to get work as a journalist and make sense of my new home, not to mention my new boyfriend—I can see it has been incredibly enriching, even if it didn't always seem so at the time. Many people find the expatriate experience makes them stronger and more adaptable. I would say in my case it's had the dual effect of making me more self-sufficient while at the same tightening the bond with Frédéric, who is not only the reason I came to France but also the person who has shared the subsequent journey. For me the experience has also been humbling. Cultural misunderstandings make for snap judgments. People I dismissed as cold and unfriendly have become friends. *It just takes time in France.* Frédéric had said so a zillion times. He was right.

It's an experience that has left me fundamentally the same—and profoundly changed. Which makes me wonder sometimes what it would be like to return to live in Australia now. Would life seem a bit dull without the tickle of tension? Would Frédéric be happy there? Would it seem like home? One day we might make the move, not in the near future but maybe later. It would be great for Frédéric to experience living in another country, because although widely travelled, he has only ever lived in France. And it would be great for me to be close again to family and friends, even if only for a few years.

Being so far away from home means you necessarily miss out on some things. You're not always there to celebrate weddings, milestone birthdays, you barely know your friends' children. I'm very lucky in that my parents come frequently to France and so do some of my close friends. And these holidays together are wonderful. But the physical distance separating us is insoluble and regular contact through phone calls and e-mails can't quite bridge it. You are no longer familiar with the intricacies of their daily lives, and neither do they know yours.

Whether or not we ever live in Australia my heart will always be tied to two places, now. Meeting Frédéric means my future is irrevocably linked to France. A decision has been made that makes that a certainty.

Epilogue

Deciding to get married fills our hearts with anticipation and excitement for the future. It also makes us laugh in wonder about the past, at the chance quality of our encounter in Bucharest. How that summer holiday—what I once feared was a flash of madness—has turned into marriage. How we stuck it out, muddling through our cultural differences and misunderstandings. Those first months in France now seem a bit unreal. 'I can't believe I came to Paris to live with a man I barely knew!' I exclaim to Frédéric, laughing but serious. 'I mean no job, no friends—what was I thinking?' But even back in those most uncertain of times it seems deep down we knew what we were doing. The same thing men and women have been doing forever. Following our hearts, not our heads.

The words of the Greek man I met on Samos island all those years ago were prescient, as it turns out. *'Once you leave your homeland nothing is ever the same,'* he'd said. Thinking back to our conversation on that luminous day, it strikes me that if we met now we'd have so much more to say to each other. Back then, his dilemma about feeling Greek in Australia and Australian in Greece didn't resonate with me. Now it does. Although our situations are very different (his wife was Greek like him whereas I'm living in France with a

Frenchman) his experiences now have meaning. His Australian-raised children teased him about his funny accent. If Frédéric and I have kids, they'll probably tease me too. Before long they'll be correcting my French — *le bouleau*, *la tondeuse à gazon* — and cringing with embarrassment at my mistakes in front of their friends.

Our decision to get married gives a new clarity to my life and future in Paris. *I might only ever be 'almost' French but France for now is home.* It is not just a matter of marrying the man I love, it is also a commitment to a new country. It deepens my sense of belonging. Silly though it may sound, it makes me feel that my place in this country is more legitimate. This is reinforced by the subtle but tangible shift in attitude towards me from Frédéric's family. They are thrilled by the news and I realise they had probably all but given up hope on us. (My family is thrilled too, although being less traditional, all that mattered to my parents was that we were happy, married or not.) But in France it seems our impending wedding means we can at last be taken seriously as a couple. It's as though a door, which had been ajar, has suddenly flung wide open. Soon after announcing our engagement we attend a family reunion, a lunch at Baincthun with those uncles and aunts whom I first met at the height of the nuclear tests furore. They congratulate us warmly, with deep sincerity and a few of them tell me in their eyes I am now a niece. I know that in northern France these ties are not taken lightly. 'I would like to take this opportunity to welcome Sarah into the family,' Frédéric's father announced, tears in his eyes. 'I am very proud.'

We decide we want a very low-key wedding. No churches, no long guest lists, no fuss, no headaches. We don't want some big bash that will unite family and friends from both hemispheres. The organisation involved is one deterrent. More importantly, though, we would rather a small, intimate celebration. Given that we live in Paris it makes sense to do the formalities here. Then in about six months time, we'll celebrate properly in Sydney with my family and friends. Under French law, religion is separated from the state and civil wedding ceremonies are obligatory, performed at local town halls which in our case means the *mairie* of the 2nd *arrondissement*. Only Frédéric's immediate family will attend, along with his cousin Gauthier, Alain's lovely Belgian girlfriend, Toinon, and Alicia and her husband Rupert, who'll be our witnesses. We plan to do it soon; there's no reason to wait when there's so little to organise.

But deciding to marry in France sends us hurtling back into space towards that familiar planet of paperwork where nothing is simple and straightforward. A blow-by-blow account of our difficulties with *l'administration française* would make for exceedingly dull reading and I will try to spare you the tedious details. In fact it was a battle with just one person—the *procureur* (magistrate) responsible for approving our *dossier*. Of course, dealing with the French bureaucracy is always terribly time consuming, I know that by now. You pray for an enlightened civil servant, one who doesn't seek to make the procedure more complicated than it is already. This time we are unlucky.

It takes a couple of months to gather the forest of documents required to get married: medical certificates, blood test results, copies of our most recent telephone and gas bills, passports, and in my case *carte de séjour* and letters from both the Australian and American embassies. We also have to supply official copies of our birth certificates. Some of the documents are not allowed to be more than three months old, others are allowed to be up to six, and the whole process seems to require the timing genius of a Parisian hostess putting on the perfect dinner party.

Eventually we're given the go-ahead to get married from the magistrate's office. We telephone Frédéric's family and fix a date with the *mairie*. Then, incredibly, the following week in a crisp, pedantic letter the *procureur* informs us we don't have permission. No apology is given for the about turn. Only the reason why approval has been finally denied. The copy of my birth certificate (which we'd waited two months for) was issued without an *apostille*.

'A what?' I ask the fellow at the town hall, my heart sinking. It sounds ominous.

'*Apostille*, it's an official stamp,' he explains. Apparently I should have asked for it to be put on the document. He lowers his voice in sympathy. 'It's a pure formality. Other *procureurs* would not insist on it, but well, it's just bad luck because this one is *très rigoureuse*.'

The infamous *apostille* arrives five weeks later and within a few days we are granted permission to marry. I don't feel so much joy as relief. Not wanting to waste any more time, we set the date for Tuesday next week. One of the reasons for rushing is that my sister, Anna, will be in Paris then—she's coming from Sydney for a two-week holiday. Her plane lands just four hours before our rendezvous at the *mairie*.

Fortunately her flight is on time. Although I haven't seen my sister for eighteen months, there's no time to chat—just a quick shower and a strong coffee to counter her jetlag and then we have to go. I am thrilled she is here to share the day. It turns out to be fitting consolation for the administrative hassles which preceded it. Alicia had insisted I be chauffeur driven to the *mairie*: low key or not, she wasn't letting our

official wedding day pass without a certain amount of ceremony. Brides must have a car, she declared. Fully nine
months pregnant with her second child, she is as energetic
and ebullient as ever. And so just before eleven, she calls
outside our apartment to pick up Anna and me. Rupert has
taken Frédéric out for a pre-wedding breakfast and they're
going to meet us at the *mairie*.

In the bright sunlight, my limousine shines like a new
plastic toy. It's not much bigger than one either. For the occasion, Alicia has taken her red Mini Cooper through the car
wash and decorated it with huge pink bows to match my pink
dress. Made by a talented Austrian designer friend, Berit, the
handprinted fabric shimmers with tiny crystals and sequins.
Alicia squeals in admiration at the sight of my shoes—high
strappy things I can hardly walk in. Giggling, we squeeze
inside: Alicia, her two-year-old daughter Lily, who is swathed
in violet tulle for the occasion, Anna and I—and Maddie and
Lou-Lou, naturally, who are both wearing pink ribbons too.
(Yes, I suspect I'm now as mad as any of those mad *mesdames*
with dogs that I meet on daily walks.) I have visions of having
to deliver a baby along the way as we dart between the fabric
delivery trucks in the Sentier's labyrinth of one-way streets,
but we make it to the *mairie* in only slightly more time than
it would have taken to walk there. Maddie and Lou-Lou trot
assuredly through the sliding glass doors past the prominent
sticker declaring 'No Dogs'.

Upstairs, the *salle des mariages* has an air of stately dignity.
It has all the French hallmarks of ceremony—pompous
portraits, chandeliers, gilded mirrors, handsome wood panelling, waxed parquet floors. Frédéric, Rupert and Gauthier
are already there and so are Alain and Toinon. Grainy shafts
of light fall through the long windows, streaking our happy

faces. The mayor won't be long, someone tells us.

About half an hour later the mayor enters the room and we all rise. Wearing a shiny tricolour sash and flanked by two other men, he sits in front of us on a raised platform like a judge presiding over a courtroom. Except that he looks about eighteen. Slim and yes, very young-looking, Jacques Boutault, our Green party mayor, is the antithesis of the portly, pipe-smoking sort of character I'd expected for some reason (probably from watching too many French films).

Civil marriage ceremonies are often purely administrative but our informal mayor precedes the paperwork with a lovely expansive message which seems to come straight from the heart. 'I am especially delighted to be conducting this wedding today,' he says softly. 'I understand the process hasn't been easy', his smile is sympathetic. 'And I am especially glad to be marrying a couple of mixed nationality. Marriages like yours are the future of France—and indeed of the whole world.' Frédéric squeezes my hand.

Five minutes later, after reading us various articles from the French civil code, the ceremony is over. Jacques Boutault hands us our *livret de famille*, a slim folder with an elegant blue cover. In France this document is more precious than a passport.

'Don't lose it; replacing it means a lot of paperwork,' he jokes.

Frédéric explains, 'It's for recording details like the births of children; you're always asked to present it.'

Opening it I'm stunned to see the headlined pages go up to *Huitième Enfant*. Eight children! They must be kidding. I'm thirty-four, for god's sake. Laughing, I say there are quite enough pages.

The mayor congratulates us warmly and shakes my hand.

'Do I call you…?'

'Turnbull,' I quickly butt in. 'I'm still Madame Turnbull.'

'Ah yes, Anglo-Saxons like to keep their own names,' he smiles.

'Anglo-Saxon women are quite feminist,' adds Frédéric, apparently pleased at being able to share this information.

They both chuckle as though this is a rich joke. More surprisingly, I laugh too. Five years ago I would have wondered what the hell was so funny about keeping my own name. It would have irritated me, being earmarked as a Radical Anglo-Saxon Feminist for something so commonplace. But now I don't feel as though I have to argue the point. The French are always laughing at what they consider Anglo-Saxon eccentricities.

Our group walks through the airy elegant arcade, Galerie Vivienne to Palais Royal, where we've booked a table for lunch at a restaurant on the edge of the gardens. First though, we want to open the champagne we've brought with us. By now it has turned into a really hot day—it must be at least thirty—and so we pull up chairs beneath the cool canopy of the sculpted lime trees. The scene is beautiful: the flower beds are radiant, a paint box of colour. It seems to me entirely appropriate to be celebrating in this most romantic of gardens where Frédéric and I have spent many lovely hours. We've just filled the plastic flutes with bubbles when a young guardian approaches. Uh oh, trouble.

'Dogs are strictly forbidden in the gardens,' he says. 'I'm sorry but you'll have to leave.'

'We just got married,' I plead.

'You can't kick them out, they're bridesmaids,' quips Frédéric. The guardian looks at Maddie and Lou-Lou. They stare brazenly back, oblivious to how ridiculous they look in their pink ribbons. The guardian allows himself a smile. 'Try to be discreet then. And congratulations.'

Now, as I sit in my office surrounded by the coffee cups and papers which have accumulated alarmingly in the writing of this book, thinking back to that encounter with the guardian makes me smile. If my love for Paris lies in the sum of little moments, then the day Frédéric and I married shines in my memory with scenes of touching Frenchness. The mayor's gentle message of openness, the way the guardian turned a blind eye with a smile and a kind word. It is moments like this that give meaning to the difficulties with the *procureur*—and to the thousands of other difficulties and challenges I've experienced here. The meaning is France itself, with all its paradoxes, its brusque aloofness and soulful warmth, its inwardness and outwardness, its paperwork and poetry, its power to fascinate and frustrate, to inspire love and anger.

That's how it seems to me now.

I stare out my office window at the shimmering rooftops and my precious patch of ever-changing sky with a strange sense of something having ended. *The adventure.* Because that's what it has been, this whole process of coming to live with Frédéric and making France my home. Not that every day has been an adrenaline rush, definitely not. It hasn't been a summit-scaling dash but rather a slow ascent. Sitting here, I am struck by another thought which stems from the knowledge that life is a chronology of different chapters.

A new adventure is just beginning.

Thanks

This book might never have been written were it not for the encouragement of my husband, Frédéric, and my parents, Jan and Murray Turnbull who gave me confidence that I had a story worth telling. I'm immensely grateful to all those who read various drafts—and in some cases several drafts—of the manuscript: Frédéric, Michael Short, Sue Quill, who believed in it right from the start and especially Alicia Drake, who couldn't have been a better critic nor a more supportive friend. My editor, Kim Swivel, helped make this story stronger by guiding me gently but firmly through my fear of writing about my own life. In the UK, I'm especially grateful to my agent Liv Blumer and my publisher Nicholas Brealey for making it all happen.

Lastly, I'd like to thank the people who appear in this book. They are all real, although some of the names have been changed for the usual reasons. It is because of them that living in France has been challenging and compelling and ultimately so rewarding.